AF761394

# Tax Policy Reforms 2020

OECD AND SELECTED PARTNER ECONOMIES

OECD
BETTER POLICIES FOR BETTER LIVES

This document, as well as any data and map included herein, are without prejudice to the status of or sovereignty over any territory, to the delimitation of international frontiers and boundaries and to the name of any territory, city or area.

The statistical data for Israel are supplied by and under the responsibility of the relevant Israeli authorities. The use of such data by the OECD is without prejudice to the status of the Golan Heights, East Jerusalem and Israeli settlements in the West Bank under the terms of international law.

**Please cite this publication as:**
OECD (2020), *Tax Policy Reforms 2020: OECD and Selected Partner Economies*, OECD Publishing, Paris, *https://doi.org/10.1787/7af51916-en*.

ISBN 978-92-64-51073-9 (print)
ISBN 978-92-64-33846-3 (pdf)

Tax Policy Reforms
ISSN 2617-3425 (print)
ISSN 2617-3433 (online)

**Photo credits:** Cover image word cloud ©Tagul.com.

Corrigenda to publications may be found on line at: *www.oecd.org/about/publishing/corrigenda.htm*.
© OECD 2020

The use of this work, whether digital or print, is governed by the Terms and Conditions to be found at *http://www.oecd.org/termsandconditions*.

# Foreword

This report was produced by the Tax Policy and Statistics Division of the OECD's Centre for Tax Policy and Administration. It was led by Sarah Perret and written jointly by Véronique Salins (Economics Department), Giulia Aliprandi, Daniel Fichmann, Sean Kennedy, Bethany Millar-Powell, Sarah Perret and Konstantinos Theodoropoulos (Centre for Tax Policy and Administration). The authors would like to thank the delegates of Working Party No.2 on Tax Policy Analysis and Tax Statistics and the Committee on Fiscal Affairs for their inputs. The authors would also like to thank David Bradbury and Bert Brys for their guidance and acknowledge the helpful contributions and comments received from Silvia Appelt, Piet Battiau, Sveinbjorn Blondal, Stéphane Buydens, Fernando Galindo-Rueda, Ana Cinta González Cabral, Tibor Hanappi, Michelle Harding, Anna Milanez, Pierce O'Reilly, Nigel Pain, Ruairi Sugrue, and Kurt Van Dender. The authors are also grateful to Karena Garnier, Natalie Lagorce and Michael Sharratt for their assistance with formatting and communication.

This report was approved by the Committee on Fiscal Affairs and Working Party No.2 on Tax Policy Analysis and Tax Statistics on 17 July 2020 and prepared for publication by the OECD Secretariat.

# Table of contents

## Tables



## Figures

## Boxes

## Follow OECD Publications on:

- http://twitter.com/OECD_Pubs
- http://www.facebook.com/OECDPublications
- http://www.linkedin.com/groups/OECD-Publications-4645871
- http://www.youtube.com/oecdilibrary
- http://www.oecd.org/oecddirect/

## This book has...

StatLinks
A service that delivers Excel® files from the printed page!

Look for the *StatLinks* at the bottom of the tables or graphs in this book. To download the matching Excel® spreadsheet, just type the link into your Internet browser, starting with the *https://doi.org* prefix, or click on the link from the e-book edition.

# Editorial

The outbreak of COVID-19 has resulted in a health crisis and a drop in economic activity that are without precedent in recent history. Containing and mitigating the spread of the virus has rightly been the first priority of public authorities to reduce the incidence of the disease and limit the pressure on healthcare systems.

Most countries have also acted rapidly and forcefully to limit the economic hardship caused by lockdowns and other containment measures. While the size of fiscal packages has varied across countries, most have been significant, and some countries have taken unprecedented action. Initial government responses focused on providing income support to households and liquidity to businesses to help them stay afloat. As the crisis has continued, many countries have expanded their initial fiscal packages. Where lockdowns and other containment measures have been eased, a number of expansionary fiscal policy measures have been implemented or announced to support economic recovery.

Uncertainty looms large, however, and continued policy adaptability will be key. There is already evidence that the recovery will not be a smooth process, with localised re-introductions of lockdowns in some countries, continued movement restrictions and risks of second and subsequent waves of infections. While some degree of stability is usually needed to strengthen confidence, given the uncertainty of the current crisis, policy flexibility and agility may be what is needed to help restore confidence.

Governments should continue to use fiscal tools to provide support to affected businesses and households. Support measures should be kept in place as long as needed to avoid scarring effects and fiscal policy should remain supportive to speed up recovery. That said, governments should make sure that policy responses are adapted: measures should be well targeted and slowly withdrawn when the situation improves.

Once recovery is locked in, governments should shift from crisis management to consideration of structural reforms, but they must be careful not to act prematurely as this could jeopardise recovery. Governments should seize the opportunity to build a greener, more inclusive and more resilient economy. Rather than simply returning to business as usual, the goal should be to "build back better" and address some of the structural weaknesses that the crisis has laid bare.

A central priority should be to accelerate environmental tax reform. Today, taxes on polluting fuels are nowhere near the levels needed to encourage a shift towards clean energy. Seventy percent of energy-related CO2 emissions from advanced and emerging economies are entirely untaxed and some of the most polluting fuels remain among the least taxed. Adjusting taxes, along with state subsidies and investment, will be unavoidable to curb carbon emissions.

Fair burden sharing will also be central going forward. The crisis has shed light on and exacerbated existing inequalities. Low-income earners, women and young people have been hit harder, while part-time, temporary and self-employed workers have accounted for up to half of the workforce in the most severely affected sectors. A number of countries have temporarily expanded sick leave or unemployment benefits to non-standard workers, but consideration should be given to strengthening their social protection in the longer run.

Once countries exit the crisis and economies recover, governments will start looking to restore public finances, but they may not be able to resort to traditional revenue-raising recipes. Raising taxes on labour and consumption, as was done in the wake of the 2008 global financial crisis, may be difficult politically and in many cases not desirable from an equity perspective. Governments will need to find alternative sources of revenues. The taxation of property and personal capital income will have an important role to play, particularly in a context of significant improvements in international tax transparency.

Global cooperation is more important than ever. The crisis has highlighted our collective vulnerability, but also the critical importance of multilateral collaboration. Rising pressure on public finances as well as increased demands for fair burden sharing should provide new impetus for reaching an agreement on digital taxation. Tax cooperation will be even more necessary to prevent tax disputes from turning into trade wars, which would harm recovery at a time when the global economy can least afford it.

Pascal Saint-Amans
Director, Centre for Tax Policy and Administration

# Executive summary

***Tax Policy Reforms: OECD and Selected Partner Economies* is an annual publication that provides comparative information on tax reforms across countries**. It tracks tax policy developments over time and gives an overview of the latest tax reform trends. This year's edition focuses on the tax reforms that came into force or were due to come into force in the second half of 2019 and 2020. However, given the significant packages of measures that were introduced in the first half of 2020 in response to the COVID-19 crisis, the report also includes a Special Feature on "Tax and Fiscal Policy Responses to the COVID-19 Crisis". This Special Feature takes stock of the tax and broader fiscal measures introduced by countries from the beginning of the virus outbreak up to mid-June 2020, largely based on countries' updates to the database[1] compiled by the OECD on tax and fiscal policy responses to the crisis.

**This year also marks the first time that China is included in the publication**. This year's report covers 40 countries including all OECD countries (with the exception of Colombia,[2] which became a member of the OECD after the primary data collection exercise had been completed), as well as Argentina, China, Indonesia and South Africa. The intention is to continue expanding the coverage of the report to additional G20 countries.

**In its assessment of the reforms adopted before the COVID-19 crisis, and due to come into force in the second half of 2019 and 2020, the report identifies a number of common tax reform trends across countries**. It should be noted that these are trends that emerged before the COVID-19 crisis and that reforms have in some cases been delayed in response to the crisis. More generally, the COVID-19 crisis should be seen as a significant intervening event and future reports will focus on the impact of the crisis on these longer-term trends. Looking at the reforms adopted before the COVID-19 crisis, the report identifies the following trends:

- **Personal income tax (PIT) reductions**, **targeted in particular at low and middle-income households, have continued**. While this trend represents a broad continuation of PIT reforms in recent years, an intensification of PIT rate cuts has been observed. PIT base narrowing measures, often targeted at families and low-income earners, have also been frequent. Regarding the taxation of household capital income, limited changes have been introduced, involving both tax increases and decreases. These measures have included changes to the taxation of rental income as well as expanded tax reliefs to support small savers.
- **Changes to social security contributions (SSCs) have been limited both in number and in scope**. Most of the reforms were aimed at lowering SSCs, but changes were generally modest. This confirms that the pace of reform in this area has slowed.
- **Corporate income tax (CIT) rate cuts have continued in 2020.** As was the case last year, the most significant CIT rate reductions have generally been introduced in countries with higher initial CIT rates, leading to further convergence in statutory CIT rates across countries. Many countries have also reinforced the generosity of their corporate tax incentives to stimulate investment, innovation and environmental sustainability.
- **With regard to international taxation, efforts to protect CIT bases against corporate tax avoidance have continued** with the adoption of significant reforms in line with the OECD/G20

Base Erosion and Profit Shifting (BEPS) project. The tax challenges arising from the digitalisation of the economy continue to represent a major concern for many countries. Efforts to achieve a consensus-based multilateral solution to address those challenges are ongoing, but a growing number of countries have announced or implemented interim measures to tax certain revenues from digital services in the meantime.

- **The stabilisation of standard value-added tax (VAT) rates observed in recent years is continuing, while VAT base changes have involved a mix of base broadening and base narrowing measures.** High standard VAT rates in many countries have limited the room for additional rate increases. Instead, many countries have concentrated their efforts on the fight against VAT fraud and on ensuring the effective taxation of cross-border online sales to raise additional revenues and strengthen the functioning of their VAT systems. On the other hand, an increasing number of countries have narrowed their VAT bases by expanding the scope of their reduced VAT rates, which suggests a slight departure from trends in previous years, where the predominant objective of VAT reforms was to raise additional revenues. A number of countries have also raised their excise taxes, in particular on tobacco products and sugar-sweetened beverages, in line with trends in previous years.
- **Environmentally related tax reforms have continued at a slow pace in 2020**. While the number of measures adopted increased compared to 2019, reforms were concentrated in a few countries and their scope remained generally limited. Most of the reforms were related to the taxation of energy use, but unlike in previous years, transport fuels were not the main focus. Instead, changes were made to carbon taxes and taxes on electricity consumption. Tax reforms in the transport sector, aside from energy use, were limited to adjustments to vehicle registration taxes and tax reductions for vehicles running on alternative fuels. There was an increase in reforms related to other environmental tax bases (e.g. plastic and waste), but their overall number remained limited.
- **There has been an increased focus on property taxation compared to previous years**. Previous editions of this report have generally shown limited changes to property taxes. This year marks a change, with an increasing number of reforms in this area. In addition, while previous years saw a mix of tax increases and decreases, this year shows a clearer trend towards increases in property taxation.

**The Special Feature on "Tax and Fiscal Policy Responses to the COVID-19 Crisis" shows that countries have taken swift and significant policy action in response to the crisis**. While the size of fiscal packages has varied across countries, most have been significant, and some countries have taken unprecedented action. The initial measures introduced by countries focused on keeping businesses and households afloat, mainly through liquidity support for businesses, job retention schemes, and income support to households. As the crisis has continued, many countries have expanded their initial response packages. Some countries have also decided to adjust some of their initial measures or to wind back or delay tax reforms that were due to come into force. The most recent measures and discussions suggest that the recovery phase will be supported by expansionary fiscal policy in many countries, including through measures to support investment and consumption and ongoing support for households and businesses.

**The report contains four chapters.** Chapter 1 discusses the macroeconomic background before the COVID-19 crisis, and provides a brief overview of the impact of the crisis on the global economy. Chapter 2 presents the latest trends in tax revenues and tax mixes. Chapter 3 gives an overview of the tax reforms entering into force or due to enter into force in the second half of 2019 and 2020. Finally, Chapter 4 provides an overview of the measures adopted by countries so far in response to the COVID-19 crisis, in the Special Feature on "Tax and Fiscal Policy Responses to the COVID-19 Crisis". The Special Feature in this year's report focuses mainly on the emergency measures announced in response to the crisis. However, the significant increases in government expenditure and the expected dramatic decline in tax revenues in the aftermath of widespread economic lockdowns are likely to present a large range of medium to longer-term fiscal challenges. In responding to these challenges, tax policy will be one of the key instruments to be relied upon by policy makers. Against this backdrop, ongoing developments in tax policy in this rapidly evolving environment will be monitored and assessed in future editions of this report.

## Notes

[1] http://www.oecd.org/tax/covid-19-tax-policy-and-other-measures.xlsm.

[2] Colombia is included in the Special Feature, but not in the other chapters of the report.

# 1 Macroeconomic background

This chapter is mainly intended to provide background on the context in which the tax reforms adopted before the COVID-19 crisis were undertaken, focusing on macroeconomic conditions in 2019. It covers trends in growth, inflation, productivity, investment, the labour market, public finances and inequality. The chapter also gives a brief overview of the early impact of the COVID-19 crisis.

**This chapter is mainly intended to provide background on the context in which the tax reforms adopted before the COVID-19 crisis were undertaken**. The COVID-19 global pandemic in 2020 is significantly changing future global economic prospects, but focusing on 2019 macroeconomic conditions helps understand preceding reforms. The chapter covers trends in growth, inflation, productivity, investment, the labour market, public finances and inequality. While the chapter is largely backward looking and focused on macroeconomic trends in 2019, Box 1.1 provides an overview of the rapidly evolving macroeconomic environment given the unprecedented nature of the economic impact from the COVID-19 crisis.

## Global growth, labour market and investment trends

### *Global growth was already weak in 2019, ahead of the large economic disruptions caused by the COVID-19 pandemic and the measures taken to contain it in 2020*

**The COVID-19 pandemic, a global public health crisis without precedent in living memory, has resulted in a sharp and sudden contraction of output around the world in the first half of 2020**. To contain the spread of the virus, most governments throughout the world imposed containment measures that led to the shutdown of many sectors and significant impairment of travel and mobility. These necessary measures have succeeded in slowing the spread of infections and reducing the death toll, but have resulted in large short-term economic disruption and job losses, compounded by falling confidence and tighter financial conditions. The global economy is now experiencing the deepest recession since the Great Depression in the 1930s, with GDP declines of more than 20% in many countries during shutdowns and a surge in unemployment (Box 1.1).

#### Box 1.1. The unprecedented early impact of the COVID-19 crisis

**The COVID-19 global pandemic has led to a sudden collapse in economic activity worldwide.** The pandemic and the necessary containment measures used to limit its spread have closed down large segments of economies around the world this year, triggering sharp and sudden contractions in output, spending and employment. Global GDP is estimated to have declined by around 3% in the first quarter of 2020, even though containment and mitigation measures were introduced only during the course of March in many countries. The full impact of the shutdowns has resulted in an even larger global output decline in the second quarter of 2020, and caused large revenue losses and a severe liquidity shock for many companies. Small and medium-sized enterprises (SMEs) have been particularly affected, with many operating in the service sectors most directly impacted by shutdowns, and having limited financial buffers to cushion sharp drops in turnover.

Figure 1.1. Global activity declined abruptly in the first quarter of 2020

Percentage change in GDP, quarter-on-quarter

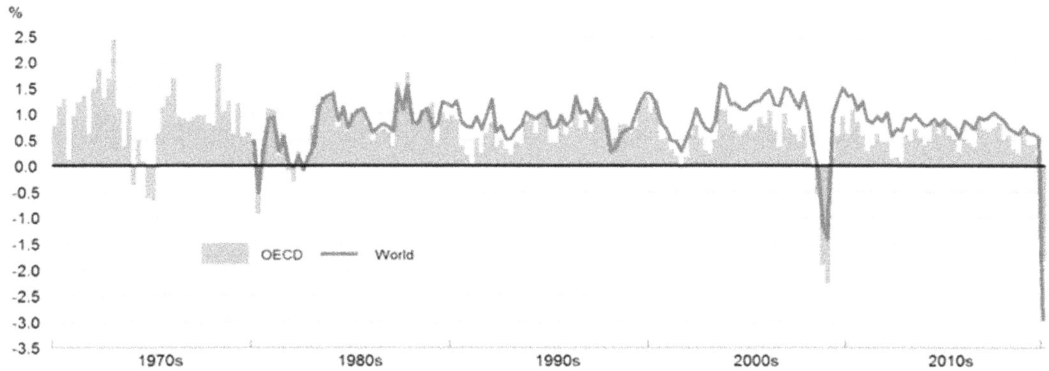


Source: OECD Economic Outlook 107 database.

StatLink https://doi.org/10.1787/888934157910

**Labour market conditions have deteriorated considerably, with unemployment claims and applications for short-time work schemes soaring, reflecting job losses and reduced work hours**. In the United States, for example, an unprecedented shock has occurred in the labour market. The unemployment rate soared, averaging 14% in April and May, the highest since the Great Depression. Extensive government-funded schemes have helped to limit the rise in unemployment in the large European economies, particularly for workers with permanent contracts, with between 20-30% of the private sector workforce being supported by short-time work or wage support schemes in the major European economies. Labour market changes have so far been less marked in Japan, reflecting differences in the timing and extent of shutdowns.

**World trade has also contracted sharply, with the volume of goods and services estimated to have fallen by 3¾ per cent in the first three months of 2020**. Aviation has been particularly hard hit, with international passenger traffic in April over 98% lower than a year earlier, and international freight traffic in April close to 30% below the level a year earlier. Disruptions to suppliers due to containment measures and the virtual cessation of international travel have added to the effects of the collapse in demand. Global export orders fell to their lowest level on record in April and remained exceptionally weak in May, with all countries reporting sizeable declines. These declines have been especially deep in Europe and some emerging-market economies, particularly India and Indonesia.

**Risk aversion in financial markets rose substantially at the beginning of the COVID-19 outbreak but has eased after prompt policy action**. The rapid spread of the pandemic and the strict containment measures adopted by governments initially prompted massive declines in financial asset prices and a spike in volatility, with some markets ceasing to function properly. In many countries, equity prices collapsed by 30-50% and at the fastest daily pace since 1987, and equity price volatility soared above the levels in the global financial crisis. Long-term government bond yields declined substantially in many advanced economies, reflecting monetary policy easing and a flight to safety, but spreads have risen on many emerging-market government bonds, amidst record high capital outflows and a substantial appreciation of the US dollar. Corporate bond spreads have also risen, particularly for the lowest rated borrowers. Rapid and sweeping responses by central banks, including through the activation of international liquidity lines, have helped to restore some stability, with a partial reversal in financial asset price moves and lower volatility.

**In most cases, governments and monetary authorities reacted remarkably quickly to the crisis, reducing the spread of the virus and preventing an even larger economic and financial collapse.** Emergency measures expanded hospital and other healthcare capacities, helped to preserve the incomes of workers and companies despite the shutdown, and guaranteed private debt on a large scale in some countries. Monetary policy has been eased, with interest rates cut, enhanced asset purchase programmes and targeted interventions in financial market segments under extreme stress. Financial policy has also been relaxed to support credit provision by financial institutions. As a result, policymakers now face exceptional challenges: government budget deficits are elevated and public debt is set to rise to exceptionally high levels in many countries, interest rates have been reduced to zero or below, and central bank balance sheets have expanded dramatically.

**The economic outlook is exceptionally uncertain**. It will depend on the evolution of the pandemic, the exit strategies from lockdown and containment measures, and the extent and impact of policy support for vulnerable sectors and workers. With the easing of the health emergency, confinement measures are being scaled back gradually. However, the recovery is likely to be hesitant, and could be interrupted by another coronavirus outbreak if targeted containment measures, notably test, track and trace (TTT) programmes, are not put in place or prove ineffective. Reflecting the unusual degree of uncertainty, the June 2020 edition of the OECD Economic Outlook presents two scenarios for each country and economy – one scenario in which a second outbreak occurs in all economies towards the end of this year and an alternative scenario where the second outbreak is avoided. In the "double-hit" scenario, global GDP is projected to decline by 7.6% this year and remain well short of its pre-crisis level at the end of 2021. In the scenario where a second outbreak is avoided, world GDP is projected to decline by 6% this year, but will have almost regained the pre-crisis level at the end of 2021. Even so, in many advanced economies, the equivalent of five years or more of per capita real income growth could be lost by 2021 (OECD, 2020[1]).

Source: (OECD, 2020[1]) OECD Economic Outlook, Volume 2020, Issue 1.

**Already, prior to the pandemic, the global outlook was becoming increasingly fragile through 2019**, with rising signs of a downturn becoming entrenched as global trade policy tensions and policy uncertainty weighed on investment, trade and output. Global GDP growth slowed further to 2.7% in 2019, from 3.4% in 2018, and remained well short of the longer-term average of 3¾ per cent seen in the two decades prior to the global financial crisis (Figure 1.2). Wage growth remained modest, despite tighter labour market conditions, checking consumer spending growth (OECD, 2019[2]). The effects of prolonged sub-par growth after the global financial crisis also continued to be reflected in subdued productivity and modest capital stock growth. Per capita GDP growth slowed in the majority of OECD economies in 2019, with the post-global financial crisis shortfalls in living standards relative to prior expectations becoming entrenched (Figure 1.3).

**The slowdown in activity was broad-based among advanced economies** (Figure 1.4). In the United States, GDP growth remained at an above-trend rate in 2019, at 2.3%, supported by solid labour markets, real wage growth and high asset prices, but rising trade tensions, waning fiscal stimulus and weaker growth in trading partners all weighed on activity and investment. GDP growth remained subdued in Japan, with the consumption tax increase in October and a series of heavy typhoons strongly affecting private domestic demand. In the euro area, GDP growth eased to 1¼ per cent in 2019, with significant policy uncertainty, including about Brexit, and export market volatility damping exports and investment (OECD, 2019[2]). The manufacturing sector was hard hit by these developments (OECD, 2019[3]) and growth in countries in which the sector represents a relatively large share of the overall activity, such as Germany and Italy, was especially affected. In Germany, the relative importance of exports and difficulties of adjusting to structural challenges in the car industry added to these factors.

**Growth also weakened in many major emerging market economies**. In China, GDP growth continued to ease slowly reflecting ongoing deleveraging efforts and escalating trade tensions with the United States. Both effects led to a sharp slowdown in Chinese import demand. Recovery in the countries strongly affected by financial turmoil in 2018 was uneven. In Turkey, growth rebounded in 2019, supported by a large fiscal and quasi-fiscal stimulus that helped strengthen private consumption. In contrast, output contracted further in Argentina, with large political uncertainty and the associated sharp depreciation of the peso weighing on domestic demand. The recovery continued in Brazil, albeit at a subdued pace with high employment falling only slowly. In Mexico, growth came to standstill as policy uncertainty and tight monetary conditions weighed on domestic demand and manufacturing activity slowed. Growth remained robust in Indonesia in 2019, but slowed in India, with stress in the shadow banking system affecting the financing of many small businesses and weighing on domestic demand.

## Figure 1.2. Real GDP growth

Year-on-year percentage changes

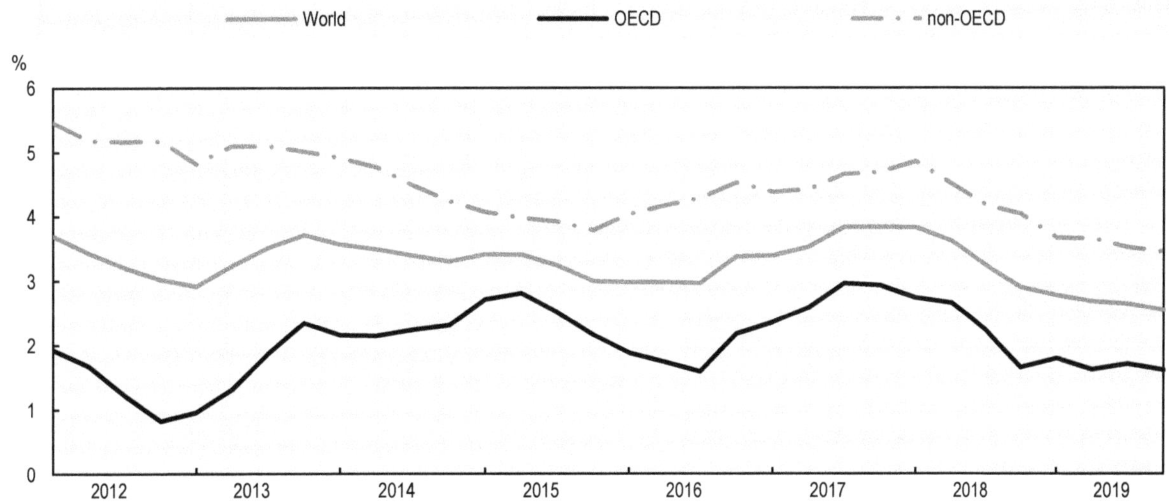


Note: GDP measured using purchasing power parities.
Source: OECD Economic Outlook database.

StatLink https://doi.org/10.1787/888934157929

## Figure 1.3. Evolution of OECD real GDP growth

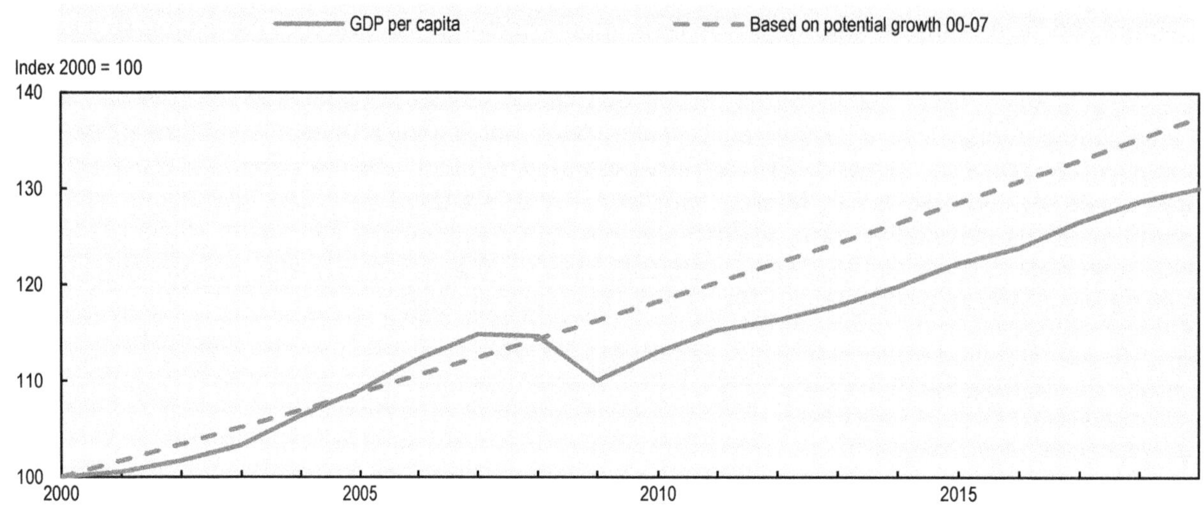


Note: The dotted line shows a linear projection based on the average annual growth rate of potential GDP per capita in the 2000-07 period.
Source: OECD Economic Outlook database; and OECD calculations.

StatLink https://doi.org/10.1787/888934157948

## Figure 1.4. Real GDP growth in OECD and selected countries

Percentage changes

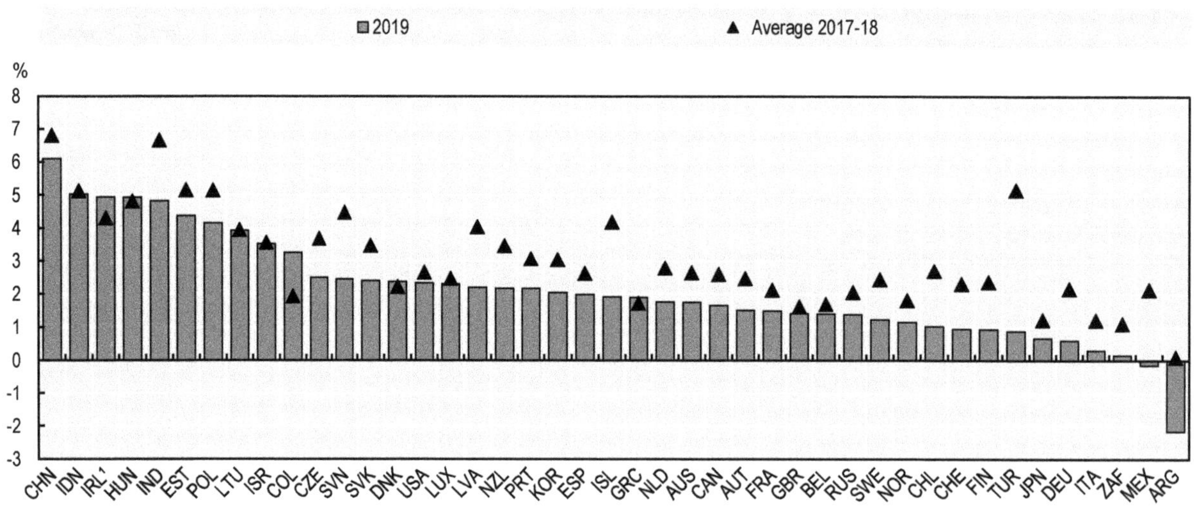


1. With growth in Ireland computed using gross value added at constant prices excluding foreign-owned multinational enterprise dominated sectors.
Source: OECD Economic Outlook database.

StatLink https://doi.org/10.1787/888934157967

### *Labour market conditions continued to improve but wage growth remained modest*

**Labour market conditions remained strong in 2019 despite moderating output growth, with record low unemployment rates** (Figure 1.5) in several OECD economies. However, some signs of easing labour market pressures became apparent towards the end of the year. In the OECD as a whole, the harmonised unemployment rate fell to 5.3% by the fourth quarter of 2019, 0.4 percentage point below the level prior to the global financial crisis and the lowest rate since 1980. Unemployment rates were below estimated longer-term sustainable rates in many economies, pointing to tight labour market conditions. However, unemployment remained high in a few countries, particularly in some euro area member countries (Figure 1.5) even after the significant declines in recent years. Employment growth slowed, especially in the United States and Japan (Figure 1.6, Panel A), hours worked started to ease and job vacancy rates started to turn down in some countries, albeit from a high level (OECD, 2019[2]). In many advanced economies, employment and labour participation rates rose above the levels prior to the global financial crisis for prime age workers (in the 25-54 age group) but remained below these levels for the youngest ones (15-24 age group).

**Long-term unemployment and the incidence of involuntary part-time employment remained elevated in some OECD economies despite declines in 2019.** Long-term unemployment (over one year) declined to represent about a quarter of total unemployment on average in the OECD economies, a level close to its pre-crisis level but it remained significantly larger in some countries, standing at 71% in Greece and 57% in Italy in 2019. The persistently high share of long-term unemployed people raises the chances of workers becoming discouraged and dropping out of the labour force. The share of involuntary part-time workers in total employment also declined in 2019, but remained above its pre-crisis level in many OECD countries. In Greece, Italy and Spain, it was still 3 to 7 percentage points above its pre-crisis level.

**Real wage growth generally remained moderate in the euro area and Japan, despite tighter labour markets but picked up in the United States where the unemployment rate fell to a fifty year low** (Figure 1.6, Panel B). In most countries, weak productivity growth and low inflation remained a drag on nominal wage developments. Longer-term factors also played a role with the spread of low-pay, non-standard jobs checking overall wage growth. In particular, there has been a significant reduction in the average earnings of part-time jobs relative to that of full-time jobs (OECD, 2018[2]; MacDonald, 2019[4]).

### Figure 1.5. Unemployment rates in OECD and selected countries

As a percentage of the labour force

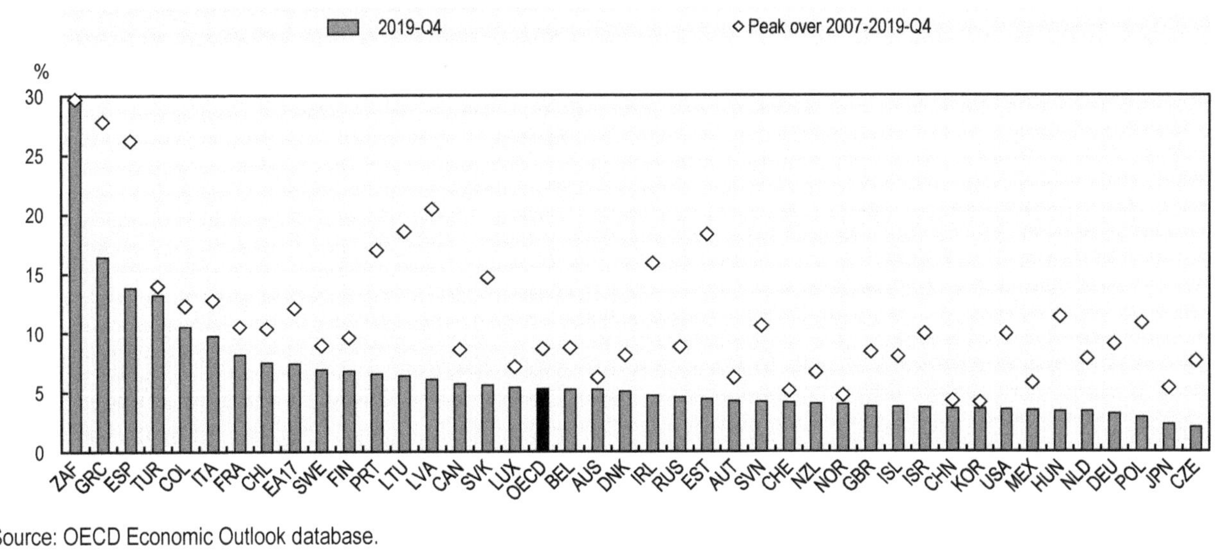


Source: OECD Economic Outlook database.

StatLink https://doi.org/10.1787/888934157986

Figure 1.6. Employment and real income growth

Year-on-year percentage changes

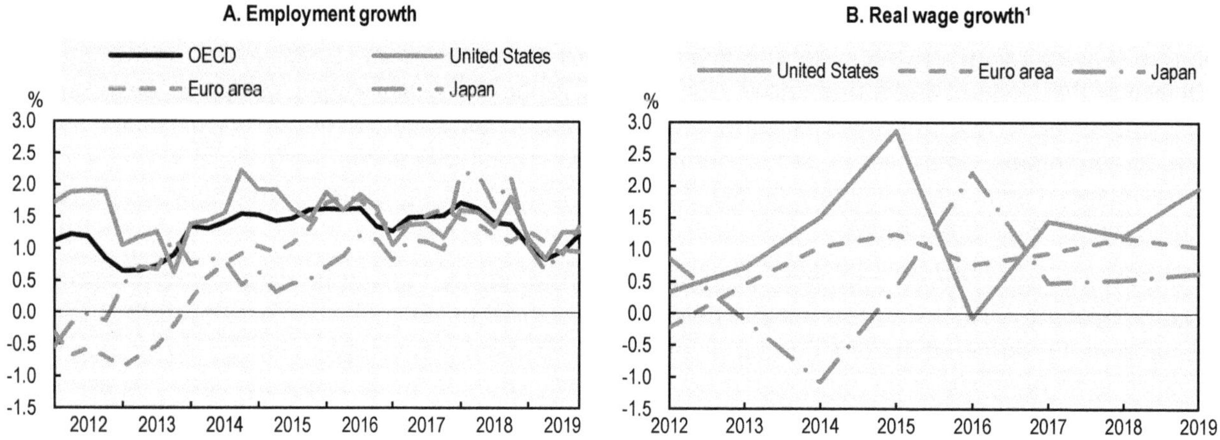


1. Labour income per employee deflated by the private consumption deflator.
Source: OECD Economic Outlook database.

StatLink https://doi.org/10.1787/888934158005

### *Subdued wage growth continued to check consumption growth and inflation in 2019*

**Private consumption growth slowed in the OECD area as a whole in 2019** (Figure 1.7, Panel A). Strong labour market outcomes, supportive financial conditions and, for some countries fiscal and regulatory measures, such as sizable increases in minimum wages in Spain, Korea, Turkey and Mexico supported household incomes. However, strong asset price growth did not result in sizeable declines in household saving ratios and soft real wage growth thus resulted in modest household spending growth in 2019 in most advanced economies. There are various possible explanations for the subdued impact of wealth effects on consumption. One possibility is that the impact of wealth effects is now much weaker than prior to the global financial crisis. This could be associated with greater wealth inequality, with wealth gains becoming more concentrated in households with a lower propensity to consume, or changes in prudential regulation that have reduced the ability of households to rising housing values as collateral for additional borrowing to finance consumption. An alternative explanation is that other factors have offset the positive effects from stronger asset prices. In particular, uncertainty about future income and employment prospects may have resulted in higher precautionary saving in some economies.

**Headline inflation eased in most OECD economies in 2019, helped by a downturn in energy price pressures** (Figure 1.7, Panel B). Oil prices declined by about 10% in 2019 to USD 64.4 per barrel on average. Supply restrictions by the Organisation of the Petroleum Exporting Countries (OPEC) and Russia, and sharp decline in production Venezuela and Iran helped to underpin prices but this effect was more than offset by weakening oil demand. In the context of moderate wage growth, underlying inflation (i.e. excluding food and energy) generally remained subdued in the major OECD economies and below official medium-term inflation objectives. In most emerging-market economies, headline inflation remained moderate as well but swine flu and adverse weather conditions kept food prices elevated in some countries, particularly in China, where annual consumer price inflation rose to 4½ per cent by the end of 2019.

Figure 1.7. Real private consumption expenditure growth and inflation

Year-on-year percentage changes

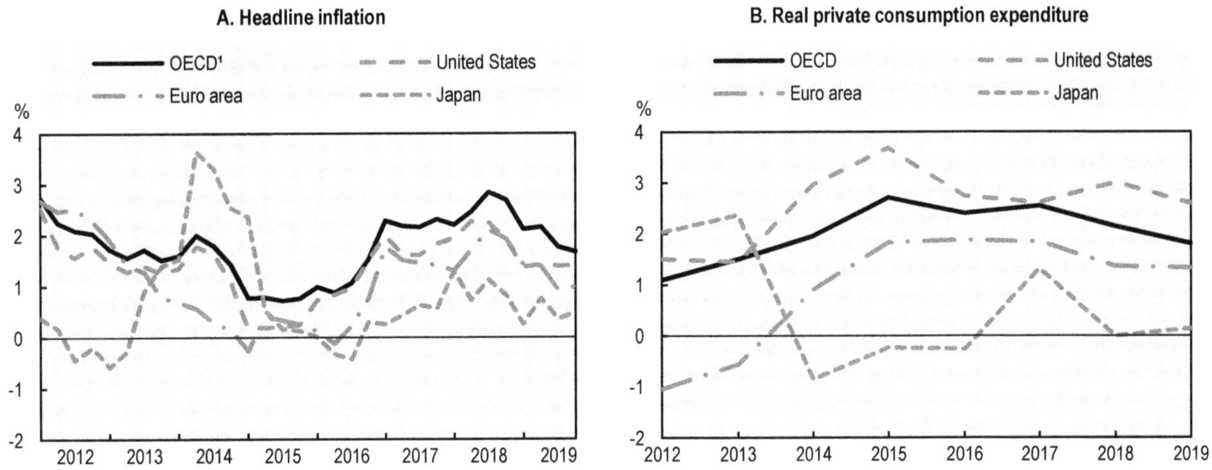


1. OECD aggregate is computed based on different indicators: United States: price index for personal consumption expenditure; euro area members and United Kingdom: harmonised index of consumer prices; and other countries: national consumer price index.
Source: OECD Economic Outlook database; and OECD calculations.

StatLink https://doi.org/10.1787/888934158024

### *Policy uncertainty and trade tensions weighed on investment and productivity growth remained low*

**Fixed capital investment slowed in most OECD economies in 2019 amid persistent trade tensions, heightened policy uncertainty and a continued decline in business confidence** (Figure 1.8). Total investment in the OECD area rose by 1.4% last year compared with 2.4% in 2018. After a decade of subdued investment, this rate remained weaker than necessary to help bring the growth of the productive capital stock back to pre-crisis levels, limiting prospects for productivity growth (OECD, 2017a). Long-term factors holding back investment include diminished long-term growth expectations and a lack of business dynamism in some economies (Calvino and Criscuolo, 2019[4]). Resources trapped in unproductive firms (Andrews, Criscuolo and Gal, 2016[5]), high corporate hurdle rates, and a slowdown in the implementation of new reforms to raise product market competition (OECD, 2019[6]) also continued to dampen investment.

**Global foreign direct investment (FDI) flows increased by 12% in 2019 (OECD, 2020c).** Nonetheless, at 1.6% of global GDP in 2019, total global FDI flows remained around 1 percentage point weaker than in 2015.[1] The 2019 rise in FDI flows was partly due to a return to positive outward FDI flows from the United States. In 2018, the end-2017 US corporate tax reform led to US parent firms repatriating earnings from foreign affiliates, resulting in large negative reinvested earnings (one component of total FDI flows) (OECD, 2020[7]). While the majority of investment policy measures taken worldwide in 2019 were designed to create more favourable conditions for both foreign and domestic investors, the usage of measures related to the screening of foreign investment for national security reasons rose (UNCTAD, 2020[8]), which may have deterred some investment. The aggregate stock of inward FDI in the OECD economies rose to a new high of 46.6% of GDP in 2019, roughly twice the size in the years immediately prior to the global financial crisis. New FDI inflows increased by 6% in 2019, largely driven by Ireland and to a lesser extent Switzerland, which both recorded negative inflows in 2018 in the aftermath of the US corporate tax reforms. In contrast, new FDI inflows declined by about 9% in the non-OECD G20 economies, notably in China.

**Labour productivity growth remained sluggish, at 0.8% in 2019 in the OECD economies,** reflecting the weak growth of productive capital per worker and the low diffusion of new ideas and technology embodied in new equipment. Labour productivity growth (output per employee) in OECD countries since the global financial crisis has generally fallen significantly below that seen in the decade prior to the crisis, checking future potential growth (Ollivaud, Guillemette and Turner, 2018[2]; Figure 1.9). Moreover, in the post-crisis period, there has been relatively weak growth in multi-factor productivity, which reflects the efficiency with which inputs are used (OECD, 2015[9]). Productivity gaps between firms have widened as frontier firms have continued to make gains but laggard firms have under-performed, contributing to rising inequality (Andrews, Criscuolo and Gal, 2016[5]). Moreover, in many countries, recent employment growth has been in activities with relatively low labour productivity, and below average wages, such as accommodation and food services, and health and residential care activities, dragging down overall labour productivity (OECD, 2019[10]). In addition to the direct drag on demand, the disruption to trade and cross-border investment and supply chains from the rise in US-China trade tensions in 2018-19 also began to harm supply and weaken medium-term growth prospects, with the induced reallocation of activities across countries and adjustment to supply chains reducing productivity. These trends, and the associated impact on wages, have led to low income growth for many households, particularly at the bottom of the income distribution, which has in turn held back aggregate consumption growth.

## Figure 1.8. Gross fixed capital formation growth in OECD countries and selected countries

Percentage changes

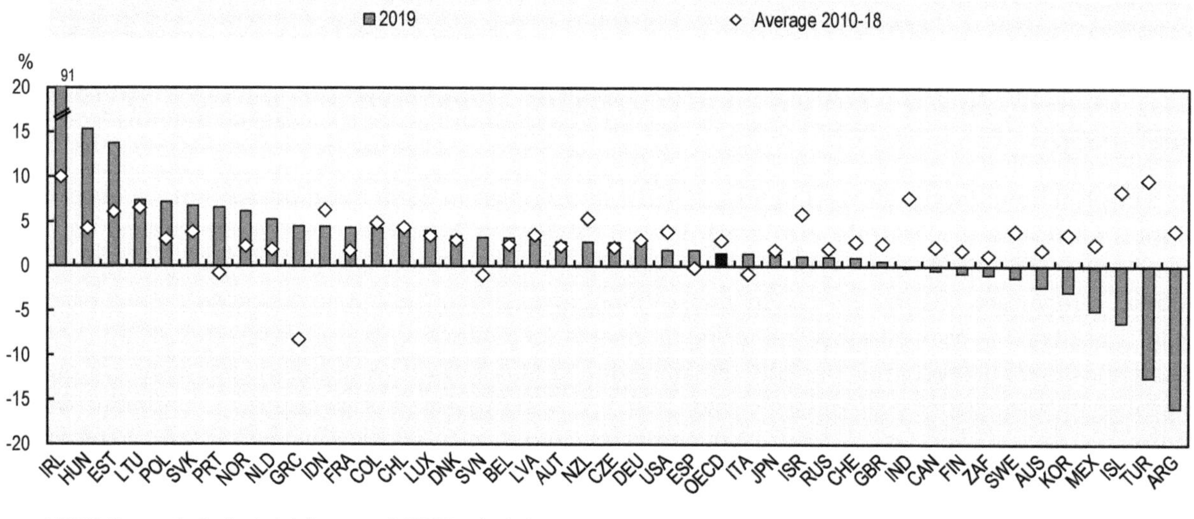


Source: OECD Economic Outlook database; and OECD calculations.

StatLink https://doi.org/10.1787/888934158043

Figure 1.9. Labour productivity in OECD countries since the global financial crisis

Percentage changes

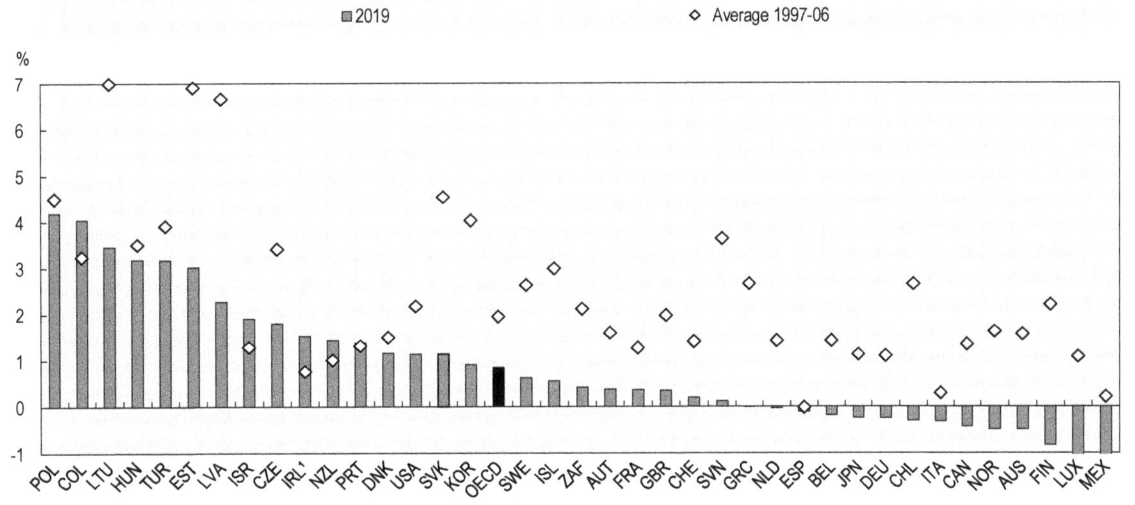


1. With growth in Ireland computed using gross value added at constant prices excluding foreign-owned multinational enterprise dominated sectors.
Source: OECD Economic Outlook database; and OECD calculations.

StatLink https://doi.org/10.1787/888934158062

## Public debt and budget balances

### *Budget balances improved and public debt ratios stabilised or declined in many countries in 2019*

**After rising rapidly in the aftermath of the global financial crisis, general government gross debt as a share of GDP has stabilised in the OECD area at a high level**. The aggregate OECD gross debt-to-GDP ratio was 110% in 2019, up from 74% in 2007 (Figure 1.10, Panel A). Across the OECD, there were wide differences in the gross debt ratio between countries in 2019, with gross general government financial liabilities (on a common national accounts definition) ranging from 13% of GDP in Estonia to an estimated 225% of GDP in Japan (Figure 1.11).

**In 2019, the overall budget deficit as a share of GDP rose for OECD economies as a whole** (Figure 1.10, Panel B) to 3.3% of GDP from 2.9% in 2018. This evolution mostly reflected a further deficit increase in the United States, to 7.3% of GDP in 2019 (from 6.7% of GDP in 2018), but deficits also rose slightly in the euro area as a whole and in Japan to respectively 0.7% of GDP and 2.6% of GDP. The overall fiscal stance, as measured by the year-on-year change in the underlying primary balance,[2] became more expansionary in 2019, by about 0.4% of GDP, in the median OECD economy. Among non-OECD G20 countries, budget deficits are also estimated to have increased in 2019, in South Africa and China but to have declined in India, Indonesia and Russia.

## Figure 1.10. General government gross debt and budget balance

As a percentage of nominal GDP

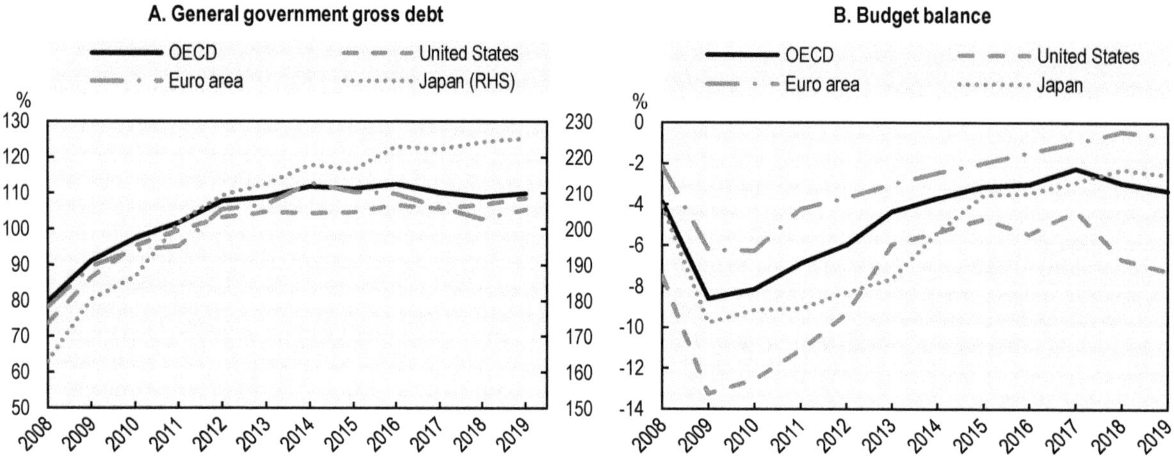


Source: OECD Economic Outlook database.

StatLink https://doi.org/10.1787/888934158081

## Figure 1.11. General government gross debt

In per cent of nominal GDP, 2019

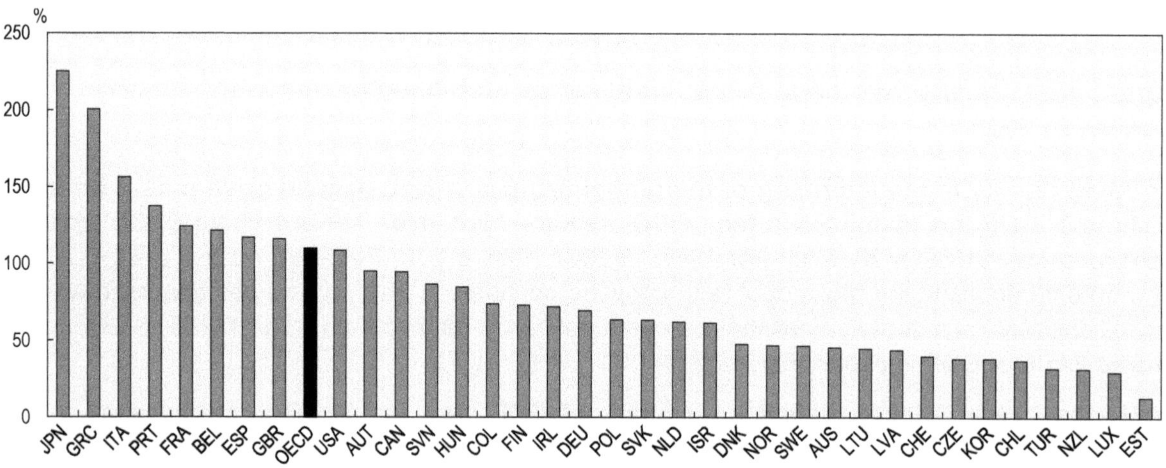


Note: These figures are from the OECD Economic Outlook Database and differ from the Maastricht definition of general government gross public debt.
Source: OECD Economic Outlook 107 database; and OECD calculations.

StatLink https://doi.org/10.1787/888934158100

Figure 1.12. General government financial balances

In per cent of nominal GDP, 2019

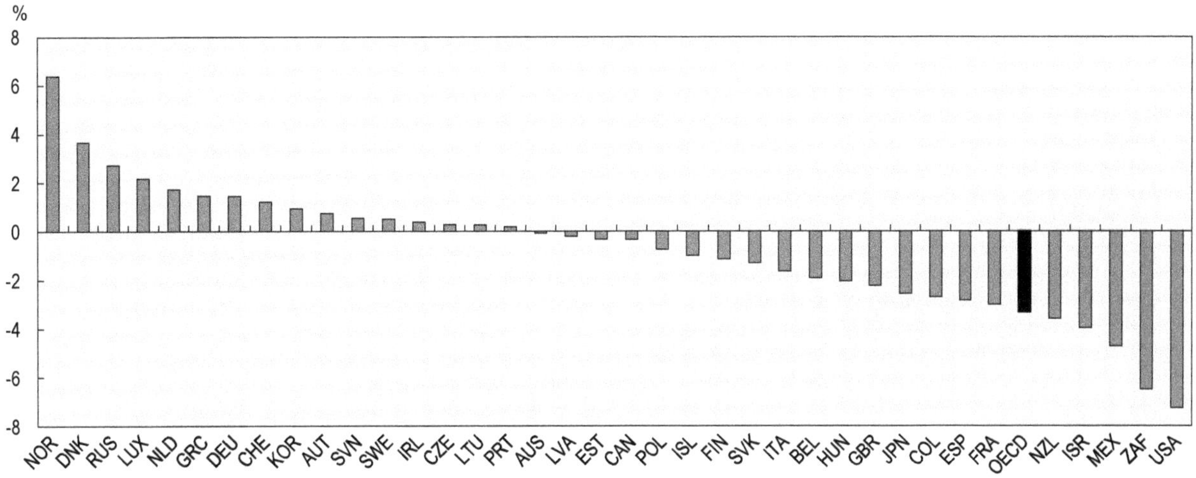


Source: OECD Economic Outlook 107 database; and OECD calculations.

StatLink https://doi.org/10.1787/888934158119

**Government bond yields declined in most economies in 2019 from already low levels.** This reflected strong demand for safer assets and expectations of monetary policy easing prompted by heightened uncertainty and a higher perceived risk of a sharp global economic slowdown. In most advanced economies, the share of outstanding government debt traded at negative yields increased further in 2019 (OECD, 2019[2]). As shown in Figure 1.13, gross government interest payments as a share of GDP generally remained below levels seen following the global financial crisis in OECD countries, despite higher debt levels, increasing fiscal space in many countries. Financial market developments varied across large emerging-market economies, but in most of them yields on long-term governments bonds in local currencies declined, helped by cuts in monetary policy interest rates. Following the severe financial shock in 2018, financial conditions improved in Turkey and interest rates declined, but the financial crisis intensified in Argentina amid increased political uncertainty.

Figure 1.13. Gross government interest payments in OECD countries and selected countries

As a percentage of nominal GDP

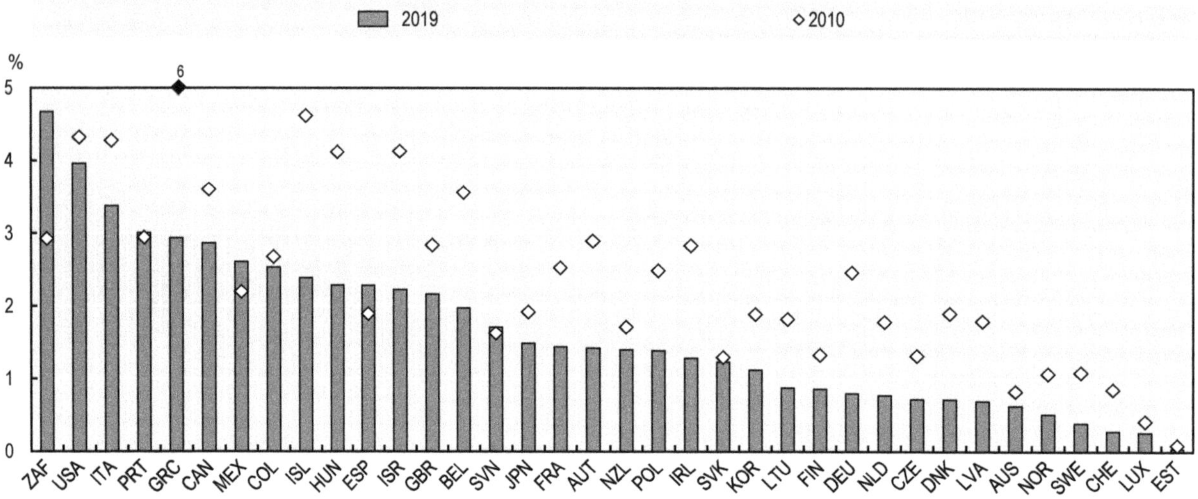


Source: OECD Economic Outlook 107 database; and OECD calculations.

StatLink https://doi.org/10.1787/888934158138

## Trends in income inequality

**Inequality in many OECD countries remained high by historical standards.** High income inequality compounds the drag on economy-wide household spending from weak income growth, as the higher-income households in which income growth has been concentrated typically have a lower marginal propensity to consume. While cross-country patterns of income inequality depend to some extent on how inequality is measured, the most widely used measure is the Gini coefficient. On this basis, inequality of market incomes (before taxes and transfers), after having increased in the aftermath of the global financial crisis, had returned to a level close to its immediate pre-crisis level in many OECD economies by end-2018 supported by strong labour market outcomes. However, inequality remained high, reflecting significant increases in most OECD economies during the three decades preceding the global financial crisis (Figure 1.14).

**Taxes reduce income inequality, but less so than transfers**: on average, over two-thirds of the reduction in inequality is due to transfers and the remaining portion is due to taxes (Figure 1.15). There are considerable differences across countries, however, with the highest redistribution in Finland and the weakest in Mexico. The impact of redistribution is even higher if non-cash transfers from governments, such as education and healthcare, are taken into account (OECD, 2016[11]). After adjusting for the impact of redistributive policies, around two third of the 28 countries for which data is available had returned to levels of disposable income inequality by 2018 that are similar or lower than immediate pre-crisis levels but inequality remained, in most cases, higher than three decades ago (Figure 1.16). The extent of redistribution via taxes and transfers has declined in many OECD countries since 2010, in part reflecting some reduction in transfers as part of post-crisis fiscal consolidation and the reduced progressivity of tax systems. In around half of the major emerging market economies, including Brazil, South Africa and China, disposable income inequality has decreased or levelled off since the mid-2000s (Balestra et al., 2018[2]). On the other hand, it has increased in India, Indonesia and Russia and generally, disposable income inequalities remained significantly larger in emerging-market economies than in the OECD countries (OECD, 2019[6]).

**Many households have seen little growth, if any, in real disposable incomes over the past decade.** Across the income distribution, some specific segments of the population may have been affected by the growing share of non-standard jobs, such as part-time work, temporary work or self-employment. Such jobs are more likely to be occupied by women and youth and pay on average less, on an hourly basis, than permanent jobs. They are also associated with poorer job quality (OECD, 2015[12]).

## Figure 1.14. Market income, Gini Coefficients

Total population

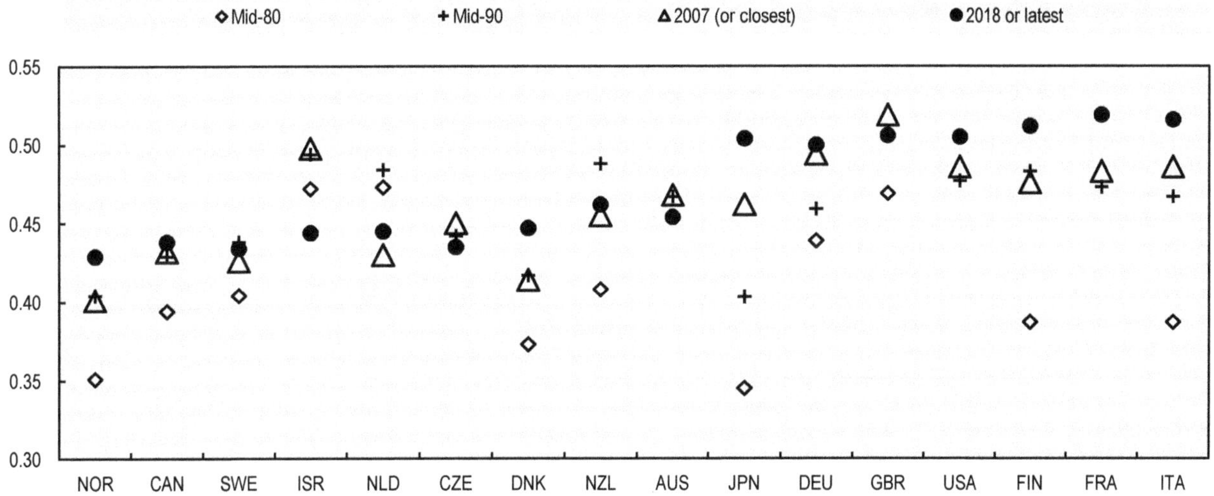


1. Mid-80 data not available/missing. There is a break in income definition starting in 2012 with all new data following the new OECD terms of reference after 2011. Compared to previous terms of reference, these include a more detail breakdown of current transfers received and paid by households as well as a revised definition of household income, including the value of goods produced for own consumption as an element of self-employed income.
Source: OECD Income Distribution Database (IDD).

StatLink https://doi.org/10.1787/888934158157

## Figure 1.15. Market income, post-transfer and disposable income Gini coefficients

2018 or latest, for total population

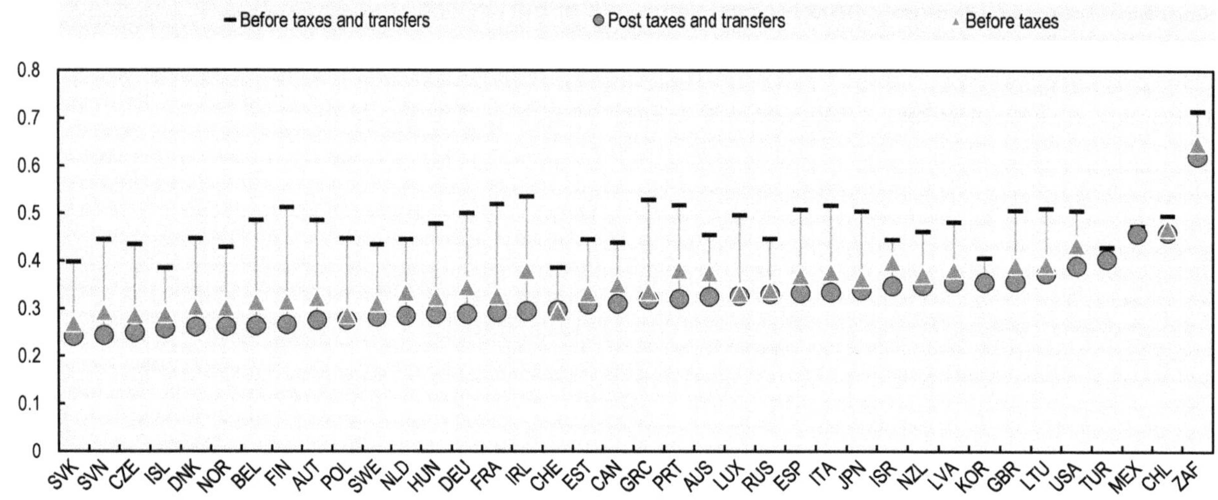


Source: OECD Income Distribution database (IDD); and OECD calculations.

StatLink https://doi.org/10.1787/888934158176

## Figure 1.16. Post taxes and transfers disposable income Gini coefficients

Total population

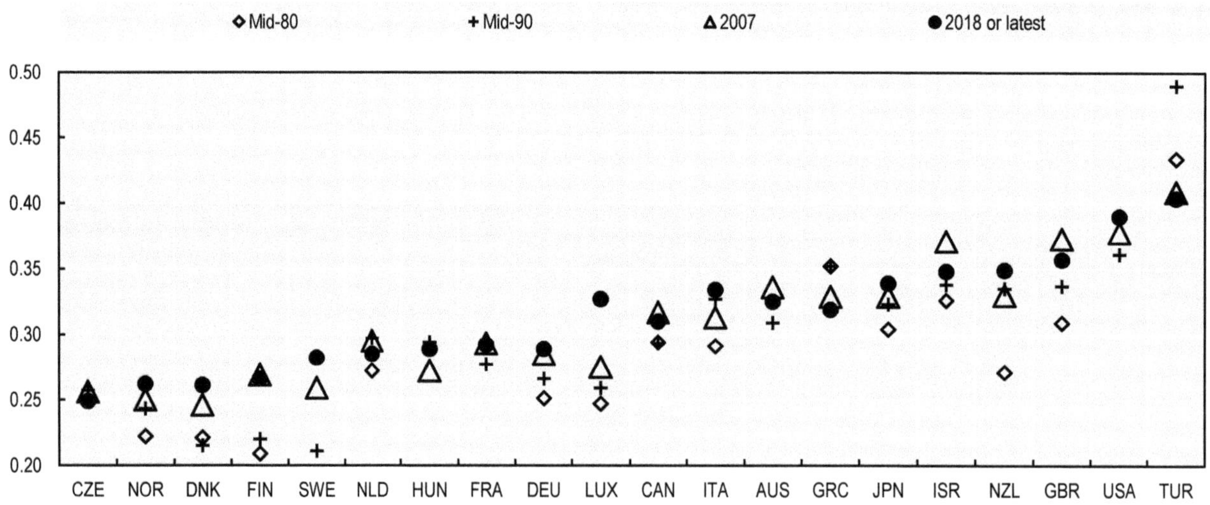


Note: There is a break in income definition starting in 2012 with all new data following the new OECD terms of reference after 2011. Compared to previous terms of reference, these include a more detail breakdown of current transfers received and paid by households as well as a revised definition of household income, including the value of goods produced for own consumption as an element of self-employed income.
Source: OECD Income Distribution Database (IDD).

StatLink https://doi.org/10.1787/888934158195

## References


Andrews, D., C. Criscuolo and P. Gal (2016), "The Global Productivity Slowdown, Technology Divergence and Public Policy: A Firm Level Perspective", *The Future of Productivity: Main Background Papers*. [5]

Calvino, F. and C. Criscuolo (2019), "Business dynamics and digitalisation", *OECD Science, Technology and Industry Policy Papers* No. 62, https://doi.org/10.1787/6e0b011a-en. [4]

OECD (2020), *FDI In Figures: April 2020*, OECD Publishing, http://www.oecd.org/investment/FDI-in-Figures-April-2020.pdf. [7]

OECD (2020), *OECD Economic Outlook, Volume 2020 Issue 1*, OECD Publishing, Paris, https://dx.doi.org/10.1787/0d1d1e2e-en. [1]

OECD (2019), *Economic Policy Reforms 2019: Going for Growth*, OECD Publishing, Paris, https://dx.doi.org/10.1787/aec5b059-en. [6]

OECD (2019), *OECD Compendium of Productivity Indicators 2019*, OECD Publishing. [10]

OECD (2019), *OECD Economic Outlook, Volume 2019 Issue 1*, OECD Publishing, Paris, https://dx.doi.org/10.1787/b2e897b0-en. [3]

OECD (2019), *OECD Economic Outlook, Volume 2019 Issue 2*, OECD Publishing, Paris, https://dx.doi.org/10.1787/9b89401b-en. [2]

OECD (2016), *Income inequality update*, https://www.oecd.org/social/OECD2016-Income-Inequality-Update.pdf (accessed on 17 July 2019). [11]

OECD (2015), *In It Together: Why Less Inequality Benefits All*, OECD Publishing, Paris, https://dx.doi.org/10.1787/9789264235120-en. [12]

OECD (2015), *The Future of Productivity*, OECD Publishing, Paris, https://dx.doi.org/10.1787/9789264248533-en. [9]

UNCTAD (2020), *Investment Policy Monitor*, https://unctad.org/en/PublicationsLibrary/diaepcbinf2020d3_en.pdf. [8]


## Notes

[1] Global FDI flows refer to the average of inward and outward FDI flows worldwide. In theory, global inward and outward FDI flows and stocks should be equal but in practice, there are statistical discrepancies between them.

[2] The underlying primary balance is the fiscal balance excluding net interest payments and adjusted for the economic cycle and for budgetary one-offs.

# 2 Tax revenue trends

This chapter describes the latest tax revenue trends, analysing both total tax-to-GDP ratios and tax structures over time and across OECD countries as well as in Argentina, Indonesia and South Africa. The analysis covers tax revenue trends until 2018, the last year for which comparable tax revenue data from the OECD Global Revenue Statistics Database is available.

**This chapter describes the latest tax revenue trends, analysing both total tax-to-GDP ratios and tax structures over time and across OECD countries as well as in Argentina, Indonesia and South Africa.**[1] The analysis covers tax revenue trends until 2018, the last year for which comparable tax revenue data from the OECD Global Revenue Statistics Database (Box 2.1) are available.[2] This overview provides useful background to the subsequent discussion on countries' latest tax reforms (Chapter 3) and partly reflects the effects of past reforms discussed in earlier editions of this annual publication.

**Overall, this chapter shows that on average tax revenues reached a plateau in 2018, with almost no increase relative to 2017.** This ends the trend of annual increases in the average OECD tax-to-GDP ratio since the global financial crisis in 2008. Over time, countries' tax-to-GDP ratios have converged closer to the OECD average, showing greater similarity in the level of tax revenues across countries and greater convergence towards an overall higher level of taxation. This chapter also identifies trends in tax structures and shows that, while on average tax levels have generally been rising, the composition of tax revenues on average across countries has remained relatively stable over time.

## Trends in tax revenue levels

### *Tax revenues vary across countries*

**Tax revenues varied significantly across the countries covered in the report, ranging from just above 10% to more than 45% of GDP in 2018**. Consistent with tax revenues in 2017, France was the country with the highest tax-to-GDP ratio in 2018 with tax revenues amounting to 46.1% of its GDP (a slight decrease from 46.2% in 2017) followed by Denmark and Belgium with tax-to-GDP ratios of 44.9%. On the other hand, and consistent with the last ten years of data, the countries with the lowest tax-to-GDP ratios in 2018 were Indonesia, with total tax revenues amounting to 11.9% of its GDP, followed by Mexico (16.1%) and Chile (21.1%). In Chile, however, the majority of social contributions are paid into privately managed funds and are not included in the tax-to-GDP ratio[3] (Figure 2.1).

Figure 2.1. Tax revenues as a share of GDP by country in 2018

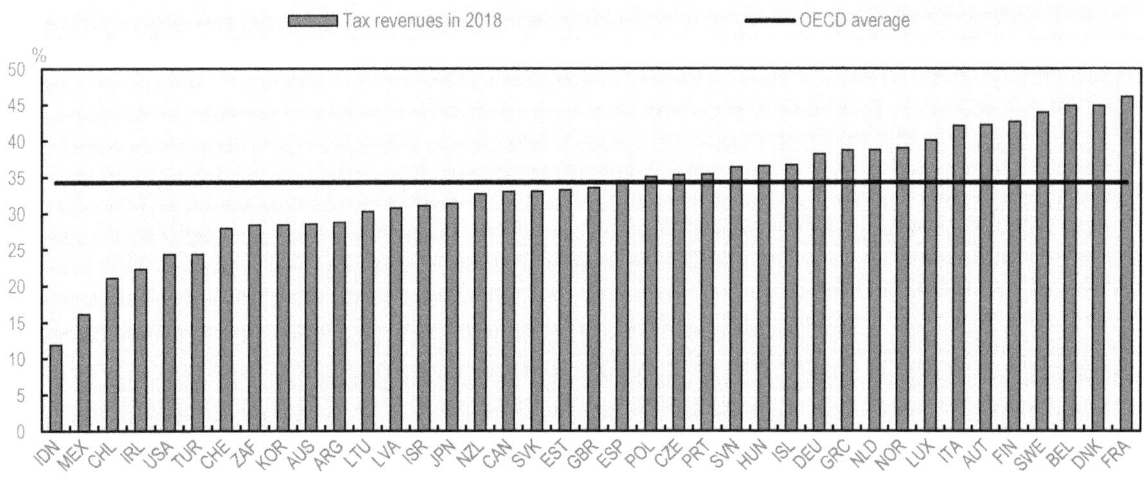


Note: For Australia, Japan and South Africa, 2017 data is used. Korea has revised its GDP figures and expects a decrease in tax-to-GDP ratios for 2017 and 2018 compared to the figures included in the 2019 edition of *OECD Revenue Statistics*.
Source: OECD Global Revenue Statistics Database.

StatLink https://doi.org/10.1787/888934158233

**Despite the wide range of tax-to-GDP ratios, there is a relatively high concentration of countries with tax-to-GDP ratios around the OECD average**. On average across OECD countries, tax revenues amounted to 34.3% of GDP in 2018 (Figure 2.1). Figure 2.2 shows a high concentration of countries that have tax revenues close to that level with 10 countries recording tax revenues between 30% and 35% of GDP and another 10 countries with tax revenues ranging from 35% to 40% of GDP. Spain, the United Kingdom and Poland were the countries closest to the OECD average. A number of countries recorded tax-to-GDP ratios further away from the OECD average: 11 had tax-to-GDP ratios below 30% and eight recorded tax revenues above 40% of GDP.

### Figure 2.2. Distribution of tax-to-GDP ratios in 2018

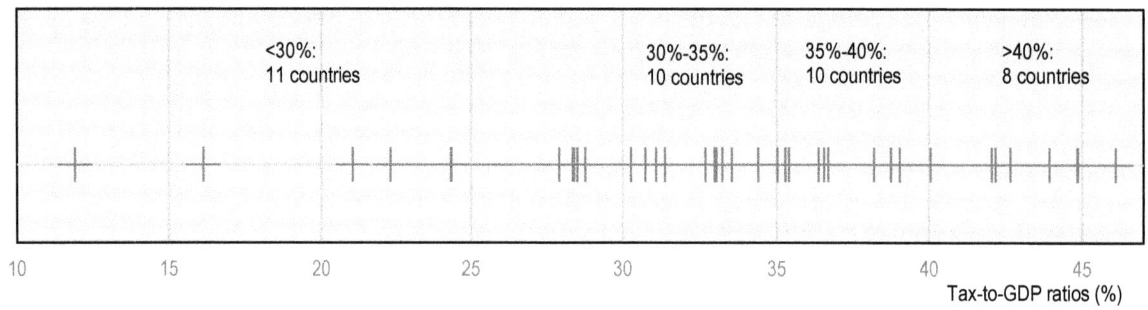


Note: Each + represents the tax-to-GDP ratio of a country in 2018 (2017 for Australia, Japan and South Africa).
Source: OECD Global Revenue Statistics Database, based on "Special feature: Convergence of tax levels and tax structures in OECD countries", in (OECD, 2018[1]).

StatLink https://doi.org/10.1787/888934158252

### Box 2.1. The OECD Global Revenue Statistics Database

The Global Revenue Statistics Database provides the world's largest public source of harmonised tax revenue data, verified by countries and regional partners. Spanning more than 100 countries in all corners of the world, the database provides a rich and accessible resource for policymakers and researchers, based on the internationally recognised OECD standard. It allows comparisons of the tax burden in these countries, measured by the tax-to-GDP ratio, as well as of the tax mix, i.e. the distribution of total tax revenues by the main types of taxes. The database presents tax revenue data in national currency and USD, and also provides information on the share of tax revenues attributed to different levels of government.

Domestic revenues are critical to efforts to fund sustainable development and to implement the Sustainable Development Goals. The database supports these efforts by measuring progress on domestic resource mobilisation, building statistical capability, and providing country-specific indicators as called for in SDG 17, in the Addis Ababa Action Agenda and by more than 55 countries and international organisations in the Addis Tax Initiative.

The database shows that countries have made strong progress toward mobilising domestic financing for development in the 21st century. Tax revenues are now higher as a percentage of GDP and their levels are more evenly distributed across countries than they were at the turn of the century. With few exceptions, the countries that recorded the lowest level of tax revenues in 2000 have increased their revenues the most.

The Global Revenue Statistics Database is updated several times a year with the latest available data from the regional Revenue Statistics publications, which cover African, Asian and Pacific, Latin American and Caribbean and OECD countries.

Access the database here: https://www.oecd.org/tax/tax-policy/global-revenue-statistics-database.htm.

**Since 2000, the concentration of countries with high tax-to-GDP ratios has increased, shifting the distribution of countries' tax revenues to the right** (Figure 2.3). Between 2000 and 2018, the number of countries with tax revenues between 35% and 40% of GDP increased from six to ten. On the other hand, the number of countries with tax-to-GDP ratios between 30% and 35% decreased from 15 in 2000 to 11 in 2018. Eight countries had tax revenues above 40% of GDP in both 2000 and 2018.

Figure 2.3. Change in the distribution of tax-to-GDP ratios from 2000 to 2018

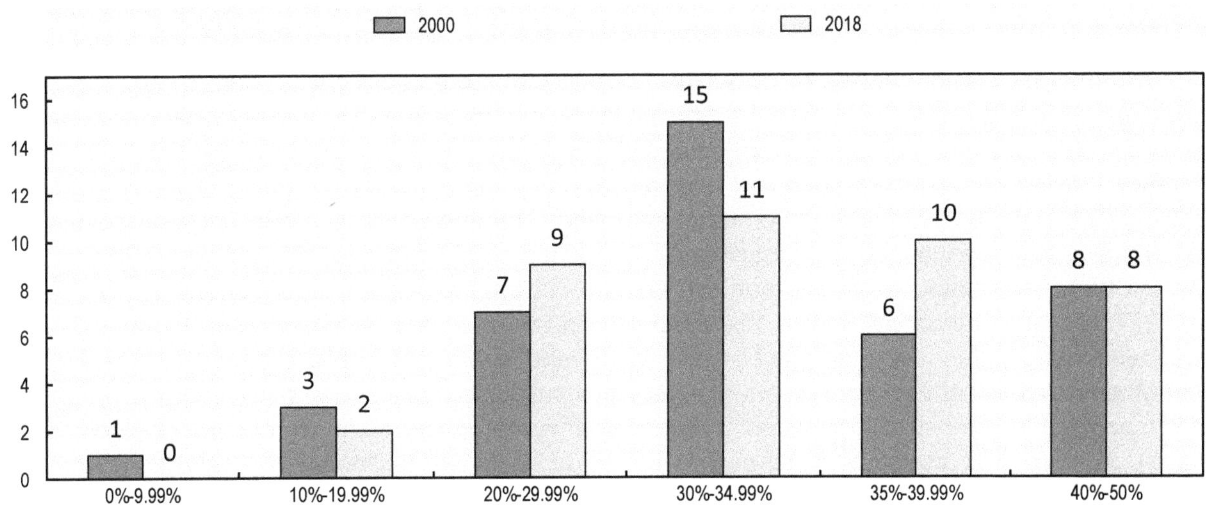


Note: The columns for 2018 are calculated with data from 2017 for Australia, Japan and South Africa.
Source: OECD Global Revenue Statistics Database.

StatLink https://doi.org/10.1787/888934158271

**As discussed in previous editions of this report, there is a positive correlation between tax-to-GDP ratios and GDP per capita levels**. Countries with lower levels of GDP per capita tend to have lower tax-to-GDP ratios (e.g. Argentina, Chile, Indonesia, Mexico, South Africa and Turkey), while high GDP per capita countries tend to have higher tax revenues as a share of their GDP (e.g. Scandinavian countries, Austria, Belgium and France) (Figure 2.4). Outliers include the United States, Switzerland and Ireland, which all have GDP per capita levels far above the average but below average tax-to-GDP ratios. There are also countries with below-average levels of GDP per capita but relatively high tax revenues as a share of GDP (e.g. some Central and Southern European countries like Greece, Hungary and Portugal). Figure 2.4 also shows that levels of tax-to-GDP ratios follow regional patterns.

## Figure 2.4. Tax revenues as a share of GDP and GDP per capita in 2018

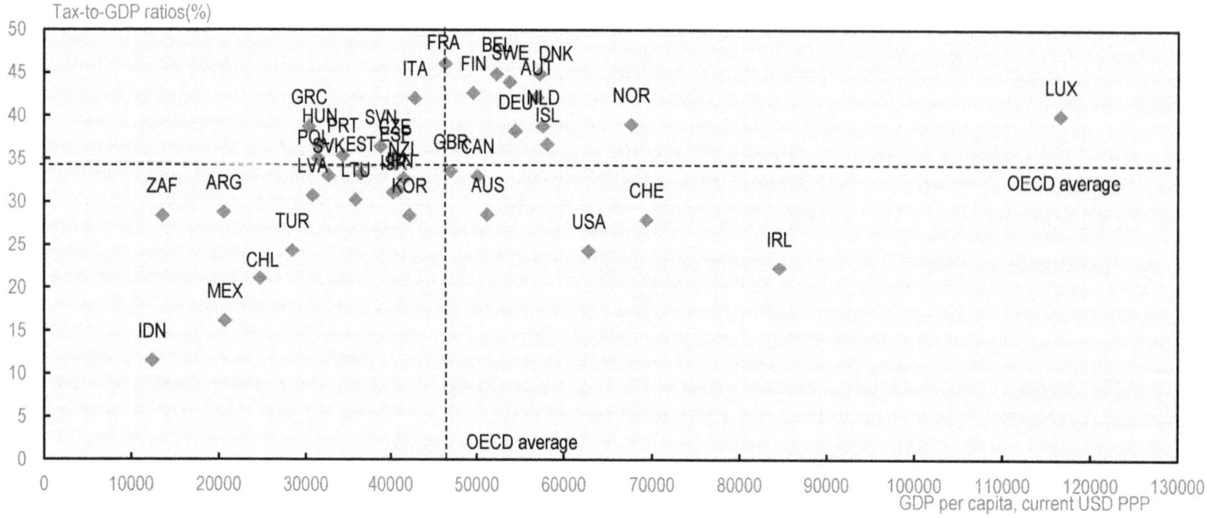


Note: For Australia, Indonesia, Japan and South Africa, 2017 data is used.
Source: OECD Global Revenue Statistics Database and OECD National Accounts Statistics.

StatLink https://doi.org/10.1787/888934158290

**Tax revenues are closely linked to countries' public expenditure levels.** Unsurprisingly, Figure 2.4 shows that there is a close link between countries' levels of public spending and their tax revenues as a share of GDP. Luxembourg, the Netherlands and Korea are the countries with the smallest relative difference between government spending and tax revenues, respectively collecting taxes amounting to 95.5%, 92.2% and 90.2% of total government spending. The largest relative gap between government spending and tax revenues, on the other hand, was observed in the United States, where the revenue collected from taxes amounts to less than two thirds (64.1%) of total government spending, followed by Israel (77.1%) and Hungary (78.3%). The level of non-tax revenues, also shown in Figure 2.5, helps understand the extent to which the gap between tax revenues and total public expenditure is financed by either other sources of government revenue or debt. In some countries, the gap between tax revenues and public spending is almost fully financed by other sources of government revenues (e.g. Finland and Poland), while in other countries a big portion of the gap between tax revenues and total government spending is financed through debt (e.g. United States). Finally, in some countries, total revenues exceed total public expenditure (e.g. Norway, Korea).

Figure 2.5. Tax revenues, total government revenues and total government spending as a share of GDP in 2018

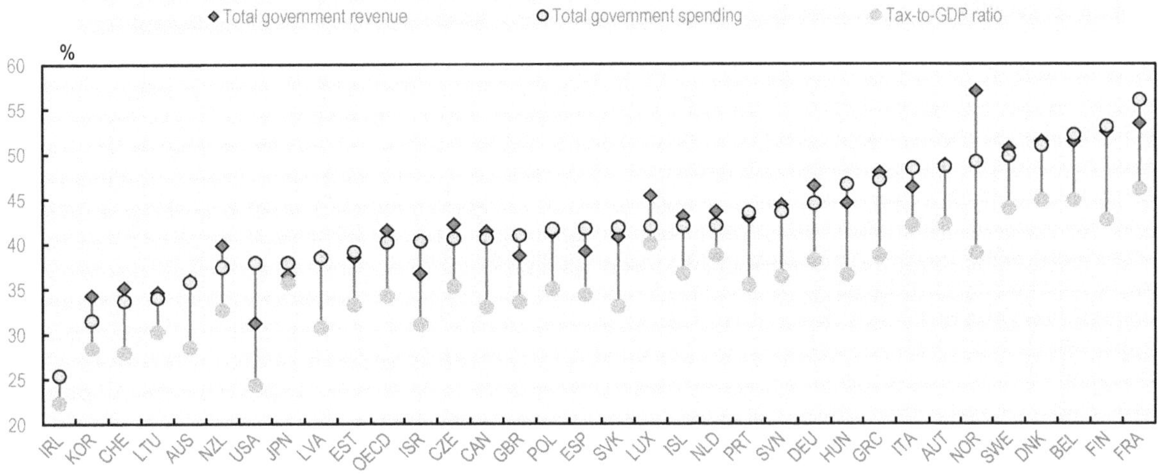


Note: No data on government spending for Argentina, Chile, Indonesia, Mexico, South Africa and Turkey; 2017 data used for Australia and Japan.
Source: OECD Global Revenue Statistics Database and OECD Economic Outlook 106 Database

StatLink https://doi.org/10.1787/888934158309

### *Recent tax revenue trends have differed across countries*

**Between 2017 and 2018, a majority of countries experienced an increase in their tax-to-GDP ratios.** 19 of the 35 countries for which 2018 data is available recorded an increase in their tax revenues as a share of GDP (Figure 2.6Figure 2.6). Between 2017 and 2018, Korea saw the largest tax-to-GDP ratio increase (1.52 percentage points) followed by Luxembourg, Chile and Portugal, which all experienced increases of close to 1 percentage point or more. For Korea, the increase in revenues was the largest it has recorded since 2000, when its tax-to-GDP ratio increased by 1.74 percentage points. The large increase in 2018 may partly reflect higher than expected earnings from stronger semiconductor sales.[4] Tax revenues in Korea have been increasing for the last five years (2014-2018) and Luxembourg's tax-to-GDP ratio has seen increases for the last three years (2016-2018) (OECD, 2019[2]). In all of the 19 countries that saw their tax-to-GDP ratio increase, nominal GDP growth and nominal tax revenue growth were positive (Figure 2.7).

Figure 2.6. Percentage point changes in tax-to-GDP ratios by country between 2017 and 2018

Changes in tax-to-GDP ratios decomposed by type of tax

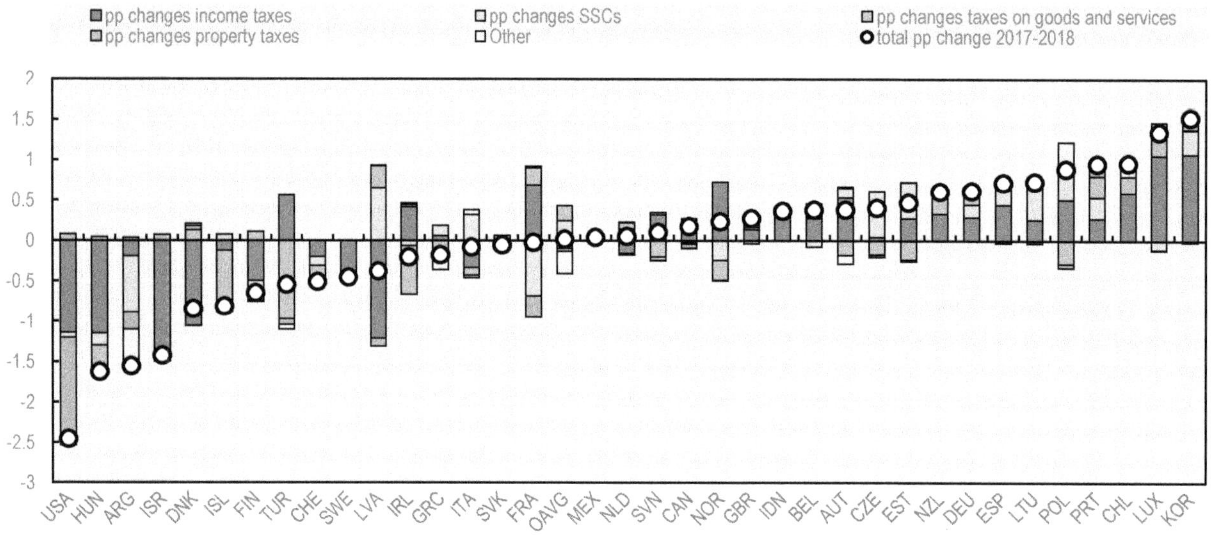


Note: No 2018 data for Australia Japan and South Africa
Source: OECD Global Revenue Statistics Database.

StatLink https://doi.org/10.1787/888934158328

**On the other hand, 16 countries experienced a decrease in their tax-to-GDP ratios in 2018 relative to 2017.** The largest tax revenue fall was recorded by the United States (2.5 percentage points) followed by Hungary (1.6 percentage points) and Israel (1.4 percentage points) (Figure 2.6). The decrease in the United States was due to the tax reforms implemented in the Tax Cuts and Jobs Act, which lowered the corporate tax rate in 2018 and also reduced the tax wedge on labour income via reductions to income tax rates and increases in the standard deduction and the child tax credit. These changes led to a 1.1 percentage point decrease in income taxation. In addition, there was a decrease in property tax revenues of 1.3 percentage points, due to the one-off deemed repatriation tax on foreign earnings under the Tax Cuts and Jobs Act, which increased property tax revenues in 2017. The decrease in Hungary was, among other things, due to a reduction in employers' SSCs rates from 22% in 2017 to 19.5% in 2018, a reduction of corporate income taxes to 9% in 2017 and a decrease in the VAT rate on selected products in 2018 (OECD, 2019[3]) (OECD, 2018[4]). In Argentina, the reduction in revenues was partly a product of a 2017 tax reform aimed at reducing distortive taxes and the tax wedge for low-income earners (OECD, 2019[5]). In Israel, the fall was driven, in part, by a temporary cut in dividend taxation from 33% to 25% for shareholders of personal service corporations, which encouraged the distribution of past retained earnings and led to a spike in revenues in 2017 and a corresponding drop in 2018 (OECD, 2018[6]). Of the 16 countries that saw their tax-to-GDP ratios decrease, only two (the United States and Israel) had negative tax revenue growth and all had positive GDP growth (Figure 2.7).

**Figure 2.7. Changes in nominal tax revenues and nominal GDP between 2017 and 2018**

Relative changes in %

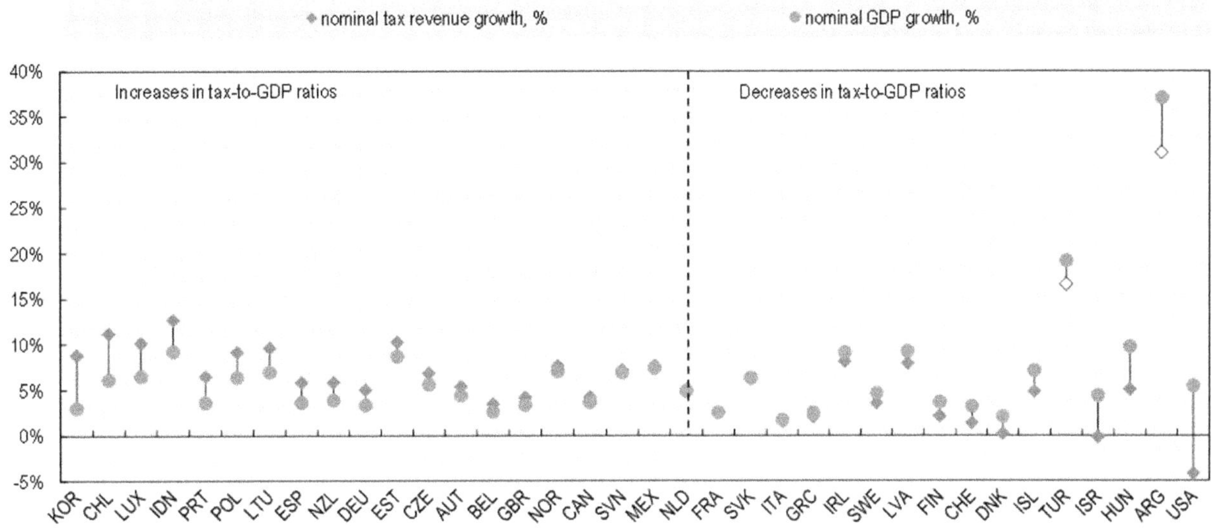


Note: No data for Australia, Japan and South Africa.
Source: OECD and Global Revenue Statistics databases.

StatLink https://doi.org/10.1787/888934158347

**Figure 2.8. Percentage point changes in tax-to-GDP ratios by country between 2008 and 2018**

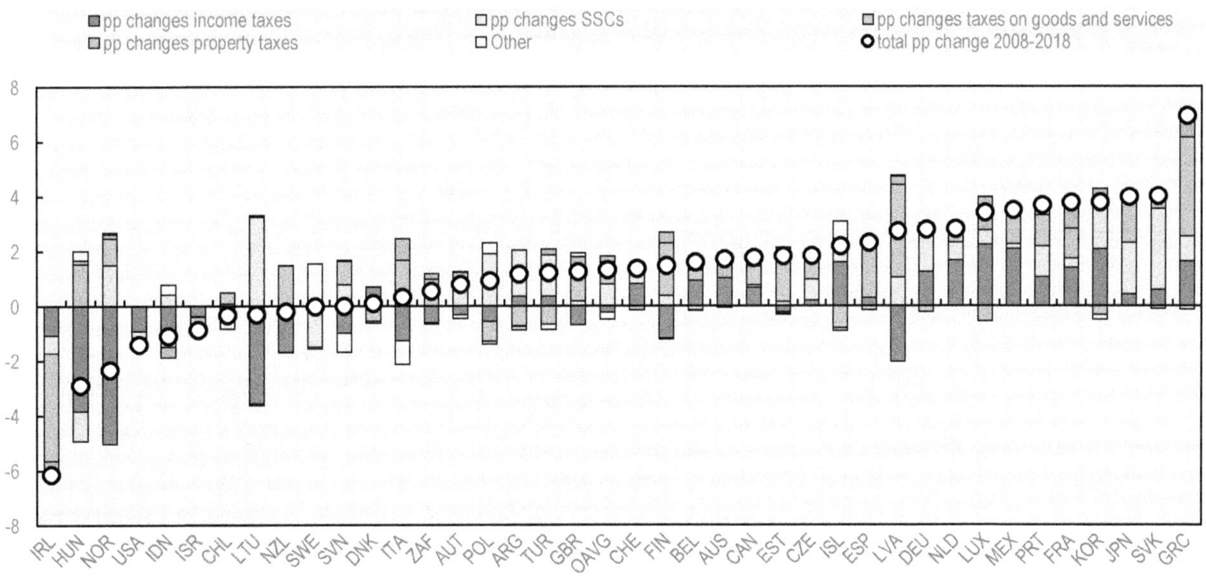


Note: Percentage point changes between 2008 and 2017 for Australia, Japan, Mexico and South Africa.
Source: OECD Global Revenue Statistics Database.

StatLink https://doi.org/10.1787/888934158366

**Looking at longer-term trends, tax-to-GDP levels are now higher than in 2008 in 28 out of 39 countries** (Figure 2.8). The largest increase over this period was recorded in Greece (6.94 percentage points). Seven other countries (the Slovak Republic, Japan, Korea, France, Portugal, Mexico and Luxembourg) experienced tax ratio increases of at least three percentage points over the same period. On the other hand, only 11 countries had lower tax-to-GDP ratios in 2018 than in 2008. The biggest fall was seen in Ireland, where revenues fell by 6.1 percentage points (from 28.5 in 2008 to 22.3 in 2018) largely due to the exceptional increase in GDP in 2015.[5] The second largest fall (2.9 percentage points) occurred in Hungary, from 39.5% in 2008 to 36.6% in 2018.

### *Tax-to-GDP ratios have converged towards higher levels over time*

**Looking at OECD countries, the average tax-to-GDP ratio has reached a plateau in 2018.** For the first time since the financial crisis in 2008 average tax revenues as a share of GDP in the OECD remained effectively unchanged in 2018. The slowing in the growth of the OECD average was predominantly driven by the impact of the significant fall in the tax-to-GDP ratio of the United States as a result of their tax reforms (OECD, 2019[2]). The average tax revenue as a share of GDP in 2018 continued to be the highest ever recorded since the OECD started collecting tax revenue data in 1965 (Figure 2.9).

Figure 2.9. Evolution of the OECD average tax-to-GDP ratio since 1965

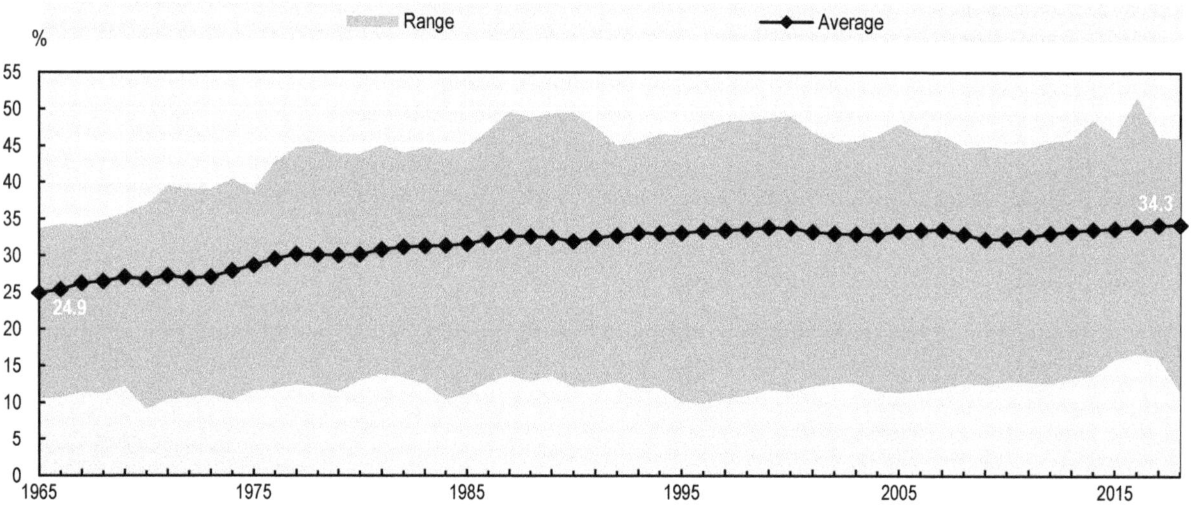


Source: OECD Revenue Statistics Database.

StatLink https://doi.org/10.1787/888934158423

**The median tax-to-GDP ratio has steadily increased over time and tax revenues as a share of GDP have gradually converged since 1990**. Accounting only for countries for which data since 1990 was available, Figure 2.10 shows that countries' tax-to-GDP ratios have gradually converged towards higher levels. In 2018, the median tax-to-GDP ratio reached a record level of 34.4% compared to 32.4% in 1990. The first and third quartile in 2018 were 28.4% and 40.1% respectively. In 1990, on the other hand, the range between the first and third quartile (25.2% and 39.3% respectively) was larger.

Figure 2.10. Dispersion box plots of tax-to-GDP ratios between 1990 and 2018

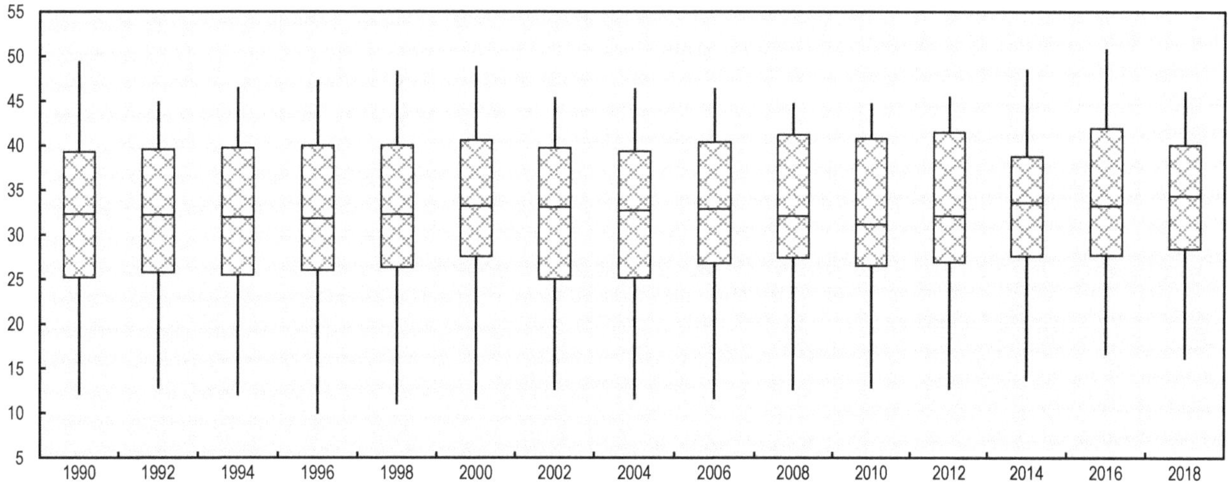


Note: Excludes countries for which there was missing data between 1990 and 2000: The Czech Republic, Estonia, Hungary, Indonesia, Israel, Lithuania, Latvia, Poland, Slovakia, and Slovenia. The box plot for 2018 includes data from 2017 for Australia, Japan, and South Africa.
Source: OECD Global Revenue Statistics.

StatLink https://doi.org/10.1787/888934158385

Figure 2.11. Evolution of tax-to-GDP ratios in low-, mid- and high-tax countries since 1990

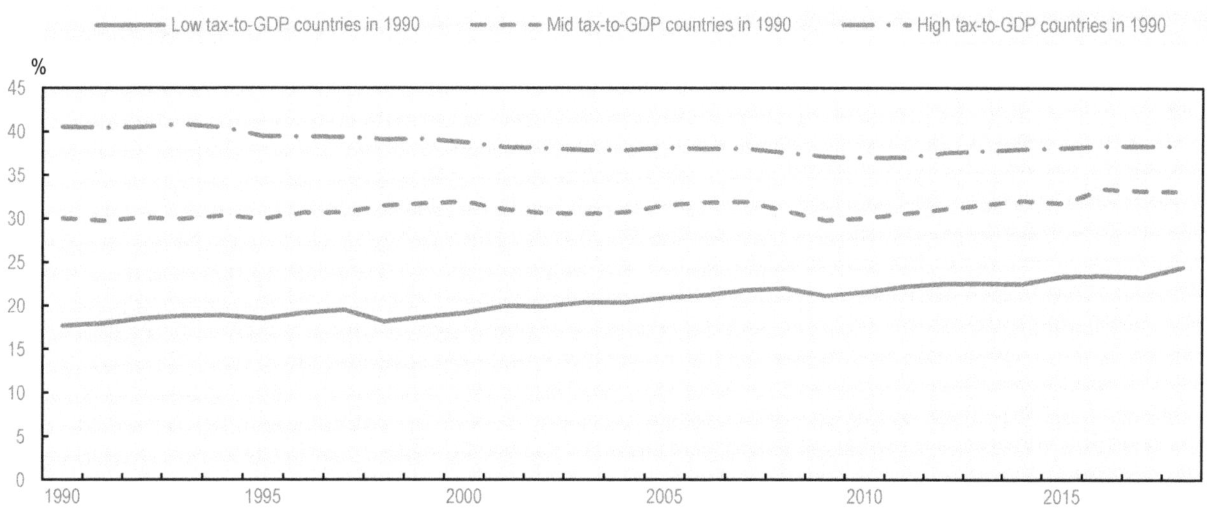


Note: Low tax-to-GDP ratio countries include all the countries covered in the report that had tax-to-GDP ratios below 25% in 1990 (8 countries); mid tax-to-GDP ratio countries include all the countries that had tax-to-GDP ratios between 25% and 35% in 1990 (12 countries); and high tax-to-GDP ratio countries include all the countries that had tax-to-GDP ratios above 35% in 1990 (18 countries).
Source: OECD Global Revenue Statistics Database.

StatLink https://doi.org/10.1787/888934158404

**Trends since the mid-1990s show that countries' tax-to-GDP ratios have become more similar.** This is apparent from the converging patterns between high- mid- and low-tax countries. Figure 2.11 breaks down OECD countries, Argentina, Indonesia and South Africa into three sub-groups: countries with high tax-to-GDP ratios in 1990, countries with mid-levels of tax-to-GDP ratios in 1990, and countries with low revenues as a share of GDP in 1990. It shows that there has been a strong increase in tax revenues on average in the countries with low-tax-to-GDP ratios in 1990, a smaller increase in countries with medium tax-to-GDP ratios, and a small decrease in the average tax to-GDP ratio of countries exhibiting high levels of tax revenues in 1990. Overall, these trends have led to a greater convergence in tax-to-GDP ratios across countries.

## Trends in the composition of tax revenues

### *The composition of tax revenues varies across countries*

**The cross-country differences in tax structures – or composition of total tax revenues – are significant.** As shown in Figure 2.12, income taxes – including both PIT and CIT – are the largest source of tax revenues in 20 countries. In Denmark, Australia, New Zealand, and South Africa, income taxes account for over 50% of total tax revenues. These four countries also collect very little or no SSCs, which partly explains the high share of revenues collected through income taxes. In 11 countries, including Central European countries and large Western European countries, SSCs are the primary source of tax revenues. In the Slovak Republic, Czech Republic, Lithuania, and Slovenia, SSCs account for over 40% of total tax revenues. Lastly, tax revenues from consumption taxes are the primary source of revenues in nine countries. Chile and Argentina collect over 45% of their tax revenues from consumption taxes while personal income taxes only account for 9.7%[6] and 7.4% respectively – the lowest shares among the 39 countries analysed.

Figure 2.12. Tax structures by country in 2017

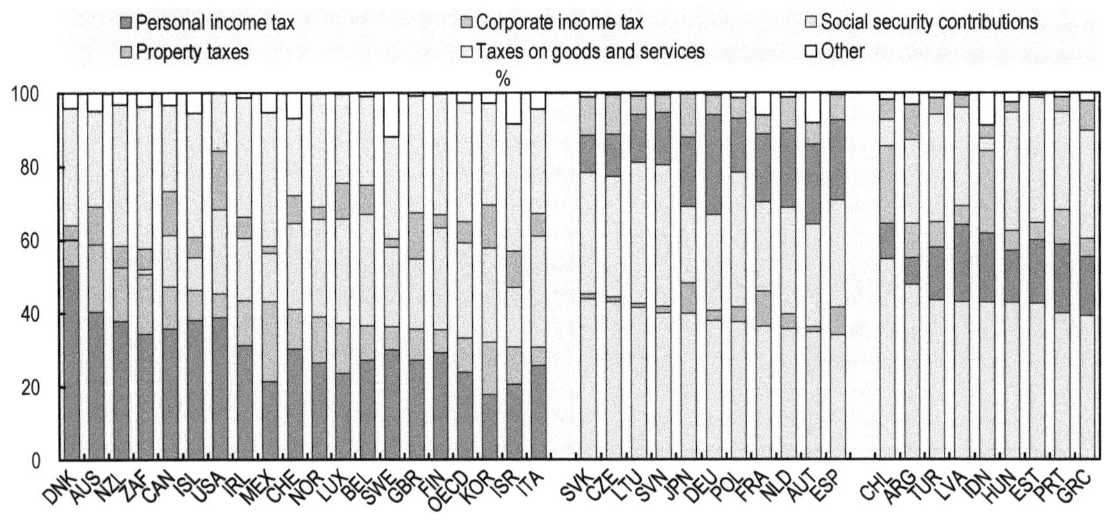


Note: Countries are grouped and ranked by those where income tax revenues (personal and corporate) form the higher share of total tax revenues, followed by those where SSCs, and taxes on goods and services form the highest share.
Source: OECD and Global Revenue Statistics database

StatLink https://doi.org/10.1787/888934158442

**As with tax-to-GDP ratios, there tends to be a link between countries' tax mixes and their GDP per capita levels.** Previous editions of this report discussed how more developed countries exhibit higher shares of tax revenues from PIT (OECD, 2018[4]). In contrast, the shares of revenues from VAT and CIT in total tax revenues tend to be lower in countries with high levels of GDP per capita (Figure 2.13 left panel).

Higher tax-to-GDP ratios also tend to be associated with lower shares of CIT and VAT in total tax revenues (Modica, Laudage and Harding, 2018[7]) (Figure 2.13 right panel).

Figure 2.13. Tax revenue as a share of total revenue, GDP per capita, and tax-to-GDP ratios in 2017

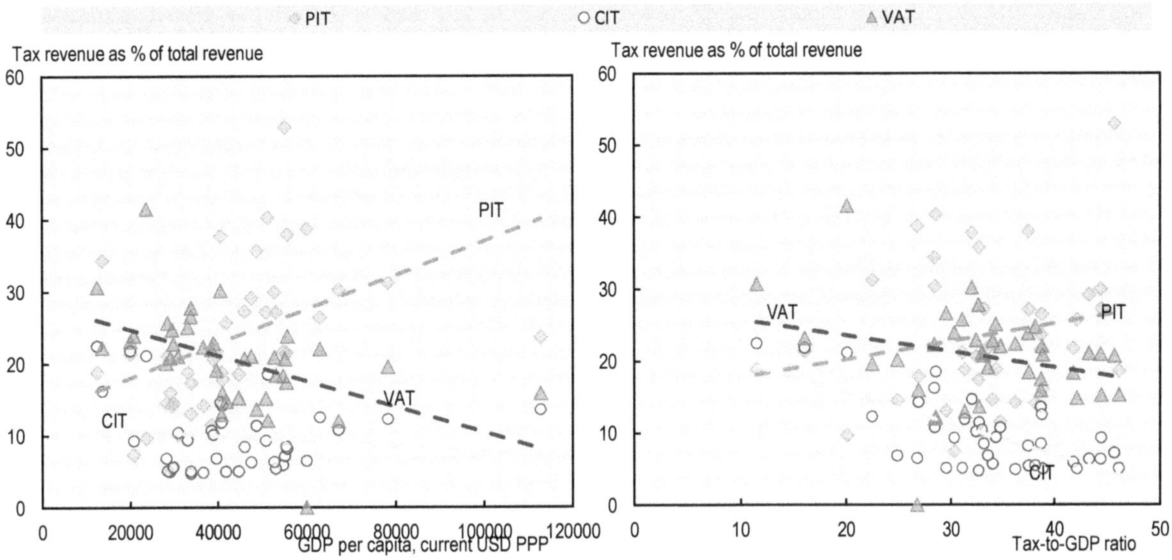


Source: OECD Global Revenue Statistics and OECD National Accounts Statistics

StatLink https://doi.org/10.1787/888934158461

### *Tax structures have remained relatively stable*

**The average tax structure across OECD countries is dominated by SSCs, PIT and VAT.** Overall, in the OECD, SSCs and payroll taxes accounted for 28.2% of total tax revenues in 2018. PIT was the second largest source of tax revenues, accounting for an average of 23.9% of total tax revenues. The VAT made up slightly over one fifth of the OECD's average tax mix in 2018, while other consumption taxes accounted for 12.0% of the tax mix. On the other hand, taxes on corporate income and property are much less significant sources of tax revenues, accounting for 8.8% and 5.5% of the OECD average tax mix in 2018 respectively (Figure 2.14).

## Figure 2.14. OECD average tax mix in 2000, 2009 and 2018

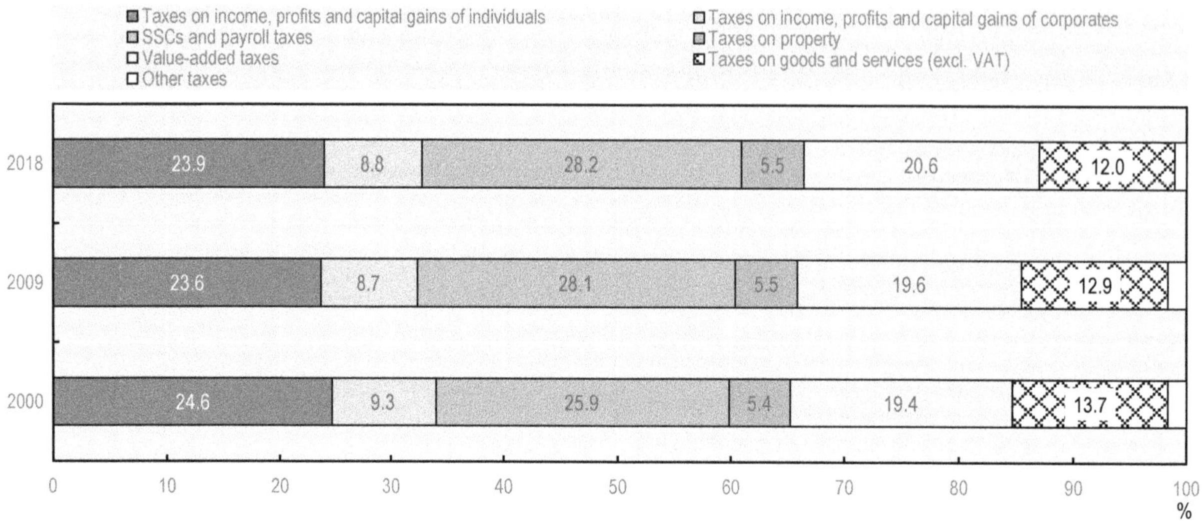


Source: OECD Revenue Statistics Database.

StatLink https://doi.org/10.1787/888934158480

**After the 2008 crisis, the OECD average shares of SSCs and VAT in total tax revenues increased.** This partly reflected the effects of the tax reforms that were introduced in response to fiscal consolidation pressures following the global financial crisis, in particular increases in SSCs and in standard VAT rates (OECD, 2016[8]).These trends also highlight the rapid revenue-raising effects of increases in SSCs and consumption taxes compared to other taxes. In 2018, the average share of total revenues collected from SSCs in OECD countries increased for the first time since 2009 (to 27%) and the average SSC revenues as a share of GDP increased slightly 0.2 percentage points (Figure 2.15) (OECD, 2019[2]). The share of VAT in the OECD average tax structure was relatively stable until it increased by 0.6 percentage points from 2016 to 2018.

**On average the share of revenues collected from CIT has fallen, after steadily increasing from 2014 to 2017.** The share of CIT in total tax revenues increased to 11.1% in 2007 and then dropped to a low of 8.7% in 2010, directly after the global financial crisis (Figure 2.15). From 2014 to 2017, the share of CIT in the OECD average tax mix steadily increased to 9.3% and then fell by 0.5 percentage points in 2018. This reversal was driven in part by Hungary and the United States, where the share of CIT in total tax revenues dropped by over two percentage points.

**The average share of PIT in total tax revenues has also increased slightly from 2017 and is now very close to its level in 2008**. Analogous to CIT, the share of PIT revenues in the OECD average tax structure initially fell after the global financial crisis, reaching a low of 22.9%. Since then, the share of PIT has fluctuated. From 2010 to 2015, PIT revenues steadily increased, partly reflecting the effects of PIT rate increases and PIT base broadening measures (OECD, 2016[8]), as well as changes in the labour share, which tends to have a countercyclical behaviour (i.e. to increase during economic downturns). The share of PIT revenues then fell by 0.6 percentage points between 2015 and 2016 and increased again between 2016 and 2018, almost reaching its pre-crisis level.

## Figure 2.15. Cumulative percentage point changes in tax revenues since 2008

OECD average, p.p. changes in tax revenues as a % of total tax revenues

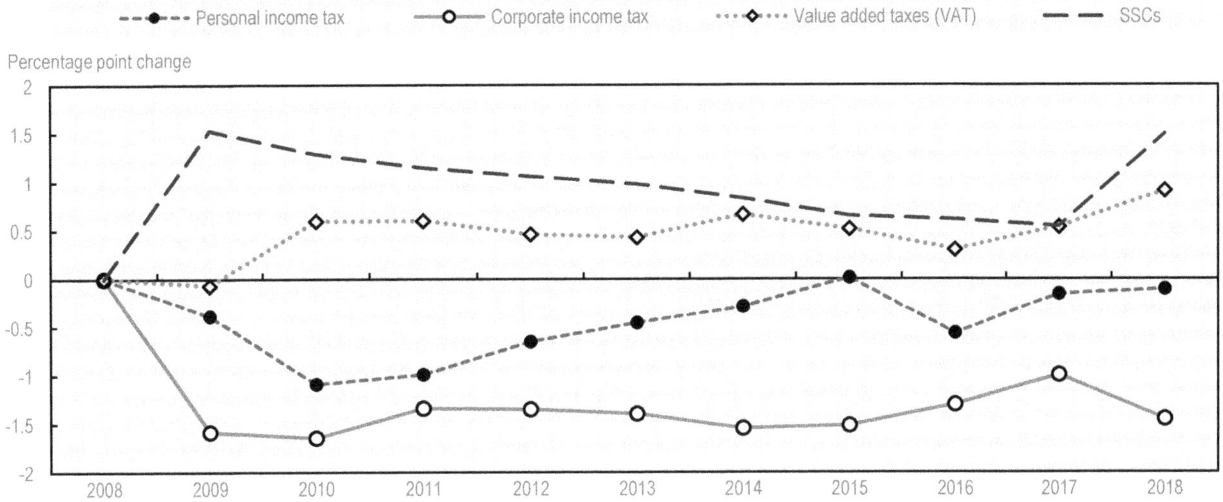


Source: OECD Revenue Statistics Database.

StatLink https://doi.org/10.1787/888934158499

## Looking ahead: potential revenue impacts of the COVID-19 crisis

**While the chapter focuses on past trends based on available data, this section considers the potential effects of the COVID-19 crisis on tax revenues, which are expected to be significant**. The COVID-19 pandemic and the policy responses linked to it will lead to a sharp reduction in tax revenues because of major reductions in economic activity and tax policy measures that reduce or waive the collection of tax liabilities.

**These revenue impacts will occur through a variety of channels:**

- The decline in economic activity and employment will reduce tax collections and social security contributions linked to personal and business income, resulting in lower CIT, PIT, SSCs and payroll tax receipts. CIT revenues may also remain depressed for some time into the future as any losses generated in 2020 will generally be available to be carried forward and applied against future income.
- The reduction in consumption, both from containment and mitigation measures and reduced consumer confidence, combined with a shift towards the consumption of necessity goods, which are often zero-rated or exempt under VAT systems, will reduce consumption tax revenues and particularly revenues from VAT, although excise and environmentally-related taxes will also be affected. Property taxes are likely to be less affected as they are not tied as directly to the economic cycle, although the various measures introduced during containment can be expected to have some impacts on property values and, therefore, taxes directly linked to property valuations may also be affected.
- A fall in tax revenue from tourism and travel is also expected, through losses in the form of reduced tourism, aviation and accommodation taxes, but also through falls in VAT revenues.

- Resource prices, notably oil, have fallen significantly, which for resource-rich countries will reduce revenues from excises and royalty payments and lead to lower revenues from corporate income taxes.
- In addition to automatic stabilisers, discretionary measures in response to the crisis will also have a significant impact on tax revenues (see Special Feature).

On average, trends in tax revenues and in GDP tend to move together, but tax revenues tend to fall faster than GDP when GDP growth is limited or negative (Belinga et al., 2014[9]). For instance, a greater decrease in tax revenues than in GDP was seen during the global financial crisis in most countries. Estimating the impact of COVID-19 on global GDP remains a highly speculative exercise, but early estimates of the impact suggest that the impact on tax revenues is likely to be significant, due to the large activity decline and the potentially even larger effect on tax revenues.

**Impacts on revenues will vary across countries and across time.** In the short-term, reductions in tax revenues are likely to be driven by the impact of confinement measures and reduced consumer confidence, as well as the direct impact of COVID-19, and will be greatest in countries with high exposure to the global economy via trade, tourism, or participation in global value chains. In the longer term, the impact on tax revenues will depend in large part on the effectiveness of policy responses taken to limit the economic impact of the crisis and on international transmission channels.

## References


Belinga, V. et al. (2014), "Tax Buoyancy in OECD Countries", No. Working Paper No. 14/110, https://www.imf.org/en/Publications/WP/Issues/2016/12/31/Tax-Buoyancy-in-OECD-Countries-41661 (accessed on 3 April 2020). [9]

Modica, E., S. Laudage and M. Harding (2018), "Domestic Revenue Mobilisation: A new database on tax levels and structures in 80 countries", *OECD Taxation Working Papers*, No. 36, OECD Publishing, Paris, https://dx.doi.org/10.1787/a87feae8-en. [7]

OECD (2019), *OECD Economic Surveys: Argentina 2019*, OECD Publishing, Paris, https://dx.doi.org/10.1787/0c7f002c-en. [5]

OECD (2019), *OECD Economic Surveys: Hungary 2019*, OECD Publishing, Paris, https://dx.doi.org/10.1787/eco_surveys-hun-2019-en. [3]

OECD (2019), *Revenue Statistics 2019*, OECD Publishing, Paris, https://dx.doi.org/10.1787/0bbc27da-en. [2]

OECD (2018), *OECD Economic Surveys: Israel 2018*, OECD Publishing, Paris, https://dx.doi.org/10.1787/eco_surveys-isr-2018-en. [6]

OECD (2018), *Revenue Statistics 2018*, OECD Publishing, Paris, https://dx.doi.org/10.1787/rev_stats-2018-en. [1]

OECD (2018), *Tax Policy Reforms 2018: OECD and Selected Partner Economies*, OECD Publishing, Paris, https://dx.doi.org/10.1787/9789264304468-en. [4]

OECD (2016), *Tax Policy Reforms in the OECD 2016*, OECD Publishing, Paris, https://dx.doi.org/10.1787/9789264260399-en. [8]

## Notes

[1] At the time of writing, China was not included in the OECD Global Revenue Statistics Database.

[2] It should be noted that the 2018 tax revenue data presented in this chapter is provisional.

[3] The majority of Chile's social contributions are paid into privately managed funds, which constitute the main part of Chile´s social security system. Accordingly, the payment of such social contributions to those managers are mandatory under the social security system of Chile, but those payments are excluded from the calculation of Chile's tax revenues as such payments are, under the definition applied, not regarded as taxes.

[4] Business Korea URL: http://www.businesskorea.co.kr/news/articleView.html?idxno=31107 (accessed 04/02/2020); Korea Times URL: http://koreatimes.co.kr/www/biz/2020/01/488_267520.html (accessed 04/02/2020)

[5] In 2015, the Irish economy experienced a nominal GDP growth of over 30%. This was, in part, due to a number of large multinational corporations reallocating their economic activities, and more specifically their underlying intellectual property, to Ireland.

[6] Chile has a dividend imputation system (either total or partial), therefore part of its revenues from personal income taxes are computed as corporate income tax revenues.

# 3 Tax reforms before the COVID-19 crisis

This chapter provides an overview of the tax reforms adopted before the COVID-19 crisis in OECD countries as well as in Argentina, China, Indonesia and South Africa. It looks at the reforms coming into force or due to come into force in the second half of 2019 and 2020. It examines trends in each category of tax including personal income taxes and social security contributions, corporate income taxes and other corporate taxes, VAT/GST and other taxes on goods and services, environmentally related taxes and property taxes.

**This chapter provides an overview of the tax reforms adopted before the COVID-19 crisis in OECD countries as well as in Argentina, China, Indonesia and South Africa**. It looks at the reforms coming into force or due to come into force in the second half of 2019 and 2020. It examines trends in each category of tax including personal income taxes and social security contributions (Section 3.1), corporate income taxes and other corporate taxes (Section 3.2), VAT/GST and other taxes on goods and services (Section 3.3), environmentally related taxes (Section 3.4) and property taxes (Section 3.5). It should be noted that some of the reforms described in this chapter have been delayed in response to the crisis. More generally, the COVID-19 crisis should be seen as a significant intervening event and future reports will focus on the impact of the crisis on longer-term tax reforms.

**The discussion in this chapter is primarily based on countries' responses to the 2020 Annual Tax Policy Reform Questionnaire**, which was completed by countries between January and February 2020. This annual questionnaire asks responding countries to describe their tax reforms as well as to provide details on their expected revenue effects and other relevant information, including the rationale for the tax measures (see Box 3.1).

### Box 3.1. The OECD Annual Tax Policy Reform Questionnaire

At the Working Party No.2 on Tax Policy Analysis and Tax Statistics (WP2) meeting in November 2009, delegates from OECD countries agreed to start collecting more systematic information on the main tax measures adopted in each country. The motivation for this proposal was to provide consistent and comparative information on tax reforms to inform policy discussions in OECD and non-OECD countries.

At the November 2010 WP2 meeting, the following criteria were agreed for deciding whether a tax policy measure was sufficiently substantial to be reported in the questionnaire:

- A significant change in a tax rate;
- A change in the tax base that is expected to change revenue from that base by more than 5% or 0.1% of GDP; and
- A politically important systemic reform.

Any central or sub-central tax policy measure that was implemented, legislated or announced in the previous calendar year which meets at least one of the criteria listed above must be reported in the questionnaire.

For each reform, the questionnaire requests information on the type of tax; the dates of entry into force, legislation or announcement; the direction of the rate and/or base change; and a detailed description of the reform. The questionnaire also asks for the rationale behind the reform and estimates of the revenue effects of the tax measures.

## Personal income tax and social security contributions

**In the area of personal income tax (PIT), the report confirms that countries are continuing to lower the tax burden on personal income**, with most of the countries that have introduced PIT reforms in 2020 opting to cut PIT rates and narrow PIT bases. The most common rationale for these reforms cited by countries is to support fairness, particularly for those on low and middle incomes. While this trend represents a broad continuation of PIT reforms in recent years, the focus on PIT rate cuts has intensified. PIT base narrowing measures have also been frequent and often targeted at families and low-income earners. Regarding the taxation of household capital income, limited changes have been introduced, involving both tax increases and decreases. These measures have included changes to the taxation of rental income as well as expanded tax reliefs to support small savers. Finally, the focus on SSC reforms has slowed compared with recent years, and most reforms have involved SSC reductions.

### *PIT and SSCs are major sources of tax revenues*

**PIT and SSCs are particularly significant sources of tax revenues in most countries.** Together, they account for half of tax revenues in OECD countries on average. PIT accounts for 24% of tax revenues in the OECD while SSCs account for 27%. As shown in Figure 3.1, in 2018, PIT, SSCs and payroll taxes accounted for over 60% of tax revenue in the United States and Germany and about 40% in Israel, New Zealand, South Africa and Mexico. In the Slovak Republic, the Czech Republic, Slovenia and Lithuania, SSCs alone accounted for at least 40% of total taxation. In Denmark, Australia and the United States, PIT alone accounted for about 40% or more of total tax revenues. PIT, SSCs and payroll taxes represent a much smaller share of tax revenues in Chile (14%), Indonesia (22%) and Argentina (29%).

Figure 3.1. PIT, SSCs and payroll taxes as a share of total tax revenues by country in 2018

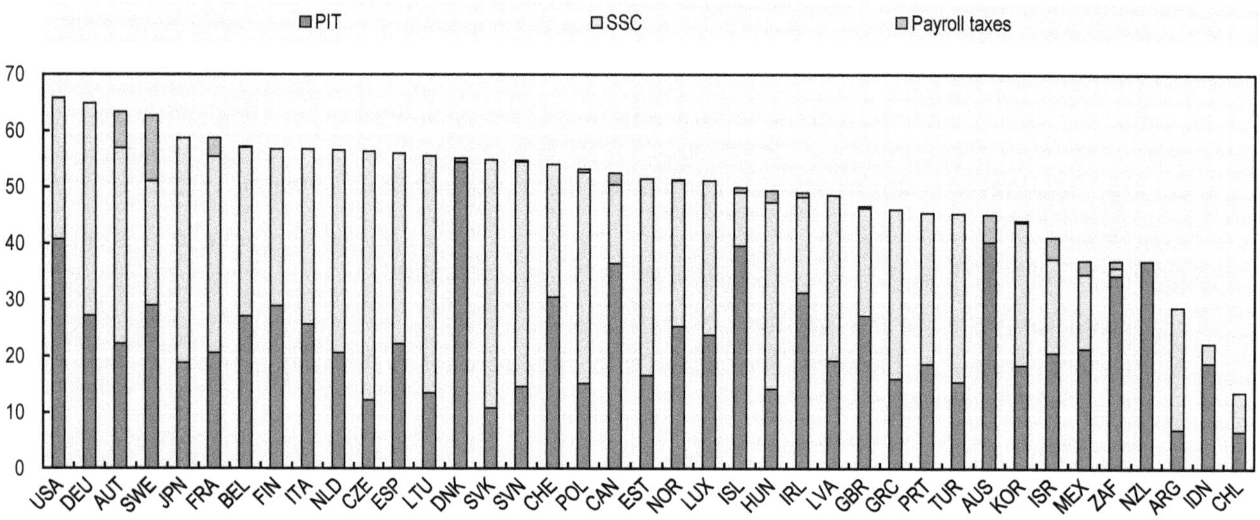


Note: 2017 data for Australia, Greece, Indonesia, Japan, Mexico and South Africa.
Source: OECD Global Revenue Statistics Database.

StatLink https://doi.org/10.1787/888934158518

**Over the past 50 years, SSCs have gradually overtaken PIT as the most important source of tax revenue in OECD countries**. The sum of PIT and SSCs has remained relatively constant over time, at around half of tax revenue, but the mix has changed. PIT has gradually declined as a share of total revenue while SSCs have gradually increased (Figure 3.2). In 1965, SSCs comprised 17.6% of tax revenues on average while PIT accounted for 26.2% of total taxation. By 1995, they were about equal at approximately 25%. By 2018, SSCs represented 27.0% of total tax revenues on average, surpassing the PIT share of 23.9%.

Figure 3.2. PIT, SSCs and payroll tax revenue as a share of total tax revenues, OECD average, 1965 - 2018

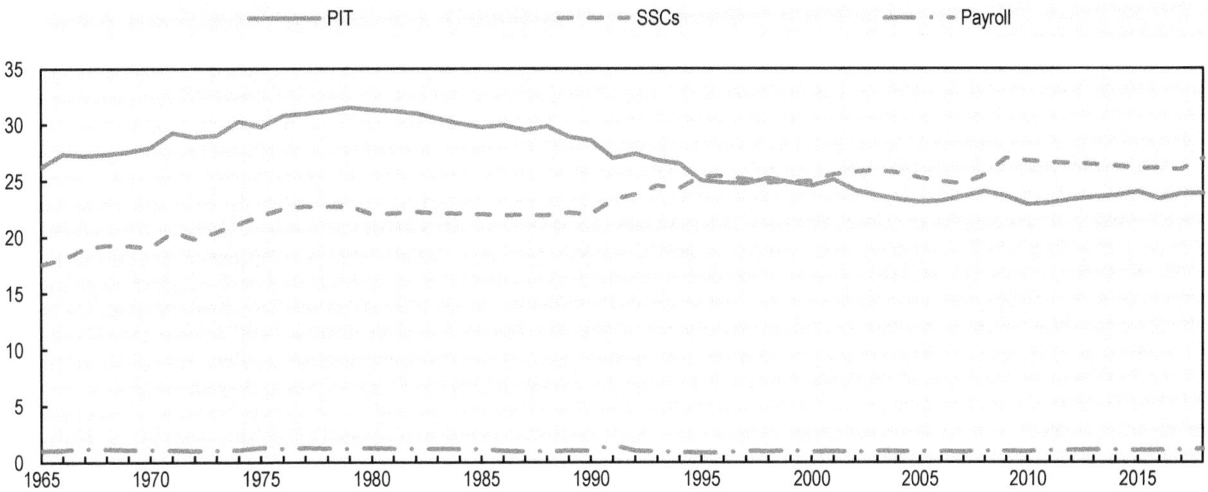


Source: OECD Revenue Statistics Database.

StatLink https://doi.org/10.1787/888934158537

### *Taxes on labour income declined on average between 2013 and 2019, after a series of increases after the global financial crisis*

**The average tax burden on labour income has been declining slowly but consistently in recent years** (Figure 3.3). Between 2009 and 2013, the OECD average tax wedge – the total tax payments on labour income as a percentage of total labour costs – for single workers earning the average wage increased by one percentage point, from 35.5% to 36.5%. This largely reflected countries' fiscal consolidation efforts at that time. Since then, the OECD average tax wedge has been declining steadily but slowly reaching 36.0% in 2018.

Figure 3.3. Evolution of the average tax wedge on labour income in the OECD between 2000 and 2019

Average tax wedge for a single person without children earning 100% of the average wage

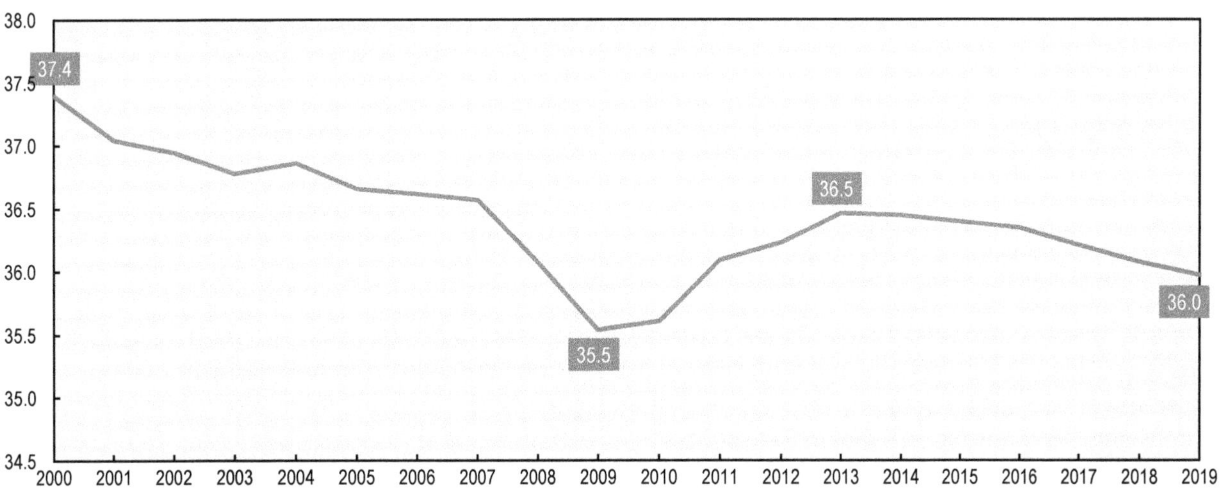


Source: OECD Taxing Wages Database.

StatLink https://doi.org/10.1787/888934158556

**Over the past 20 years, tax burdens have declined, particularly for families with children**. In the early 2000s, the tax burden declined across family types. Between 2009 and 2019, in the years following the global financial crisis, average tax wedges rose modestly for many family types, for example for one-earner married couples with children and single persons at 100% of average earnings with no children. However, tax wedges declined for single persons at 67% of the average wage with children. Overall, tax wedges remain lower than in 2000 across family types despite modest increases in the past decade (Figure 3.4).

### *PIT rate cuts have intensified*

**PIT reforms are important tools for governments to achieve different policy objectives**, including raising tax revenues, stimulating economic growth or enhancing the redistributive impact of the tax system. These reforms involve the upward or downward adjustment of PIT rates and the broadening or narrowing of PIT bases. These policy choices often involve a trade-off between equity and efficiency. For instance, while PIT rate increases on the upper income brackets strengthen progressivity and fairness, they might also reduce economic incentives to work, save and invest. This section looks at the PIT reforms that were recently introduced in OECD countries, Argentina, China, Indonesia and South Africa, beginning with PIT rate reforms followed by PIT base changes.

Figure 3.4. Changes in labour income tax wedges in OECD countries before and after the financial crisis by family type

Percentage point changes

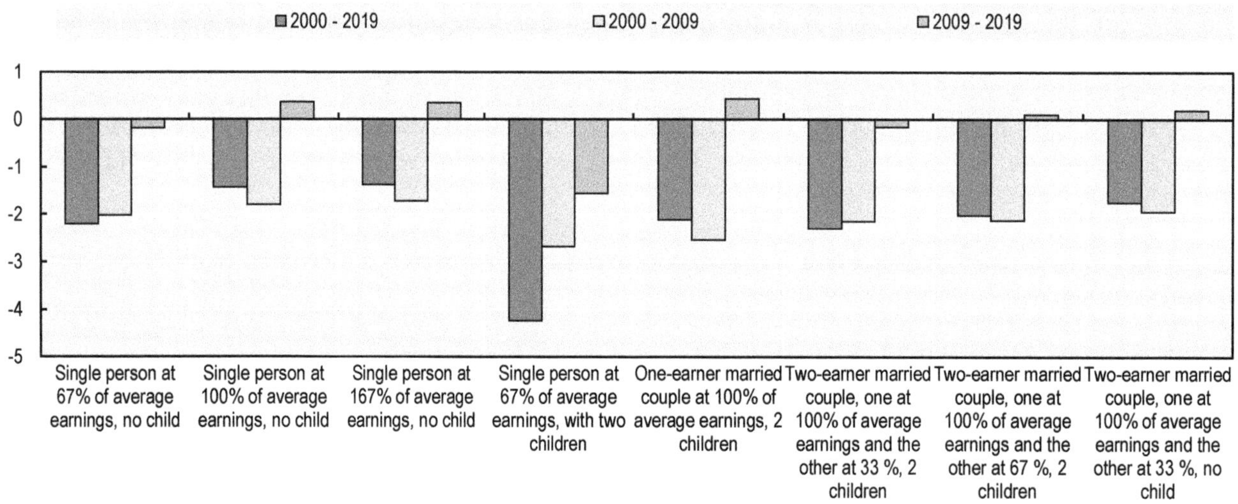


Source: OECD Taxing Wages Database.

StatLink https://doi.org/10.1787/888934158575

#### *Fewer countries have made changes to their top PIT rates compared to previous years*

**Of the countries undertaking top PIT rate reforms, three involved cuts while two involved increases** (Table 3.1). This marks a decline in the number of top PIT rate changes compared to recent years. There are also fewer countries increasing their top PIT rates compared to previous years. For instance, in 2018, four countries reported top PIT rate increases, and in 2019, three countries raised their top PIT rates and Poland introduced a solidarity levy on taxpayers whose total income in the fiscal year exceeds PLN 1 million, levied at a rate of 4% on the excess of this amount.

**Greece, the Netherlands and Sweden have lowered their top PIT rates.** As part of its Annual Tax Plan 2020, the Netherlands is accelerating the introduction of its two bracket PIT (to replace the previous three bracket PIT rate schedule) by introducing it in 2020 rather than in 2021 as had previously been envisaged. As part of this reform, the rate of the top PIT bracket is decreased to 49.5% in 2020 from 51.75% in 2019. Sweden abolished its top PIT rate in 2020, which had previously added a 5% surtax on higher incomes above SEK 703 000. In Greece, the PIT rate on the highest income bracket for business, employment and farming income above EUR 40 001 is reduced modestly to 44% from 2020.

**While several countries had increased top rates in recent years, only Chile and Turkey have done so in 2020, with both countries introducing a new highest income tax bracket with a PIT rate of 40%.** In Chile, the previous highest tax rate was 35%. In Turkey, the new top PIT bracket applies to those earning over TRY 500 000 annually (the second highest bracket is 35%). The stated objective of both reforms is to raise revenues and enhance progressivity.

## Table 3.1. Changes to personal income tax rates

| | Rate ⇧ | | Rate ⇩ | |
|---|---|---|---|---|
| *Into effect in* | **2019** | **2020 or later** | **2019** | **2020 or later** |
| Top PIT rate | ESP LTU NOR | CHL TUR | NLD NOR | GRC (NLD) SWE[1] |
| Non-top PIT rate | DNK ESP LTU | (ISL)[4] ITA LTU (NLD) GRC[3] | AUS IRLNLD NOR POL | AUS[5] DNK FRA (DEU)[2] GRC ISL SVN SVK[6] |

Note: Countries in brackets have only announced reforms.
1. In Sweden, the top PIT rate which adds a 5% surtax on higher income exceeding SEK 703,000 is abolished.
2. In Germany, it is proposed that the solidarity charge is to be abolished for most taxpayers.
3. In Greece, a previous proposal to cut the first PIT bracket is repealed.
4. In Iceland, it is proposed that the middle PIT bracket is increased in 2021.
5. In Australia, the 32.5% PIT rate will be lowered to 30% in 2024/2025.
6. In the Slovak Republic, the PIT rate is cut for self-employed workers.
Source: OECD Annual Tax Policy Reform Questionnaire.

### *More countries are focusing on tax rate cuts targeted at low and middle-income earners*

**Similar to the top PIT rate reforms, non-top PIT rate reforms have involved more rate cuts than increases**. Nine countries reported non-top PIT rate cuts and five reported non-top PIT rate increases in 2020. In 2019, there was a more even split between non-top PIT rate cuts and increases (four countries undertook non-top PIT rate cuts and three undertook increases). The current reforms are more closely aligned with 2017 and 2018 where most countries that undertook non-top PIT rate reforms introduced tax cuts targeted at low and middle-income earners (although these were small).

**A few countries are increasing PIT rates on lower and middle-income brackets.** Of the countries increasing non-top PIT rates, Lithuania increased the rate on its second PIT bracket from 27% to 32% in 2020. This PIT rate increase follows from a significant reform undertaken in Lithuania in 2019 when a new progressive PIT system was introduced to replace the previous flat-rate system. The Netherlands also increased its lowest rate modestly to 37.1% in 2020, up from 36.65% in 2019. In Iceland, it is proposed that the PIT rate on the middle bracket will be increased from 22.75% to 23.5% in 2021. In Greece, a number of previously proposed PIT reforms due to commence in 2020 were repealed including a previous proposal to cut the 22% PIT rate to 20% in January 2020. In Italy, the 20% substitute PIT rate for self-employed and entrepreneurs with incomes from EUR 65 000 to EUR 100 000 has been abolished. The regime, which had been due to come into force in 2020, allowed for the application of a different PIT rate than the ordinary progressive PIT rates.

**Several countries are undertaking non-top PIT rate cuts to support low and middle-income earners.** In Iceland, as part of the second phase of a three-phase PIT reform between 2019 and 2021, several non-top PIT rate changes are being introduced to reduce the tax burden on low and middle-income families.

The lowest PIT rate bracket is reduced from 22.5% to 20.6% in January 2020; the middle-income bracket is 22.75% and the top bracket remains unchanged (although the threshold is adjusted for inflation). Furthermore, it is proposed that the lowest PIT rate will be further reduced to 17% in 2021. In Greece, non-top PIT rates are also being cut modestly in 2020 through several adjustments across the PIT rate schedule. A new lowest bracket is introduced with a PIT rate of 9% up to EUR 10 000 and the PIT rate has been reduced by one percentage point for incomes above EUR 10 000. Consequently, the new PIT rate schedule in Greece is as follows: 9% from EUR 0 – 10 000; 22% from EUR 10 001 – 20 000; 28% from EUR 20 001 – 30 000 and 36% from EUR 30 001 – 40 000 and 44% above EUR 40 001. In France, to support fairness, the first bracket of the PIT schedule is reduced from 14% to 11% from January 2020. Similarly, in Poland, as part of the Act on Personal Income Tax in mid-2019, the lowest PIT rate was reduced from 18% to 17% in October 2019. In Slovenia, the PIT rate is reduced modestly by one percentage point on both the second and third brackets to 26% and 33% respectively from 2020. In Germany, the solidarity charge, which amounts to 5.5% of the income tax, is proposed to be abolished for the majority of taxpayers and reduced for certain higher income earners from 2021. The rationale for the tax cut is to lower the tax on lower and middle incomes. In the Slovak Republic, for self-employed workers with incomes below EUR 100,000 per year, the PIT rate is reduced from 21% to 15%. In Denmark, the lowest PIT bracket is reduced slightly to 12.11% effective for 2020 and 2021. In Australia, a decrease in the 32.5% marginal tax rate to 30% in 2024/2025 was legislated.

### *PIT base narrowing reforms have continued*

**The trend among countries in recent years to narrow PIT bases has continued**. A majority of PIT base reforms in 2020 have been aimed at supporting those on low incomes and families (Table 3.2). Overall, these measures are expected to reduce tax revenues. Of the countries undertaking PIT base reforms, 33 were base narrowing and three were base broadening. This policy preference for PIT base narrowing rather than base broadening follows the trend observed in recent years.

Table 3.2. Changes to personal income tax bases

| | Base ⇧ | | Base ⇩ | |
|---|---|---|---|---|
| *Into effect in* | **2019** | **2020 or later** | **2019** | **2020 or later** |
| Personal allowances, credits, tax brackets | | ISL | AUS BEL DEU DNK FIN GBR ISL LTU NLD SWE ZAF | AUS DEU FIN IRL[1] ITA LTU NLD SVK SVN |
| Provisions targeted at low-income earners, EITCs and other in-work benefits | | | DKN ESP FIN IRL NLD SWE | IRL ITA FIN NLD |
| Children & other dependents | | | AUT DEU ESP IRL | CAN DEU GRC LTU (PRT) SVK IRE JPN |
| Elderly & disabled | | | AUS FIN FRA HUN LAT NLD SWE | FIN GRC LTU SWE |
| Self-employed & unincorporated business | GBR NLD | NLD | GBR DNK IND ITA | SVK |
| Miscellaneous expenses, deductions & credits | NOR SWE | FIN ITA NLD[2] | POL NOR SWE USA | |

Note: Countries in brackets have only announced reforms.
1. Ireland raised the income ceiling of its universal social charge (USC).
2. In the Netherlands, the deductibility of education costs will be abolished from 2021 and replaced with a subsidy.
Source: OECD Annual Tax Policy Reform Questionnaire.

**PIT base narrowing reforms have been aimed at supporting those on low incomes and families with children.** Ten reforms involved increases in personal tax allowances, tax credits and tax brackets to support low-income earners and employment. Eight reforms were aimed at supporting children and other dependents. PIT base reforms targeted at supporting the elderly have been less frequent than in 2019. Four countries have expanded the scope of their earned income tax credits (EITCs) or other in-work benefits.

### *Personal tax allowances, tax credits and tax brackets*

**Many countries have increased the generosity of their general tax allowances and tax credits.** These reforms, which are targeted at supporting low-income earners, are expected to increase after-tax incomes but also to reduce tax revenues.

**In Australia, a number of significant reforms were introduced in mid-2019 to reduce PIT on individuals over the coming years**. The stated objective of the reform is to make PIT lower, fairer and simpler. To increase tax relief for low incomes, a new 'low and middle-income tax offset' was introduced to provide tax relief of up to AUD 1 080 between 2018 and 2022. Entitlement to this new offset is in addition to the existing "low income tax offset". From 2022, a new "low income tax offset" will replace both the current "low income tax offset" and the "low and middle-income tax offset". This new "low income tax offset" will increase from AUD 445 to AUD 700. In addition, the top threshold of the 19% tax bracket will increase from AUD 37 000 to AUD 45 000 in 2022. Australia has also legislated an increase in the threshold at which the top marginal PIT rate is levied from AUD 180 000 to AUD 200 000 from the 2024–25 income year.

**Five countries have increased their basic tax allowances**. In Germany, the basic allowance has been increased modestly to EUR 9 408 in 2020 (it was EUR 9 168 in 2019 and EUR 9 000 in 2018). In Lithuania, with the similar objective of reducing the tax burden on low-income workers, the basic monthly tax allowance is increased to EUR 350 in 2020 and the authorities have proposed to increase it further to EUR 400 in 2021. Similarly, Slovenia increased the annual basic tax allowance from EUR 3 303 to EUR 3 500 in 2020. An additional tax allowance in Slovenia is also available for residents where taxable income does not exceed EUR 13 317 and the tax allowance for income from student work has been increased. In Finland, the basic allowance for earned income is increased to EUR 18 100 in 2020 from EUR 17 600 in 2019. In the Slovak Republic, the basic allowance for employees (and self-employed workers) is increased from 19.2 to 21 times the living minimum (of EUR 210) in 2020.

**Several countries have narrowed the PIT base through increased tax credits**. In the Netherlands, the general tax credit will be increased gradually over two years by EUR 80 in total starting in 2020. This adds to increases in the general tax credit in 2019. In Italy, tax credits increased in 2020 to reduce PIT on labour income and encourage consumption. In Iceland, on the other hand, the personal tax credit is decreased to ISK 655,538 annually, based on an adjustment for inflation and taking account of the decrease in the bottom rate.

**In some countries, tax brackets have been shifted upwards.** In Slovenia, the threshold for the highest income bracket, which has a rate of 50%, has been raised to EUR 72 000. In Ireland, the income ceiling for the Universal Social Charge (USC) in the second tax bracket, which has a tax rate of 2%, has been raised from EUR 19 874 in 2019 to EUR 20 484 from February 2020. In Finland, the temporary highest income bracket of the progressive income tax schedule (the so-called 'solidarity tax') will remain in effect until the end of 2023.

### *Children and other dependents*

**Greece, Germany and Canada have introduced several PIT measures aimed at supporting families and children.** In Greece, the tax credit for those earning employment, pension and farm income has been increased for married persons with dependents but decreased for those on higher incomes from January 2020. In addition, a cut in child tax credits to start from 2020 has been repealed. In Germany, a number of family benefits increased in January 2020. For example, the tax-free allowance for parents with children will increase to EUR 7 812 in 2020, up from EUR 7 620 in 2019. In addition, the child benefit was increased to EUR 204 per month in mid-2019 (the amount depends on the number of children). In Canada, a number of measures are being introduced to support families and children throughout 2019 and 2020. In British Columbia, a new child opportunity benefit is introduced in late 2020 to be combined with the existing childhood tax benefit. In Ontario, a new tax credit for childcare is introduced which provides families with an income-tested refundable tax credit of up to 75% of eligible childcare expenses.

**Other countries have increased tax deductions and credits for children and other dependents.** In Portugal, the draft budget proposes an increase in the tax credits from 2020 for households with small children to EUR 300 and an additional EUR 150 for the second child onwards when there are two or more children under three years of age. In Lithuania, the child benefit will also increase from EUR 50 to EUR 60 and from EUR 70 to EUR 100 for larger families. In the Slovak Republic, the child tax credit for children up to six years of age was increased to EUR 45.44 in mid-2019. In Japan, the deduction of JPY 350 000 for single parents with a dependent child was reviewed. The deduction now applies regardless of the marital status or gender of the parents. In addition, the deduction for widows and widowers with dependents other than a child is set to remain at JPY 270 000, for those with taxable income up to JPY 5 million. In Ireland, the home carer tax credit, where one spouse (or civil partner) works in the home caring for a dependent person, is increased to EUR 1 600 in 2020, up from EUR 1 500 in 2019 and EUR 1 200 in 2018.

### *EITCs and other in-work tax benefits*

**A number of changes to EITCs and other in-work benefits were introduced in the Netherlands, Ireland, Finland and Italy**. When designed correctly, such measures have the potential to improve labour market participation and reduce poverty. The number of EITC reforms has declined compared to recent years. In the Netherlands, to support employment, the maximum of the income dependent EITC will be increased gradually over three years by a total of EUR 285 starting in 2020 (this follows a previous increase of EUR 150 in 2019). In Ireland, for self-employed workers, the EITC is increased by EUR 150 to EUR 1 500 in 2020. This adds to a consecutive set of increases in recent years including in 2019 (when it was EUR 1,350), 2018 (EUR 1 150) and 2017 (EUR 950). In Finland, for municipal taxation, the deduction for earned income has been increased to EUR 1 770 in 2020, up from EUR 1 630 in 2019 and EUR 1 540 in 2018. In Italy, the monthly tax credit is increased from EUR 80 to EUR 100 for employees with an income up to EUR 28 000 from July 2020 (the measure is only for employees with a tax liability). In addition, Italy introduced a temporary non-refundable tax credit of EUR 600 for employees with PIT income above EUR 28 000 from July 2020 and the amount of the tax credit is gradually decreased for higher incomes up to EUR 40 000. The tax credit is due to be phased out by December 2020.

### *Elderly and disabled*

**In 2020, PIT reforms to support the elderly have slowed**. Supporting low-income older people continues to be an important policy rationale for age-related tax concessions (OECD, 2011[1]). A number of countries have undertaken PIT reforms to support low-income retirees in recent years. In 2020, two countries undertook such reforms. In Sweden, to reduce the tax burden on older workers, the basic personal allowance has been increased for people above 65 years of age from 2020. Finland is increasing the pension income deduction in both central and local government taxation in 2020 with the aim of reducing the tax burden on low-income taxpayers.

**Two countries reported PIT measures to support the disabled**. In Greece, taxpayers with certain disabilities are exempt from the solidarity surcharge from 2020. In Lithuania, the basic monthly tax allowance for disabled persons is increased to between EUR 600 and EUR 645, depending on the extent of disability from 2020.

### *Other employment and skills-related tax provisions*

**Several reforms were made to other tax provisions related to employment, skills and young workers**. In Portugal, to support employment, the draft budget includes a partial exemption from PIT on employment income earned by certain young workers with income not exceeding EUR 25 000 from 2020 onwards. The PIT relief is applicable to a reducing fraction of taxable income in the first three years after completing education (30% in the first year, 20% in the second year and 10% in the third year). In Poland, PIT on employment income is exempt for those aged under 26 years age up to a limit of PLN 85 528 starting from August 2019. In Quebec in Canada, a tax credit for career extension is introduced to encourage experienced workers to remain in the labour market. In Estonia, to support employment, the compensation of employees' public transport costs between home and work are not taxed as fringe benefits from 2020. In Turkey, non-taxable employer provided transport benefits have been expanded in 2020. In the Slovak Republic, certain daily allowances, such as business trips, are tax-exempt for employee salaries above 1.65 times the minimum wage from 2020, an increase from 1.3 times the minimum wage in 2019.

### *Tax reforms for the self-employed*

**Some countries reported PIT base reforms for the self-employed and unincorporated businesses**. In the Netherlands, the allowance for the self-employed will be cut from EUR 7 280 in 2020 in consecutive annual steps until it reaches EUR 5 000 in 2028. In the Slovak Republic, to support the self-employed, the monthly exemption from PIT and SSCs for accommodation and transport costs are to be increased in 2020 and 2021 respectively. In addition in the Slovak Republic, a new category of taxpayers ('micro-taxpayers') will be introduced in 2021 under the Income Act, defined as individuals that generate income from business or self-employment activities not exceeding the threshold for VAT registration. These taxpayers will be entitled to several tax benefits including related to tax depreciation of movable property.

### *Other PIT deductions and credits*

**Regarding other types of PIT deductions and tax credits, a few base broadening measures were introduced**. In the Netherlands, to simplify the tax system, the deductibility of education costs will be abolished from 2021 and replaced with a subsidy. The reform is expected to increase PIT revenues. In Finland, to increase tax revenues, the tax credit for domestic household expenses will be decreased in 2020. In Italy, the tax credit of 19% for certain personal expenses (such as expenses and mortgage interest on owner-occupied houses) is capped in 2020 at taxable incomes of EUR 120 000.

## *Changes to personal capital income taxation have been limited*

**Overall, changes to the taxation of household capital income have been limited**. The two main rationales for the reforms to personal capital income cited by countries were to encourage savings on the one hand and to raise revenues on the other. Among others, reforms have included a mix of tax rate cuts and increases on rental income and expanded tax relief for financial income to support small savers.

**Three countries have cut tax rates on personal capital income** (Table 3.3). In Portugal, the tax rate on long-term housing rentals is reduced substantially from 28% to 10% starting January 2020. Similarly, in Italy, rental income is subject to a reduced 10% substitution rate from January 2020, under certain conditions (the rate had previously been proposed to be 15%). In Greece, to support investment, the tax rate on dividends is reduced from 10% to 5% for distributed dividends in 2020.

**Two countries have increased tax rates on personal capital income**. In Slovenia, the capital gains tax rate was increased from 25% to 27.5% for holding periods below five years. For holding periods greater than five years, the capital gains tax rate was increased to 20% between 5 and 10 years, to 15% between 10 and 15 years and to 10% between 15 and 20 years (for holding periods greater than 20 years, capital gains are exempt). In addition, in Slovenia, the tax rate on rental income was raised from 25% to 27.5%. In Chile, the increased 40% PIT rate (see above) is applicable to all types of ordinary income, including dividends and capital gains. In addition, dividends distributed to higher earners residents in Chile by companies under the Partial Imputation Regime are subject to an effective PIT rate of 44.45%. Finally, a new fixed 40% tax applies to disproportionate dividends (i.e. that do not correspond to the shareholder´s equity participation) that have no business or commercial justification and are distributed as a way to reduce the PIT burden of related-party shareholders (with family ties).

## Table 3.3. Changes to tax rates on personal capital income

| | Rate ⇧ | | Rate ⇩ | |
|---|---|---|---|---|
| *Into effect in* | 2019 | 2020 or later | 2019 | 2020 or later |
| Dividend or interest income/equity or bond investment | LTU | CHL | | GRE |
| Capital gains | NOR POL | SVN | | |
| Rental income | | SVN | | ITA POR |
| Tax treatment of pensions and savings account | (ESP) | | | |
| Employee share acquisition deductions | | | | |

Note: Countries in brackets have only announced reforms.
Source: OECD Annual Tax Policy Reform Questionnaire.

**Some countries have introduced base narrowing measures** (Table 3.4). In Argentina, the tax on certain financial income, including interest on fixed term deposits, government securities and corporate bonds, has been abolished from 2020. In Hungary, a tax exemption was introduced for interest income from retail treasury bonds to encourage households to buy these bonds. In Japan, the 'General NISA' and 'Installment-type NISA' individual savings account programme, which provides certain tax-exempt benefits, was extended by five years. In Sweden, the coupon tax, which is withheld when a dividend is paid and no tax return is submitted, can be deferred in some cases under a new system introduced in 2020.

**Two countries have reported measures broadening personal capital income tax bases**. In Chile, a new one-year period limitation was introduced for the capital gains tax exemption on the sale of stocks or quotas in the capital market when the sale is made under a market maker agreement. In Finland, the deductibility of mortgage interest payments will be limited from 25% to 15% in 2020 and then further until it reaches zero in 2023.

## Table 3.4. Changes to personal capital income tax bases

| | Base ⇧ | | Base ⇩ | |
|---|---|---|---|---|
| *Into effect in* | 2019 | 2020 or later | 2019 | 2020 or later |
| Dividend or interest income/equity or bond investment | | FIN | BEL | ARG HUN SWE |
| Capital gains | | CHL | GRC | |
| Rental income | ITA NLD | | IRL | |
| Tax treatment of pensions and savings accounts | | | DKN NOR | JPN |
| Employee share acquisition deductions | | | | |

Note: Countries in brackets have only announced reforms.
Source: OECD Annual Tax Policy Reform Questionnaire.

### *SSC reforms have slowed compared with recent years*

**There have been fewer SSC reforms compared to previous years, and they have almost all involved SSC reductions**, both through rate cuts and base narrowing. Overall, however, SSC reforms have been modest and SSCs remain high in many countries. In some countries, high SSCs have distortive effects and more comprehensive tax reforms will be needed to rebalance the tax mix towards less distortive and potentially more progressive taxes.

### *Changes to SSC rates have been limited*

**Three countries undertook SSC rate cuts in 2020, and one reported rate increases** (Table 3.5). In Estonia, the rate of employer SSCs was cut from 33% to 20% for recipients of the parental allowance and disabled workers. In Hungary, employer SSCs were cut from 19.5% to 17.5% in mid-2019. In addition, with the stated objective of simplifying the tax system, employee SSCs, which currently consist of four separate items, will be integrated into a single SSC in mid-2020. In Sweden, a number of SSC reforms have been introduced with the aim of supporting employment and skills. For example, SSC contributions for new entrants to the labour market and younger workers have been reduced. Germany has undertaken a reform involving a mix of SSC rate increases and cuts. These reforms are introduced across the four types of social insurance in Germany: pension, unemployment, health and long-term care. The rationale for the reform is to reduce the tax burden on labour but also to address demographic requirements, for instance through the financing long-term care. Argentina was the only country to report an increase in SSC rates: a proposed SSC employer rate of 19.5% has been abolished and replaced with new SSC employer rates ranging from 18% to 20.4%, depending on the type of employer, with the objective of raising revenues.

Table 3.5. Changes to social security contribution rates

| | Rate ⇧ | | Rate ⇩ | |
|---|---|---|---|---|
| *Into effect in* | **2019** | **2020 or later** | **2019** | **2020 or later** |
| Employers SSCs | DEU | ARG | DEU ISL LTU | EST HUN |
| Employees SSCs | DEU LTU | | DEU LTU | SWE |
| Self-employed | | | DEU GRC | |
| Payroll taxes | | | | |

Note: Countries in brackets have only announced reforms.
Source: OECD Annual Tax Policy Reform Questionnaire.

### *Countries have continued to narrow employer SSC bases, but reforms have been limited*

**All SSC base reforms, with one exception, involved SSC reductions, generally focused on employer SSCs** (Table 3.6). In Sweden, to support research and development (R&D), the tax relief on the total SSCs paid by companies for individuals who work in R&D was increased from 10% to 20% in 2020. In Slovenia, the holiday allowance, which is paid by employers to employees, will be exempt from SSC contributions up to 100% of the average monthly minimum wage. In Argentina, the monthly deductible amount for employers from the employer contribution base is increased to ARS 12 000 per employee in some sectors and will remain in place until 2022. In Lithuania, the SSC ceiling is reduced to 84 times the average monthly salary from 2020. In addition, Lithuania's tax-free salary threshold is increased from 1.3 to 1.65 minimum wages from January 2020. In Ireland, the weekly income threshold for the higher rate of employers pay related social insurance (PRSI) is increased to EUR 395 in 2020 (previously it was EUR 386 in 2019 and EUR 276 in 2018). Base narrowing measures related to employees and self-employed SSCs and payroll taxes were also introduced. In Austria, where certain SSCs can be partly reimbursed, the maximum SSC reimbursement for low-income earners is increased from EUR 400 to EUR 700 annually. The maximum SSC reimbursement for retirees is also increased from EUR 110 to EUR 300. In Poland, to reduce the tax burden on micro-entrepreneurs whose income in the previous calendar year was less than PLN 120 000, the minimum monthly SSC base has been set at 30% of the minimum monthly salary (MMS, equal to PLN 2 600 in January 2020), compared to the standard minimum of 60% of the MMS. In Quebec in Canada, to encourage the employment and retention of older workers, payroll taxes are reduced for SMEs that employ older workers through a tax credit (by 50% for workers aged 60 to 64 and 75% for workers aged 65 and over).

**Only one country broadened its SSC base, which represents a marked decline compared with recent years.** In France, employers benefit from a general reduction in employer SSCs due on the remuneration of their employees earning less than 1.6 times the minimum wage. As of January 1, 2020, the parameters for calculating this SSC reduction have been modified and is now capped for employees benefiting from a specific flat-rate deduction for professional expenses.

Table 3.6. Changes to social security contribution bases

| | Base ⇧ | | Base ⇩ | |
|---|---|---|---|---|
| *Into effect in* | **2019** | **2020 or later** | **2019** | **2020 or later** |
| Employers SSCs | ESP | FRA | HUN IRL LTU SVK | ARG IRL LTU SVN SWE |
| Employees SSCs | ESP GBR | | HUN FRA SVK | AUT |
| Self-employed | GBR GRC | | ESP POL | POL |
| Payroll taxes | GBR | | | CAN |

Note: Countries in brackets have only announced reforms.
Source: OECD Annual Tax Policy Reform Questionnaire.

## Corporate income taxes and other corporate taxes

**The downward trend in statutory corporate income tax (CIT) rates is continuing.** The most significant CIT rate reductions have generally been introduced in countries with higher initial CIT rates, leading to further convergence in CIT rates across countries. Many countries have also reinforced the generosity of their corporate tax incentives to stimulate investment and innovation. With regard to international taxation, efforts to protect CIT bases against corporate tax avoidance have continued with the adoption of significant reforms in line with the OECD/G20 Base Erosion and Profit Shifting (BEPS) project. The tax challenges arising from the increasing digitalisation of the economy are another major concern for many countries. Efforts to achieve a consensus-based multilateral solution to address those challenges are ongoing, but some countries have announced or implemented interim measures to tax certain revenues from digital services in the meantime.

### *Trends in CIT revenues have varied across countries*

**The CIT to GDP ratio and CIT revenues as a share of total tax revenues vary across countries**. CIT revenues ranged from 1.0% of GDP in Latvia[1] to 6.0% of GDP in Norway in 2018 (Figure 3.5). As a share of total tax revenues, CIT ranged from 3.2% of total taxation in Hungary to 22.5% of total tax revenues in Indonesia (Figure 3.6). Multiple factors can explain differences in revenues from CIT including statutory CIT rates, the breadth of the CIT base, the degree to which firms are incorporated, the phase in the economic cycle and the degree of cyclicality of the corporate tax system, as well as countries' reliance on other taxes. These factors may have also contributed to the large differences in revenues between 2000 and 2018 observed in several countries including Chile, Greece and Finland. Figure 3.6 shows that CIT tends to represent a larger share of revenue in countries with significant natural resources and in emerging and developing economies. In the case of emerging and developing economies, total tax revenues are generally lower as a percentage of GDP and personal income tax revenues tend to play a smaller role than the CIT.

Figure 3.5. Corporate income tax revenues as a share of GDP in 2000 and 2018

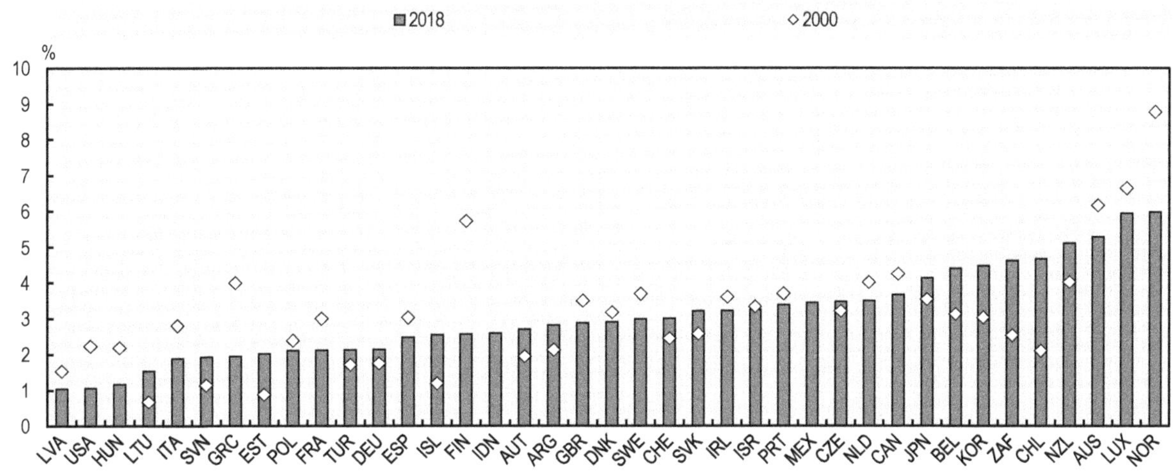


Note: 2017 data was used for Argentina, Australia, Greece, Indonesia and South Africa. No 2000 data were available for Indonesia and Mexico.
Source: OECD Global Revenue Statistics Database.

StatLink https://doi.org/10.1787/888934158594

Figure 3.6. Corporate income tax revenues as a share of total tax revenues in 2000 and 2018

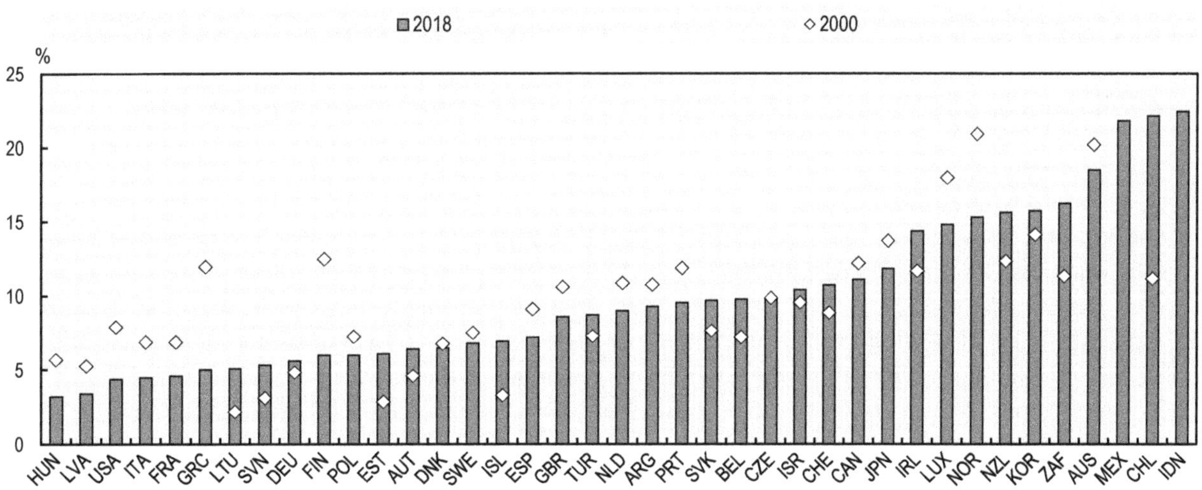


Note: 2017 data was used for Argentina, Australia, Greece, Indonesia, Japan, Mexico and South Africa. No 2000 data were available for Indonesia and Mexico.
Source: OECD Global Revenue Statistics Database.

StatLink https://doi.org/10.1787/888934158613

**On average, CIT revenues have held up as a share of GDP over the last two decades**. Across OECD countries, after a peak in 2007 and a subsequent fall following the global financial crisis, CIT revenues have remained relatively stable since 2009 on average, slightly picking up from 2015 onwards. Average CIT revenues as a share of GDP are now back to a level slightly below their 2000 level (Figure 3.7). They seem to have been relatively unaffected by the progressive decline in statutory CIT rates, which is also shown in Figure 3.7, and discussed in the following section. Various factors may have contributed to this apparent paradox between declining CIT rates and relatively stable CIT revenues, including the rise in corporate profits, the broadening of CIT bases, the incorporation of businesses, and the decline in borrowing costs as a result of low interest rates.

Figure 3.7. Evolution of the average combined statutory CIT rate and average CIT revenues in OECD countries since 2000

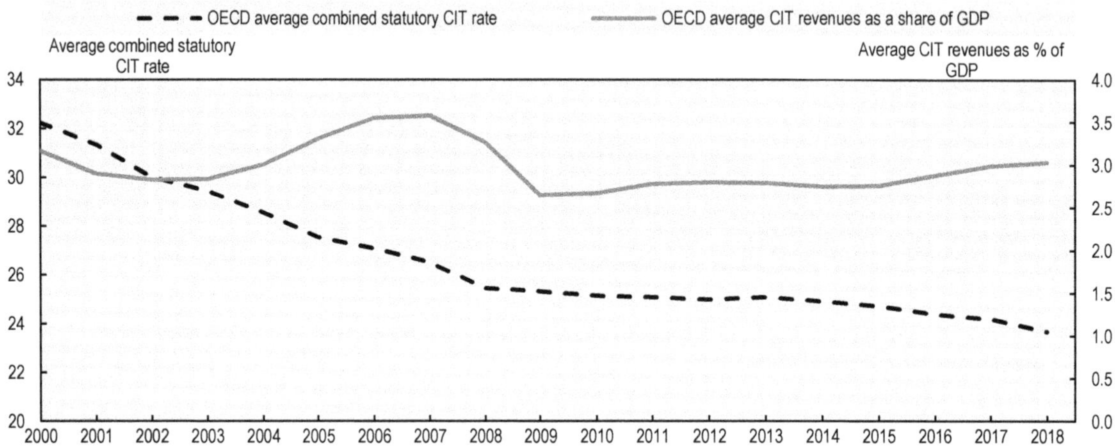


Note: Combined statutory CIT rates refer to central and sub-central statutory CIT rates.
Source: OECD Revenue Statistics Database and OECD Tax Database.

StatLink https://doi.org/10.1787/888934158632

### *There has been a steady and widespread decline in corporate income tax rates*

#### *Standard CIT rates*

**The decline in CIT rates has been a steady and widespread trend.** Figure 3.8 shows the changes in the distribution of CIT rates between 2000 and 2020 across the countries covered in the report and highlights major shifts in the CIT landscape. In 2020, there were only two countries with CIT rates above 30%, against 23 in 2000. Meanwhile, the number of countries with CIT rates below 20% increased from two in 2000 to 11 in 2020. Overall, in the OECD, the average combined (central and sub-central) CIT rate has declined from 32.2% in 2000 to 23.5% in 2020 and OECD countries' CIT rates have become slightly less dispersed (Figure 3.9).

**From 2015 onwards, the decline in average CIT rates has been driven by high-tax countries.** In Figure 3.9, three main phases in the decline of OECD statutory CIT rates can be distinguished. First, there was a rapid decline in the OECD average CIT rate from 2000 to 2008 from 32.2% to 25.4%, driven by decreases in countries with both high and low CIT rates. This decline was followed by a more stable phase where the average CIT rate remained relatively stable, at around 25%. Finally, starting in 2015, the decline in the average CIT rate started accelerating again, declining from 24.9% in 2014 to 23.2% in 2020. This decline has been driven by a decrease in countries with relatively high tax rates as indicated by the evolution of the 75$^{th}$ percentile, which dropped from 29.9% in 2014 to 27.2% in 2020. In the same period, countries with relatively low CIT rates remained constant in the majority of cases, with the 25$^{th}$ percentile remaining at 20%. The only exception was Hungary where the CIT rate was cut to 9% in 2017.

## Figure 3.8. The distribution of combined statutory CIT rates in 2000 and 2020

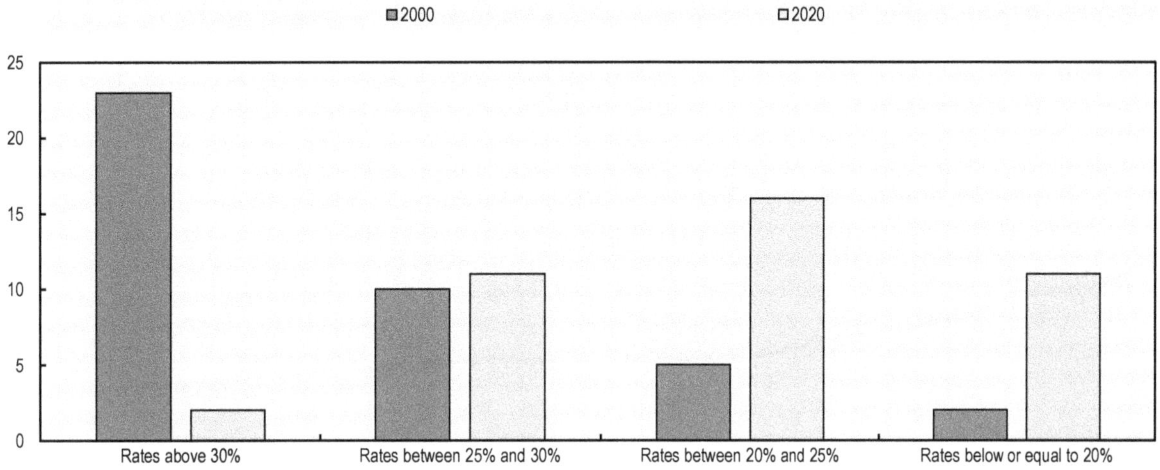


Source: OECD Corporate Tax Statistics Database, OECD Tax Database and OECD Annual Tax Policy Reform Questionnaire.

StatLink https://doi.org/10.1787/888934158651

## Figure 3.9. Evolution of the OECD average combined statutory CIT rate and dispersion of OECD CIT rates between 2000 and 2020

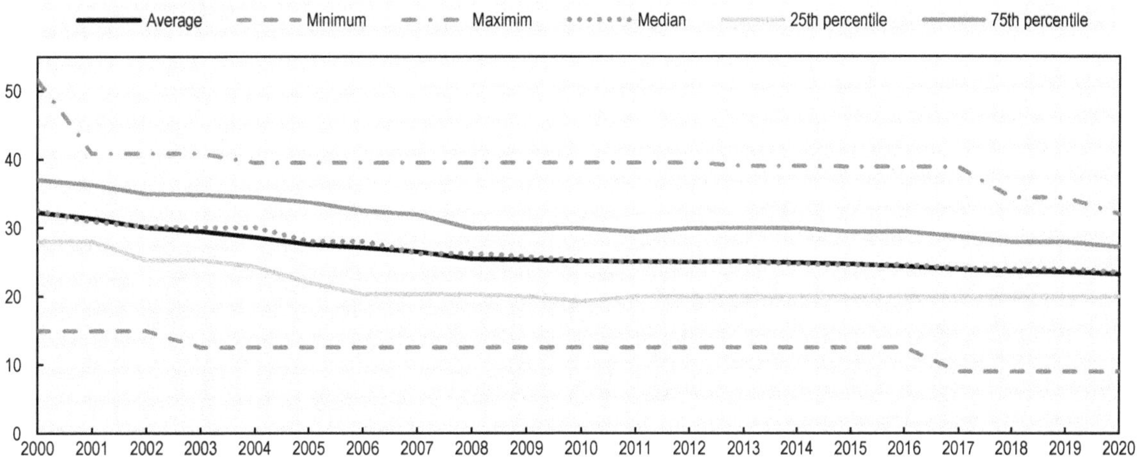


Source: OECD Tax Database and OECD Annual Tax Policy Reform Questionnaire.

StatLink https://doi.org/10.1787/888934158670

**CIT rate reductions have been particularly pronounced in G7 countries.** G7 countries had significantly higher CIT rates than other countries in the early 2000s and, on average, experienced the strongest average CIT rate reduction between 2000 and 2020, amounting to 13.2 percentage points. In comparison, the average decline for OECD countries that are not G7 members was about 8.0 percentage points (Figure 3.10). With the exception of the United Kingdom, the combined statutory CIT rates of G7 members remain among the highest in the OECD (Figure 3.11). The non-OECD countries covered in the report (Argentina, China, Indonesia and South Africa) have also seen a decline in their CIT rates, but not to the same extent as OECD countries, and their CIT rates remain higher than the OECD average (Figure 3.10).

## Figure 3.10. Evolution of average combined statutory CIT rates in different groups of countries

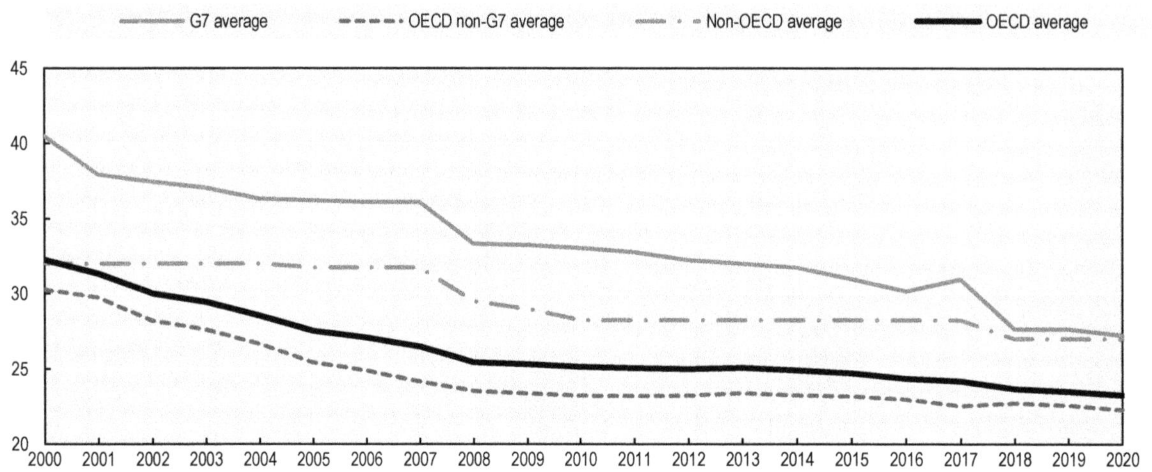


Note: The non-OECD average refers to the average of the four non-OECD countries covered in this publication: Argentina, China, Indonesia and South Africa.

Source: OECD Corporate Tax Statistics Database, OECD Tax Database and OECD Annual Tax Policy Reform Questionnaire.

StatLink https://doi.org/10.1787/888934158689

## Figure 3.11. Combined statutory CIT rates by country in 2000, 2008 and 2020

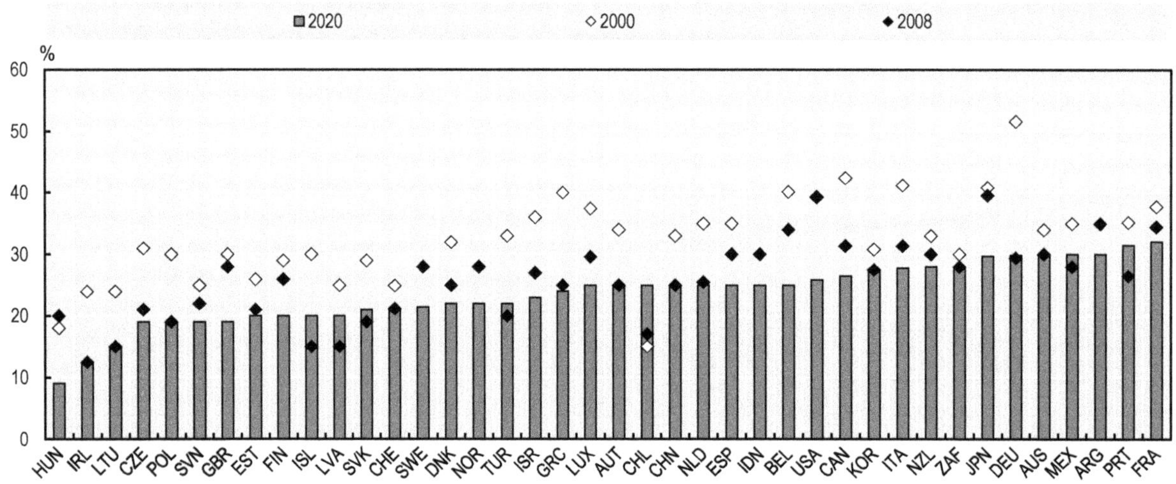


Note: Statutory CIT rates as of January 2020

Source: OECD Corporate Tax Statistics Database, OECD Tax Database and OECD Annual Tax Policy Reform Questionnaire.

StatLink https://doi.org/10.1787/888934158708

**In 2020, reductions in standard CIT rates were introduced in Belgium, Canada (Alberta), France, Greece and Indonesia** (Table 3.7). In Belgium, the standard CIT rate was lowered to 25% as part of the Corporate Income Tax Reform Act of 2017. In France, the standard CIT rate was lowered to 31% (except for companies with an annual turnover exceeding EUR 250 million), as part of a previously legislated CIT rate reduction, which is expected to progressively bring the CIT rate down to 25% by 2022. In Canada, the region of Alberta implemented the Job Creation Tax Cut, which provides for reductions in the general CIT rate from 12% to 8% over four years. The rate was reduced from 12% to 11% on 1 July 2019 and will be reduced by one percentage point on 1 January of each year until it reaches 8% in 2022. In Greece, from tax year 2019 onwards, the CIT rate has been reduced from 28% to 24%. Indonesia has accelerated the decrease in its statutory CIT rate, initially planned to start in 2021. Indonesia's CIT rate is now lowered from 25% to 22% in 2020 and 2021, and will be further decreased to 20% in 2022. Overall, the CIT rate cuts introduced in 2020 have been more sizeable than in 2019, with an average combined CIT rate reduction across the countries that introduced CIT rate cuts of around 3 percentage points, compared to an average decrease of around 1 percentage point in 2019.

**Standard CIT rate reductions are also set to come into force in 2021.** In the Netherlands, the originally planned reduction of the CIT rate applying to income exceeding EUR 200 000, was partly reversed; the CIT rate was not decreased to 22.55% in 2020 as originally planned; instead it remains at 25% in 2020 and will be lowered to 21.7% instead of 20.50% in 2021. Argentina also revised its scheduled CIT rate reduction: the planned reduction of its CIT rate from 30% to 25% in 2020 has been postponed until 2021 (Figure 3.12). Argentina's distributed dividend tax will also increase from 7% to 13% in 2021. In Sweden, the statutory CIT rate remains at 21.4% in 2020 and will be cut to 20.6% in 2021.

Table 3.7. Changes in corporate income tax rates

| | Rate ⇧ | | Rate ⇩ | |
|---|---|---|---|---|
| Into effect in | 2019 | 2020 or later | 2019 | 2020 or later |
| Standard CIT rate | | | GRC LUX NOR SWE | ARG BEL FRA GRC IDN NLD NOR SWE |
| SME CIT rate | | | AUS CAN NLD POL | HUN NLD SVK |
| | | | | |
| Patent box/IP regime rate | NLD | | FRA POL | CHE1 |

1. Switzerland introduced an IP regime requiring cantons to tax at least 10% of the eligible income.
Source: OECD Annual Tax Policy Reform Questionnaire.

### *SME CIT rates*

**Reduced CIT rates for SMEs are common across OECD countries.** A number of countries provide reduced CIT rates for SMEs, although the design of these reduced tax rates varies significantly. Some countries apply lower tax rates on the first tranche(s) of profits, regardless of total income levels; some have reduced CIT rates for corporations with income below a certain level; and others determine eligibility for small business tax rates based on non-income criteria (e.g. turnover or assets) instead of or in addition to income criteria.

Figure 3.12. Selected corporate income tax rate reductions

Central government corporate income tax rates, %

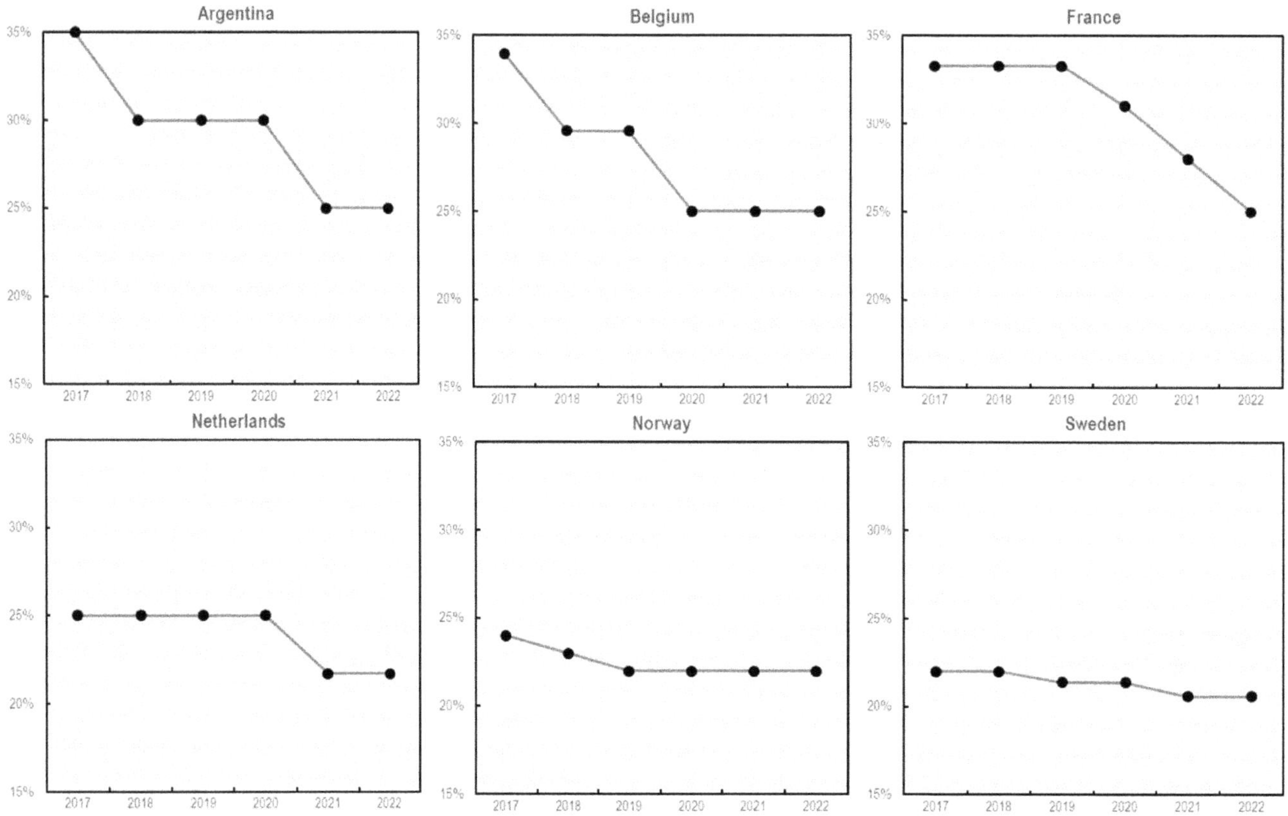


Source: OECD Annual Tax Policy Reform Questionnaire.

StatLink https://doi.org/10.1787/888934158727

**A few countries have reduced their SME CIT rates**. In the Netherlands, as planned, the lower CIT rate that applies to taxable income up to EUR 200,000 was cut from 19% to 16.5% in 2020 and will be further reduced to 15% in 2021. To simplify its tax system and reduce the tax burden on SMEs, Hungary abolished the Simplified Business Tax (EVA) while reducing the rate of small business tax (KIVA) by 1 percentage point from 13% to 12%. The Slovak Republic has lowered the CIT rate from 21% to 15% for all corporations with a turnover below EUR 100 000 per year. In Portugal, the taxable income subject to the reduced CIT rate of 17% has been increased from EUR 15 000 to EUR 25 000 and, in the case of SMEs that carry out their activities in inland regions, the taxable income subject to the reduced CIT rate of 12.5% has also been raised from EUR 15 000 to EUR 25 000. In Poland, the definition of "small taxpayer" for CIT and PIT purposes was increased to include companies with revenues not exceeding the equivalent of EUR 2 million in the previous tax year (until 2019 this threshold was equal to EUR 1.2 million). This measure is aimed at bringing more companies into the SME regime.

### *Taxes on the financial sector*

**A few countries are introducing changes to financial sector taxes.** Taxes on the financial sector gained attention in the aftermath of the global financial crisis. They are generally collected on top of ordinary corporate taxes and can be applied on different bases (e.g. bank deposits, capital assets, risk-weighted assets). The Slovak Republic first introduced a bank levy in 2012. The tax was initially introduced for a limited period and was expected to be repealed by 2020. However, the government approved its extension in November 2019, doubling the tax rate from 0.2% to 0.4% of banks' liabilities net of equity. In Iceland, a bank levy was introduced in 2011 at a rate of 0.041% on financial institutions' debt. In 2014, the rate was raised to 0.376% to finance the government's household debt relief programme. This tax is scheduled to be lowered in four steps to reach 0.145% by 2023. In Sweden, a tax on the financial sector, which is scheduled to take effect in 2022, has been announced. Lithuania has introduced an additional CIT rate of 5% on top of the standard rate of 15% on the taxable profits of credit institutions.

*Intellectual property regimes*

**Intellectual property (IP) tax regimes allow income from the exploitation of IP to be taxed at a lower rate than other income**. IP regimes have been introduced in an increasing number of countries, and these usually involve a significant reduction in the tax rate applicable to IP-related income compared to the tax rate that would otherwise apply (Figure 3.13).

Figure 3.13. Reduced CIT rates under selected non-harmful intellectual property regimes in 2019

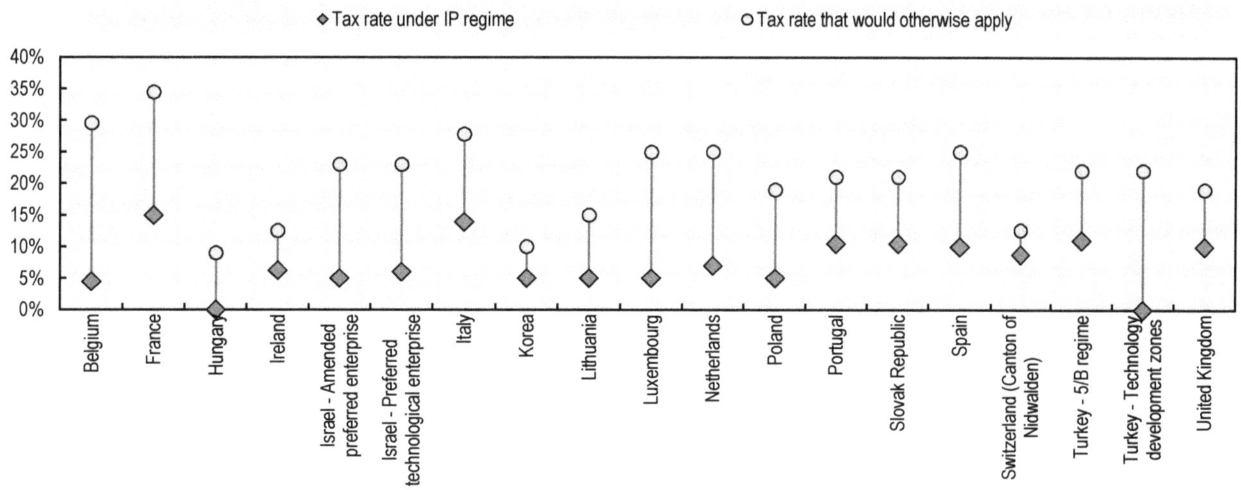


Source: OECD (2020), Corporate Tax Statistics Database.

StatLink https://doi.org/10.1787/888934158746

**A number of IP regimes were revised to comply with BEPS Action 5 and Poland introduced a new IP regime.** Countries need to align their IP regimes with Action 5 of the OECD/G20 BEPS project, which aims at addressing harmful tax practices, including IP regimes where certain substance requirements are not met. In the past, IP regimes could be designed in a way that incentivised firms to locate their IP assets in a jurisdiction regardless of where the underlying R&D was undertaken. The modified nexus approach under Action 5 now requires that substantial economic activity is undertaken in the country offering the favourable tax regime and that the amount of income eligible for benefits in an IP regime is proportional to the amount of expenditures undertaken by the taxpayer to develop the IP. Action 5, which is a peer-reviewed minimum standard of the OECD/G20 BEPS package, has led many countries to align their IP regimes with these new requirements (see section 3.2.4). As noted in last year's report, Poland introduced an IP regime for the first time, designed to be in line with the modified nexus approach. Starting from January 2019, under the Polish IP box regime, profits from qualifying IP are taxed at the preferential rate of 5%. Luxembourg replaced its previous IP regime, abolished in 2016, with a new one that is in line with the modified nexus approach. France also introduced a revised IP regime in line with the modified nexus approach as of 1 January 2019. The income benefitting from this regime is taxed at a 10% rate. In Switzerland, a significant tax reform, approved by Parliament and adopted after a referendum in May 2019, includes mandatory patent boxes at the cantonal level effective starting from January 2020 (Box 3.2).

### Box 3.2. The Swiss tax reform

In Switzerland, the Federal Act on Tax Reform and AHV (old age and survivors' insurance) Financing (TRAF) was approved in a referendum on 19 May 2019. The reform aims to maintain the competitiveness of Switzerland as a business location while securing jobs and tax receipts in the Confederation, cantons and communes. Mandatory measures of the TRAF entered into effect on 1 January 2020 at the federal level. Some of the cantonal measures are optional and cantons can tailor the majority of measures to their specific circumstances and needs within certain boundaries.

The tax reform brings the replacement of certain preferential tax regimes in line with a new set of internationally accepted measures. The central part of this package is the elimination of cantonal tax privileges for status companies (i.e. those that would benefit from the mixed, domiciliary, holding or principal company regimes, or the Swiss finance branch regime), which is compensated by the creation of patent boxes and the possibility for cantons to introduce additional deductions for R&D. Finally, it entails an increase in the cantonal share of federal direct tax revenues, a rebalancing of the national financial equalisation scheme, and increased AHV financing.

**Abolition of cantonal tax privileges (mandatory)**

The reform abolished the tax privilege of status companies that previously paid a reduced or null CIT at cantonal level. At the federal level, status companies continue to be subject to the regular CIT rate.

**Patent box (mandatory)**

The reform introduces a patent box regime intended to comply with OECD standards. Net profits from domestic and foreign patents and similar rights are to be taxed separately with a maximum reduction of 90% to be set at cantonal discretion.

**Additional deductions for research and development (voluntary)**

The cantons may give a higher weighting to R&D expenditure to promote research and development. The enhanced R&D deduction at the cantonal level can reach a maximum of 50% (on top of the 100% baseline tax deduction) of the effective qualifying expenses, at the discretion of cantons. The value of tax allowances will depend on the canton specific CIT rate.

#### *Other business taxes*

**Poland has reduced the tax rate on the extraction of copper and silver by 15%.** This measure aims to reduce the burden on businesses engaging in mining activities subject to the Law on Taxation of Extraction of Certain Metals introduced in 2012.

**A new levy is charged on all Greek-owned fishing ships and boats**, as well as tug boats, which operate in maritime transport or shipping services for a time period that does not exceed 50% of their total operating time. Lifeguard vessels that perform exclusively rescue and maritime relief operations are excluded. Depending on the type of boat, the duty is calculated based on the horsepower or length of the vessel.

### *Many countries have increased the generosity of their corporate tax incentives*

**Most countries have CIT base narrowing provisions that lower companies' effective tax burdens**. Corporate tax systems differ across jurisdictions with regard to provisions that affect the tax base. Forward-looking effective tax rates (ETRs) capture information on corporate tax rates and bases as well as other relevant provisions within a single framework, providing a basis to compare corporate tax systems across jurisdictions. In particular, effective marginal tax rates (EMTRs) measure the extent to which taxation increases the pre-tax rate of return required by investors to break even. This indicator is used to analyse how taxes affect the incentive to expand existing investments given a fixed location.

**EMTRs can diverge considerably from statutory tax rates.** When fiscal depreciation is generous compared to true economic depreciation or if there are other significant base narrowing provisions, the EMTRs will be lower than the statutory tax rate. On the contrary, if tax depreciation does not cover the full effects of true economic depreciation, effective taxation will be higher. The EMTRs reported in Figure 3.14 show the effects of fiscal depreciation and other allowances and deductions (e.g., allowances for corporate equity, half-year conventions, inventory valuation methods). These CIT base narrowing provisions lower corporate EMTRs compared to statutory CIT rates in the majority of countries, reflecting their positive effects on businesses' incentives to expand investments. Certain CIT base narrowing provisions, in particular allowances for corporate equity (in Italy, Belgium, Portugal and Poland in 2019) and generous accelerated depreciation rules considerably reduce EMTRs, which end up reaching negative values.

Figure 3.14. Composite marginal effective tax rates in 2019

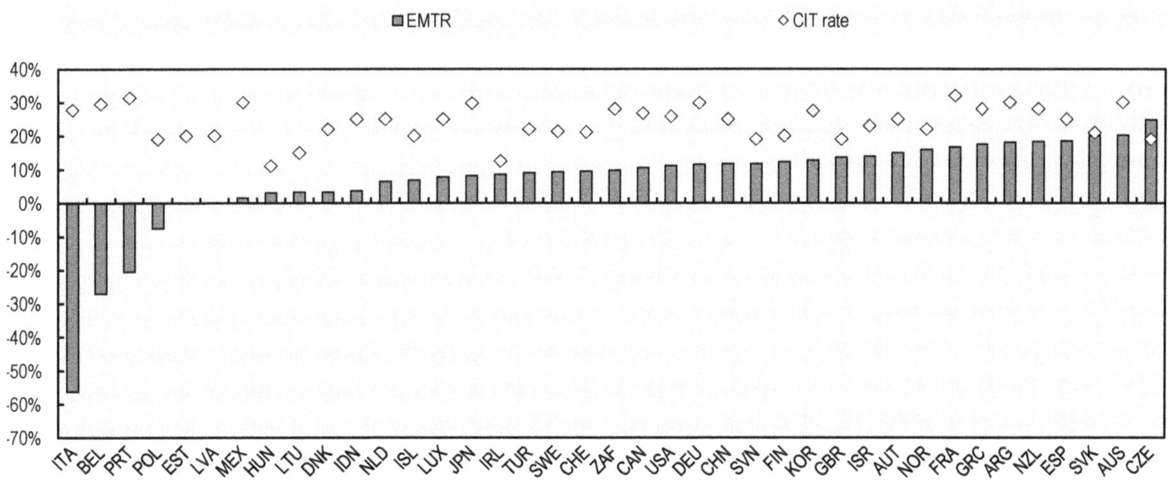


Note: The results are based on the macroeconomic scenario with constant 3% interest and 1% inflation rates. The composite Effective Marginal Tax Rate (EMTR) is constructed as a weighted average across finance- and asset-specific EMTRs. It is a synthetic tax policy indicator measuring the extent to which taxation increases the pre-tax rate of return required by investors to break even on their investment. This indicator is used to analyse how taxes affect the incentive to expand existing investments given a fixed location (along the intensive margin).
Source: OECD Corporate Tax Statistics Database.

StatLink https://doi.org/10.1787/888934158765

**Countries have generally increased the generosity of their tax incentives through tax reforms affecting CIT bases.** Several countries have increased the generosity of their CIT incentives to stimulate investment, innovation and environmental sustainability (Table 3.8). These measures will contribute to further reducing corporate EMTRs. Significant CIT base changes have also been introduced in Chile as part of its comprehensive 2020 tax reform (Box 3.3).

## Table 3.8. Changes to corporate tax bases

| | Base ⇧ | | Base ⇩ | |
|---|---|---|---|---|
| Into effect in | 2019 | 2020 or later | 2019 | 2020 or later |
| Capital allowances and general incentives | | | AUS CAN GBR HUN | AUS CHL DEU FIN ITA USA |
| Loss carryover provisions | BEL GBR KOR NLD | | | SVK |
| SME-related tax base changes | | | HUN | HUN POL SVK |
| R&D tax incentives and patent box regimes | | | CHE DNK KOR ISL NZL TUR | IRL ITA SVK |
| Notional interest deductions | | | POL | ITA |
| Environmentally-related tax incentives | | ITA USA | IRL | ISL ITA SVK |
| Other tax incentives | | | ITA KOR LTU MEX POL | |

Note: Countries in brackets have only announced reforms.
Source: OECD Annual Tax Policy Reform Questionnaire.

### Box 3.3. Chile´s 2020 Tax Reform: The Tax Modernisation Law

Chile's Tax Modernisation Law (Nº 21.210) was approved by Congress on 29 January 2020. Its main provisions entered into effect retroactively on 1 January 2020. It is a comprehensive tax reform that aims to support investment and growth and to modernise the relationship between taxpayers and the tax authority, trough enhanced tax certainty and digitalisation. It also includes measures to strengthen the progressivity of the tax system.

#### Investment and growth

The reform implements the return to a single general Corporate Income Tax regime (which consists of a Partially Integrated System) and an enhanced fully integrated regime for SMEs. Under the Partially Integrated System, the CIT rate is 27% and shareholders receive a 65% tax credit for the underlying CIT paid. SMEs benefit from a reduced CIT rate of 25% and a full dividend imputation credit. The accruals based corporate tax regime has been abolished. Small businesses whose shareholders are liable to the PIT can now opt to be taxed under the PIT and no longer first under the CIT and then under the PIT. Given the implementation difficulties of the previous system, the 2020 tax reform reduces complexity and tax compliance costs and delivers greater tax certainty. Other measures supporting increased levels of capital investment are described in the Report (e.g., accelerated tax depreciation, faster reimbursement of VAT).

#### Enhanced tax certainty

The reform contains a range of measures intended to provide greater tax certainty to taxpayers. These include new transparency rules on administrative requests to the tax authority, new rules for the deductibility of business expenses and for the use of foreign tax credits. The reform also implements a domestic permanent establishment concept that is consistent with OECD standards. For the first time, a tax ombudsman is incorporated in Chile and an entirely new set of rules have been added to the taxpayers' charter of rights. The taxable event of the Green Tax is amended, as the requirement of a minimum thermal power capacity of the polluting facilities is removed, focusing now on the volume of emissions (and new tax offsetting possibilities through effective mitigation measures are introduced).

**Digitalisation**

With the objective of facilitating and enhancing tax compliance, the tax reform further digitalises the relationship between taxpayers and the tax authority, including a new digital folder with historical taxpayer records and additional online filings for all types of taxes. It also implements mandatory electronic VAT receipts (in addition to the e-invoices established mandatorily in 2014), which are designed to simplify and modernise VAT procedures and further reduce VAT and income tax evasion. The reform also implements a new VAT simplified registration and compliance regime for non-resident suppliers to facilitate compliance on B2C digital transactions, in accordance with OECD Guidelines.

**Strengthening the progressivity of the tax system**

The reform will have the effect of modifying the Chilean tax structure. Once in full effect, the reform is projected to increase tax revenues by USD 2 204 million, of which more than 55% (USD 1 222 million) will be derived from high-income taxpayers. Many of these progressivity-enhancing measures are described in the Report (e.g. the new progressive property tax on high-value property added to the ordinary property tax; the highest income tax bracket with a top PIT rate of 40%). Additionally, the reform extended the residential property tax rebate for the elderly low-income taxpayers.

### *Increases in capital allowances*

**Several countries introduced (often temporary) measures increasing the generosity of their capital allowances.** In Finland, new temporary measures were introduced to support investment in new machinery and equipment. For these assets, the rate of annual depreciation was increased from 25% to 50% until the end of 2023. Temporary measures were also introduced in Chile, where new or imported fixed assets acquired between October 2019 and December 2021 can be expensed for 50% of their value and depreciated at an accelerated rate the remaining part. More generous allowances were introduced in Araucania, a region in the south of Chile, where new and imported fixed assets can benefit from full expensing. In Australia, the threshold for the ‘instant’ asset write-off was temporarily increased from AUD 20 000 to AUD 30 000, and access was expanded to businesses with an annual turnover below AUD 50 million (up from AUD 10 million) prior to the COVID-19 pandemic. In Germany, the construction of new rented flats is encouraged through special temporary depreciation rules until the end of 2026. Immediate expensing was introduced in the Slovak Republic for micro taxpayer corporations (i.e. with yearly turnover below EUR 49 790). Under this provision, micro taxpayers can benefit from a 100% deduction of all tangible assets except cars costing more than EUR 48 000. Japan introduced a 30% depreciation (or, alternatively, a 15% tax credit) for investments in 5G-related equipment.

**A few countries introduced more generous depreciation schemes to encourage the transition to environmentally friendly vehicles.** In Italy, the deductibility of company vehicle costs was tied to carbon emissions such that deductibility decreases as carbon emissions increase. The Slovak Republic introduced a shorter two-year depreciation period for battery and plug-in hybrid vehicles, as compared to the usual four-year depreciation period generally applied to motor vehicles. In Greece, a 130% super deduction was introduced for corporate passenger car expenses with low (up to 50 grams of $CO_2$/km) or zero emissions and a maximum retail price before tax of EUR 40 000, for expenses incurred for public transportation tickets, and for expenses related to the installation and operation of charging points for low-emission cars. Finally, in Iceland, eco-friendly business vehicles can benefit from accelerated annual tax depreciation.

### *Increase in the generosity of R&D tax incentives*

**Many countries incentivise business investment in R&D through tax incentives.**[2] R&D tax incentives have become a widely used policy tool to promote business R&D. The number of OECD countries offering tax relief for R&D expenditures increased from 19 in 2000 to 30 in 2019, with the design and scale of R&D

tax reliefs differing across countries.[3] As shown in Figure 3.15, up until the onset of the global financial crisis, the marginal rate of R&D tax subsidy estimated for large profitable firms[4] on average increased across OECD countries. This trend stabilised around 2014, with average implied subsidy rates remaining relatively constant thereafter. Figure 3.16 compares the implied tax subsidy rates on R&D expenditures for large profitable firms across countries and years (2000, 2009 and 2019). In 2019, R&D tax incentives were particularly generous for large profitable firms in France, Portugal, Chile and Spain, with the largest increases in generosity compared to 2000 being observed in Chile, France, and Lithuania. These changes reflect the introduction of new R&D tax incentives and the increasing generosity of existing R&D tax relief provisions.

Figure 3.15. Implied tax subsidy rates on R&D expenditure: aggregate trends, 2000-19

1-B-Index, large profitable firms

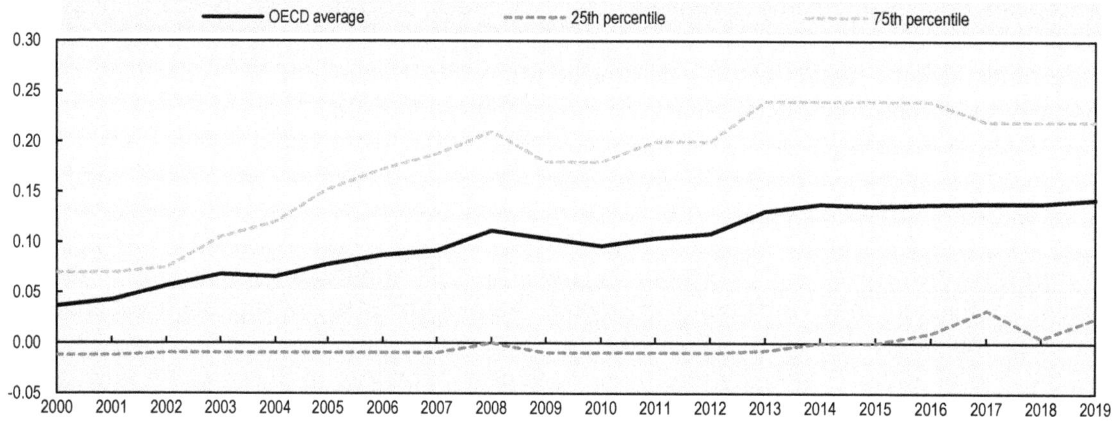


Note: Information on B-Index methodology can be found here: http://www.oecd.org/sti/b-index.pdf.
Source: OECD R&D Tax Incentive Database, https://oe.cd/rdtax, December 2019, Data and notes: https://oc.cd/ds/rdtax.

StatLink https://doi.org/10.1787/888934158784

Figure 3.16. Implied tax subsidy rates on R&D expenditures, 2000, 2009 and 2019

1-B-Index, large profitable firms

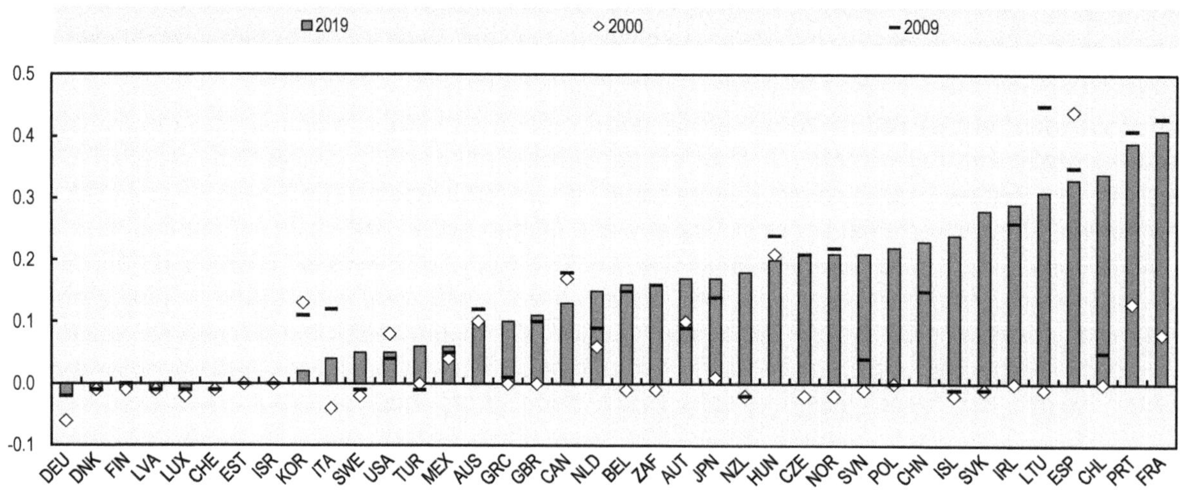


Note: Information on B-Index methodology can be found here: http://www.oecd.org/sti/b-index.pdf
Source: OECD R&D Tax Incentive Database, https://oe.cd/rdtax, December 2019, Data and notes: https://oc.cd/ds/rdtax

StatLink https://doi.org/10.1787/888934158803

**Germany implemented a new R&D tax credit to complement its business R&D support policies.** This new incentive, effective in January 2020, is made available for a broad range of R&D activities, complementing Germany's direct support measures (e.g. R&D grants, government procurement of R&D services) targeting specific R&D investments. It consists of a 25% R&D tax credit, applicable to R&D salaries and eligible contract research expenses up to EUR 2 million, and entails a maximum level of R&D tax support of EUR 500 000 per year per company. Funding is open to activities carried out in-house or by an external R&D service provider.[5] In the case of expenses incurred for contract R&D activities, 60% of the overall expenses that are paid for such activities are considered eligible expenses. The R&D tax credit itself is not subject to taxation and is refundable when it exceeds the taxpayer's tax liability.

**In Ireland, the current R&D tax credit is to be enhanced for micro and small companies,** subject to state aid approval from the European Commission. For these companies, the rate of the tax credit will be increased from 25% to 30%. As was the case previously, the measure can also support loss-making companies, since unused tax credits in any year are payable[6] or may alternatively be carried back to the previous accounting period or carried forward indefinitely. An additional feature allows micro and small companies to claim credits for qualifying pre-trading R&D expenditures. Before a company begins to trade, the credit may be offset against VAT and payroll taxes. Additional measures to enhance R&D incentives for all companies have been introduced. In particular, the amount of a company's qualifying R&D expenditure that can be outsourced to third-level institutions was increased from 5% to 15% to increase collaboration between companies and the education sector.

**Other countries have increased the generosity of their tax incentives for R&D and innovation.** In the Slovak Republic, the amount of deductible costs has increased. For financial years starting on or after 1 January 2019, the volume-based and incremental rate of the R&D tax allowance was retrospectively increased from 100% to 150%, while for fiscal years starting on or after 1 January 2020, these rates have been increased to 200%. Finally, the new R&D tax credit announced in New Zealand in 2018 became effective in July 2019, providing a refundable tax credit[7] of 15% of eligible R&D expenditures with a minimum R&D expense of NZD 50 000 and a ceiling on total eligible R&D expenditure of NZD 120 million.

**In Italy, the R&D tax credit that was available in 2019 has been modified and extended to apply to expenses in the innovation and design fields**. The R&D tax credit is computed by taking into account eligible expenses incurred in the fiscal year 2020 and depends on two factors that will need to be multiplied to compute the amount of the tax credit. These two factors are the type of expense incurred and the type of activity. For expenses such as research labour costs and contract R&D, up to 150% of the actual expenditure is considered. For costs such as materials, technical expertise and depreciation expenses, 20% to 30% of the incurred costs is considered. The factor depending on the type of activity ranges from 12% of eligible expenses for R&D activities to 6% for design activities. The tax relief ceiling was decreased from EUR 10 million in 2019 to EUR 3 million for R&D expenditures and EUR 1.5 million for the remaining activities.[8]

*Other tax incentives*

**In the United States, several existing business tax credits were further extended, mainly to promote environmental sustainability**. The existing tax credits for biodiesel and renewable diesel, electricity produced from certain renewable sources and alternative fuels were extended. Also, to boost economic growth and support investment, existing tax credits for new markets, work opportunities and railroad track maintenance were extended.

**Incentives for investments in small enterprises were introduced in Hungary, Chile and Japan**. In Hungary, the development tax incentive allows companies to deduct up to 80% of their CIT in the year of investment and over the following 12 years. The minimum present value of investments required to obtain the allowance will be reduced in the case of SMEs, which makes the tax incentive more widely available. Also, investments in start-ups are incentivised through an increase in the maximum limit of tax allowances related to angel investments. Chile enhanced profit reinvestment incentives for SMEs with the introduction of a measure allowing a tax base reduction of up to 50% of reinvested profits. The maximum deduction allowed is of UF 5 000 (approximately EUR 165 000). Japan introduced corporate income deductions equivalent to 25% of the investment carried out in innovative start-ups.

**Temporary tax incentives to improve productivity were introduced in Korea**. From January until December 2020, tax credits granted for investments made in qualifying facilities were increased from 1% to 2% for large companies, from 3% to 5% for medium-scale enterprises and from 7% to 10% for SMEs.

**In Mexico, tax incentives to specific regions are being reoriented**. The tax relief granted to the Special Economic Zones (SEZs)[9] was repealed. Going forward, tax policies will focus on fundamental projects targeting southern regions (e.g. the Mayan Train and the Isthmus of Tehuantepec) and on tax benefits available for activities in the northern border area.

**In Japan, eligibility conditions for tax credits and tax allowances were revised to encourage large enterprises to increase salaries and investments**. More specifically, large corporations where the average salary does not exceed that of the previous year and the amount of domestic capital investment does not exceed 30% of the depreciation expenses in the current year, cannot benefit from R&D tax measures and other tax credits. In addition, large companies where the average wage growth was less than 3% or domestic capital investment was less than 95% of the depreciation costs incurred during the financial year cannot benefit from the tax credit equivalent to 15% of the wage increase.

**Indonesia has expanded the scope of its tax allowance regime to encourage investment**. Indonesia's tax incentive schemes, which were kept unchanged, include additional deductions, the accelerated depreciation of fixed tangible assets, the accelerated amortisation of intangible assets, as well as enhanced loss carry forward provisions (from five to ten years). The new rules have expanded the number of sectors eligible for the incentives and have removed many of the existing geographical restrictions on eligible investments.

### *Deductions for reinvested earnings in Portugal*

**Portugal has broadened the deduction for the reinvestment of retained earnings.** The reinvestment of retained earnings ("DLRR – Dedução por Lucros Retidos e Reinvestidos") is a tax incentive for micro, small and medium-sized companies that provides the right to a CIT deduction equivalent to 10% of the retained and reinvested earnings used for the acquisition of relevant assets.[10] In the 2020 State Budget Law, the reinvestment period for retained earnings was increased from three to four years and the maximum amount of retained earnings that can be reinvested was raised from EUR 10 million to EUR 12 million. Intangible assets are also eligible if they are eligible for amortisation for tax purposes and are not acquired from related parties.

### *Notional interest deductions*

**The Italian allowance for corporate equity (ACE) was reintroduced.** The Italian ACE consists of a notional interest deduction from the CIT base, equal to the net increase in new equity employed in the entity (i.e. the equity generated after 2010) multiplied by a rate determined every year. In its 2019 budget, the Italian government abolished the ACE, compensating its removal by introducing several measures aimed at supporting investment, including a reduced CIT rate for reinvested profits. With the elimination of the tax reduction for reinvested earnings, the ACE was reintroduced from 2019 and its notional return rate was decreased from 1.5% in 2018 to 1.3% in 2019.

### *Loss carryover provisions*

**Contrary to the trend observed in recent years, where countries were limiting loss carryover provisions, the Slovak Republic increased the generosity of its loss carry-forward provisions.** The carry-forward period was extended from four to five years and the volume limit changed from 25% of accumulated losses to 50% of the tax base. For corporations in the category of micro-taxpayers (i.e. with turnover below EUR 49 790), a similar measure was introduced: the carry-forward period was extended from four to five years but no volume limits apply.

## *Fight against corporate tax avoidance*

**The past year has seen further progress on the implementation of the OECD/G20 BEPS package.** The OECD/G20 BEPS package, which includes 15 Actions aimed at addressing tax planning strategies that artificially shift profits to low or no-tax jurisdictions, was delivered in October 2015. The BEPS package sets out a variety of measures, including four minimum standards (Actions 5, 6, 13 and 14), common approaches that will facilitate the convergence of national practices, and guidance drawing on best practices. Countries are carrying out the implementation of the BEPS package through the Inclusive Framework on BEPS, which brings together more than 135 jurisdictions.

**As of March 2020, the provisions of the Multilateral Instrument to Implement Tax Treaty Related Measures to Prevent BEPS (MLI) had taken effect for about 300 tax agreements.** The MLI, concluded by over 100 jurisdictions in November 2016, allows jurisdictions to swiftly implement measures to strengthen existing tax treaties and protect governments against tax avoidance strategies that inappropriately use tax treaties to artificially shift profits to low or no-tax jurisdictions. The MLI includes measures against hybrid mismatch arrangements (Action 2), treaty abuse (Action 6), a strengthened definition of permanent establishment (Action 7) and measures to make mutual agreement procedures (MAP) more effective (Action 14). The MLI entered into force on 1 July 2018 and its provisions started to take effect from 1 January 2019. As of 15 March 2020, the MLI covered 94 jurisdictions[11] and 43 jurisdictions had deposited their instrument of ratification, acceptance or approval. Overall, it covers over 1650 tax agreements, which will be modified by the MLI once its provisions take effect for each of these agreements. More jurisdictions are expected to deposit their instrument of ratification, acceptance or approval of the MLI in 2020.

### *BEPS minimum standards*

**The MLI has allowed significant progress on the implementation of the Action 6 minimum standard on treaty shopping**. Action 6 calls for the adoption of treaty provisions to prevent the granting of treaty benefits in inappropriate circumstances and to put an end to treaty shopping. The 2019 peer review report, which was approved by the BEPS Inclusive Framework at its January 2020 meeting and which covers all comprehensive tax agreements concluded by each of the 129 jurisdictions that were members of the Inclusive Framework as at June 2019, shows substantial progress in the implementation of the Action 6 minimum standard. The peer review also confirms the success of the MLI, which has been the preferred tool of jurisdictions for implementing Action 6.

**Significant progress has also been made on Action 5 in addressing harmful tax practices**. Since the start of the BEPS Project, the Forum on Harmful Tax Practices (FHTP) has reviewed a total of 287 preferential tax regimes against the standard for harmful tax regimes. The results to date show that all IP regimes have been, with one exception, either abolished or amended to comply with the modified nexus approach, which requires that substantial economic activity is undertaken in the country offering the favourable tax regime and that the amount of income that is eligible for benefits in an IP regime is proportional to the amount of expenditures undertaken by the taxpayer to develop the IP. Where necessary, other changes have been made to comply with the standard (e.g., removal of ring-fencing features designed to attract investment while protecting the domestic tax base).

**In addition to the review of preferential tax regimes, there was a review of the substantial activities factor for "no or only nominal jurisdictions".** After agreeing the new substantial activities standard for "no or only nominal tax jurisdictions" in November 2018, the 12 "no or only nominal tax jurisdictions" identified by the FHTP introduced the necessary domestic legal framework to meet the standard. The standard requires that for certain highly mobile sectors of business activity, the core income generating activities must be conducted with qualified employees and operating expenditure in the jurisdiction. The FHTP has now reviewed the new domestic laws of the 12 no or only nominal tax jurisdictions. For 11 of these jurisdictions, the FHTP concluded that the domestic legal framework is in line with the standard and therefore "not harmful." Regarding the remaining jurisdiction reviewed by the FHTP (United Arab Emirates), the FHTP concluded that the legal framework was in line with the standard but with one technical point outstanding, and the jurisdiction is now in the process of amending the relevant law.

**On transparency in tax rulings, the second pillar of Action 5, progress has been achieved towards the compulsory spontaneous exchange of information on tax rulings**. So far, almost 18 000 tax rulings have been identified and close to 30 000 exchanges of information have taken place. Eighty jurisdictions have now successfully implemented the standard and have not received any recommendations for improvement.

**In line with Action 13, the first automatic exchanges of country-by-country (CbC) reports started in 2018.** Action 13 requires the ultimate parent entity of an MNE group to file a CbC report in its jurisdiction, providing information (on turnover, profits, employees, taxes paid, etc.) for each of the jurisdictions in which it operates. The tax administration of the country where the ultimate parent entity is a tax resident will then exchange this data with the tax authorities of other countries. As of January 2020, there were over 2 400 bilateral exchange relationships activated with respect to jurisdictions committed to exchanging CbC reports. These include exchanges between the 84 signatories[12] to the CbC Multilateral Competent Authority Agreement, between EU Member States under EU Council Directive 2016/881/EU and between signatories to bilateral competent authority agreements for exchanges under Double Tax Conventions or Tax Information Exchange Agreements, including 41 bilateral agreements with the United States. Jurisdictions continue to negotiate arrangements for the exchange of CbC reports.

**Action 14, which deals with the improvement of mutual agreement procedures (MAP), has also seen significant progress**. Action 14 aims at improving mechanisms to resolve tax treaty-related disputes to make them more effective. The MAP peer review process is conducted in two stages. Under Stage 1, the implementation of the Action 14 minimum standard is evaluated for Inclusive Framework members. Stage 2 focuses on monitoring the follow-up of any recommendations resulting from the Stage 1 peer reviews. As of October 2019, six rounds of Stage 1 peer review reports covering 45 jurisdictions had been released. The OECD will continue to publish Stage 1 peer review reports in batches in accordance with the Action 14 peer review assessment schedule.[13] In addition, MAP country profiles for more than 80 countries have been published to increase transparency of the MAP processes.

### *BEPS beyond minimum standards*

**Beyond the BEPS minimum standards, BEPS Actions 2, 3 and 4 have been rapidly adopted by a large number of countries**. These actions include common approaches to neutralising hybrid mismatches (Action 2) and to limiting excessive interest deductions (Action 4) as well as best practices in the design of effective controlled foreign company (CFC) rules (Action 3).

**For EU countries, the adoption of the recommendations under BEPS Actions 2, 3 and 4 was agreed by the EU Council**. The Council adopted the Anti-Tax Avoidance Directive (ATAD) as amended by ATAD II requiring Member States to implement domestic legislation in accordance with the provisions of ATAD for interest limitation and CFC rules with effect from 1 January 2019 and anti-hybrid rules with effect from 1 January 2020 (with the exception of the reverse hybrid mismatch rule, which will apply from 1 January 2022). In January 2020, the European Commission issued letters of formal notice to selected jurisdictions under Article 258 of the Treaty on the Functioning of the EU, where these letters serve as the first step in an infringement procedure. In the second stage of the procedure, the Commission may send a formal request to comply with EU law if it concludes that a member state is failing to fulfil its obligations under EU law.

**Progress has also been made outside of the EU**. In particular, Mexico adopted a reform that took effect in January 2020 to bring its tax legislation in line with recommendations from the OECD/G20 BEPS project (Box 3.4). Chile also adopted changes that took effect in January 2020, introducing a new special anti-avoidance rule that prevents the application of a reduced (4%) withholding tax on interest paid to a foreign financial institution if the lender institution is not the beneficial owner of the interest payments. In addition, Chile included new substance requirements for an entity to be qualified as a foreign financial institution and therefore be entitled to the reduced (4%) withholding tax on interest.

**Actions 8 to 10 contain transfer pricing guidance to ensure that transfer pricing outcomes are in line with value creation in relation to intangibles and other high-risk transactions**. Through this work, the OECD Transfer Pricing Guidelines have been modernised, and a new edition was published in July 2017. In June 2018, guidance on the application of the transactional profit split method and additional guidance addressed to tax administrations on the application of the approach on hard-to-value intangibles were approved, and have been incorporated into the OECD Transfer Pricing Guidelines. The implementation of Actions 8 to 10 has varied across countries. For a number of countries, changes to the OECD Transfer Pricing Guidelines resulted in domestic laws containing a direct reference to the Guidelines. In other countries, changes have consisted of clarifications, rather than substantive modifications to transfer pricing practices. Many other OECD and Inclusive Framework countries have introduced new legislation or regulations to implement domestically all or part of the guidance developed under BEPS Actions 8 to 10 (e.g. Argentina, Japan, Italy, Poland).

**As recommended by BEPS Action 11, significant work has been undertaken to improve the quality of available corporate tax statistics,** which is a critical step towards strengthening the Inclusive Framework's ongoing efforts to measure and monitor BEPS and the impact of the BEPS package. New data collection processes and analytical tools have been developed. A new dataset – the *OECD Corporate Tax Statistics Database* – was released for the first time in January 2019, with the second edition published in July 2020. The second edition includes anonymised and aggregated CbC report statistics for 2016, to provide a more complete view of the largest MNEs' global activities and improve the statistical and economic analysis of BEPS.

**Finally, many countries have indicated that they plan to introduce or expand mandatory disclosure rules, in line with BEPS Action 12.** BEPS Action 12 contains recommendations regarding the design of mandatory disclosure rules for aggressive tax planning schemes, taking into consideration the need to avoid disproportionate administrative and compliance costs and drawing on the experiences of the increasing number of countries that have such rules. EU countries are required to implement the rules as part of the EU Council Directive 2018/822 of 25 May 2018 (also known as DAC 6). While not all EU member states adhered to the implementation deadline of 31 December 2019, it is expected that DAC 6 will be transposed into the domestic laws of EU member states in 2020, with mandatory disclosure rules entering into force no later than 1 July 2020. Non-EU countries that have adopted mandatory disclosure rules include Canada, Israel, Mexico, Norway, Russia, South Africa, the United Kingdom and the United States.

### Box 3.4. Mexico's 2020 Tax Reform

In Mexico, a tax reform was approved by Congress on 30 October 2019 and entered into effect on 1 January 2020. This box provides an overview of the numerous changes intended to bring Mexico's tax legislation in line with recommendations from the OECD/G20 BEPS project.

**Anti-hybrid mismatch arrangements**

In order to address BEPS risks from hybrid mismatch arrangements, legislation was amended to follow the recommendations of Action 2 of the OECD/G20 BEPS project. In particular, the reform modified a rule that disallows the deduction of any payment if the same taxpayer can claim a deduction on the same payment in a different jurisdiction by reason of dual residency or if the same payment is also deductible for a related party. In addition, a pre-existing rule that disallowed the deduction of payments made between related parties to preferential tax regimes was modified in order to incorporate the recommendations of the Final Report on Action 2 related to deduction/no inclusion outcomes. Moreover, rules were introduced to disallow foreign tax credits based on recommendations 2.1 and 2.2 of the Final Report on Action 2.

**Controlled foreign corporation rules**

The pre-existing rules regarding controlled foreign corporations subject to preferential tax regimes were redrafted to adopt several of the recommendations of the Final Report on Action 3 of the OECD/G20 BEPS project and to further clarify the application of the rules. One of the most important changes was a new definition of control that now includes other types of control such as economic control, *de facto* control and control based on consolidation.

**Interest expense deduction limit**

To address tax base erosion taking place through the use of debt mechanisms, new interest deductibility limitation rules were implemented based on Action 4 of the OECD/G20 BEPS project. The deductibility of interest payments was restricted by disallowing any net interest in excess of 30% of EBITDA. Under specific circumstances, a ten-year carry forward is applicable to payments not deducted during a specific tax year. Furthermore, the reform introduced a *de minimis* exception as well as certain exemptions regarding specific industries (e.g. related to energy and water projects).

**Permanent establishment**

Following Action 7 of the OECD/G20 BEPS project, the definition of a permanent establishment (PE) in domestic law was modified to incorporate the changes made to Article 5 of the OECD Model Tax Convention. These changes address the artificial avoidance of a PE through commissionaire arrangements and specific activities that are excluded from the PE definition, among others.

**Mandatory Disclosure Rules**

Mexico introduced mandatory disclosure rules based on the Final Report of Action 12. The new legislation requires promoters and/or taxpayers to disclose specific tax schemes. The promoters are required to provide a reference number of the tax scheme (issued by the tax authority) to the users. The users are required to provide this reference number in their tax return. Promoters must also provide the tax authorities with a list of clients to whom they provided tax advice with respect to a reportable tax scheme. In certain cases, taxpayers are required to report their tax scheme directly to the tax authorities. The first disclosure returns are expected to be submitted in 2021 with respect to tax schemes that have tax effects in 2020 or in later years.

**Mutual Agreement Procedure implementation**

The second sentence of Article 25 (2) of the OECD Model Tax Convention says that any agreement shall be implemented notwithstanding the time limits in the domestic law of the Contracting States. In order to avoid any differences between the domestic law and their tax treaties, Mexico introduced a provision that says that the time limits in the Tax Code shall not affect the implementation of any agreement reached in a Mutual Agreement Procedure.

**General Anti-Avoidance Rule**

Mexico introduced a general anti-avoidance rule that says that legal arrangements without a business reason that create tax benefits should have the tax effects that correspond to those arrangements that would have been carried out to obtain the economic outcome expected by the taxpayer. The rule includes a procedure on how tax authorities can apply this provision.

## *Progress is being made towards a long-term multilateral solution to address the tax challenges arising from digitalisation*

**Efforts to address the tax challenges arising from digitalisation have been ongoing under the auspices of the Inclusive Framework**. Digitalisation has led to the emergence of new business models and these changes have put pressure on some of the key principles underlying the international tax system. In January 2019, the Inclusive Framework agreed on a Policy Note that grouped proposals to address these tax challenges under two "pillars" and set out to examine them as a possible basis for consensus (OECD, 2019[2]) Pillar One examines nexus and profit allocation rules, and Pillar Two seeks to ensure a minimum level of taxation. Building on the note, the Inclusive Framework delivered a detailed Programme of Work in May 2019, which was endorsed by the G20 Finance Ministers and Leaders in June 2019. In January 2020, the Inclusive Framework at its plenary meeting reaffirmed its commitment to reach a consensus-based long-term solution by approving the "Statement by the OECD/G20 Inclusive Framework on BEPS on the Two Pillar Approach to Address the Tax Challenges Arising from the Digitalisation of the Economy".

**Pillar One aims to expand the taxing rights of market jurisdictions over certain defined business activities in exchange for improved tax certainty.** For some business models, the market jurisdiction is the jurisdiction where the user is located. To achieve this result, a new taxing right would be created, largely unconstrained by physical presence requirements, focusing on large MNEs providing automated digital services or selling goods or services to consumers (i.e. consumer facing businesses). This reallocation of taxing rights would stem from a recognition that the profits from sustained and remote participation of a business in the economy of a market jurisdiction should give rise to some taxing rights in that jurisdiction. The amount of this reallocation of profits would be determined through a formula and based on the consolidated financial accounts of MNE groups.

**Pillar Two is also referred to as the Global Anti-Base Erosion proposal or "GLoBE" proposal**. It focuses on the remaining BEPS risks and seeks to develop rules that would provide jurisdictions with a right to "tax back" where other jurisdictions have not exercised their primary taxing rights, or where the payment is otherwise subject to low levels of effective taxation. The GLoBE proposal would be composed of four rules: a) the income inclusion rule; b) the switch-over rule; c) the undertaxed payment rule; and d) the subject to tax rule.

**The technical work on various aspects of the two-pillar approach is underway in a range of Working Parties within the OECD**. The objective is to deliver the key policy features of the Pillar One and Pillar Two solutions for a political agreement by the end of 2020. The Inclusive Framework also agreed to continue ongoing work on the economic analysis of the proposals (Box 3.5).

### Box 3.5. Economic Analysis of the Digital Proposals

Recent economic analysis suggests that the proposed two-pillar solution would have a significant positive impact on global tax revenues. The revenue gains are broadly similar across high-, middle-, and low-income economies, as a share of corporate tax revenues.

The economic analysis and impact assessment of the Pillar One and Pillar Two proposals is being undertaken to inform key decisions on the design and parameters of the tax reform to be agreed by Inclusive Framework members. The analysis covers data from more than 200 jurisdictions, including all members of the Inclusive Framework, and more than 27,000 MNE groups. Assumptions in the preliminary analysis are illustrative, and do not pre-judge decisions to be taken by the Inclusive Framework.

The analysis shows that the Pillar One reform would bring a small tax revenue gain for most jurisdictions. Under Pillar One, low- and middle-income economies are expected to gain relatively more revenue than advanced economies, with investment hubs experiencing some loss in tax revenues. More than half of the profit re-allocated would come from 100 large MNE groups.

The analysis shows that Pillar Two could raise a significant amount of additional tax revenues. By reducing the tax rate differentials between jurisdictions, the reform is expected to lead to a significant reduction in profit shifting by MNEs. This will be important for developing economies as they tend to be more adversely affected by profit shifting than high-income economies.

The overall direct effect on investment costs is expected to be small in most countries, as the reforms target firms with high levels of profitability and low effective tax rates. The reforms would also reduce the influence of corporate taxes on investment location decisions. In addition, failure to reach a consensus-based solution would likely lead to further unilateral measures and greater uncertainty.

**In the meantime, some countries have taken unilateral action on digital taxation**. During the period covered by this report, a number of countries have explored, announced, or implemented digital services taxes (DSTs), typically defined as sectoral turnover taxes targeted at (or including) revenue from online activity, such as advertising services, digital transactions, or online and physical distribution of audio-visual content (OECD, 2018[3]) (Table 3.9). Some countries have also implemented or proposed other measures such as withholding taxes on digital services (Turkey), measures to provide for a digital permanent establishment (Indonesia), and taxes on advertising revenues (Hungary).

**The DSTs that have been proposed or implemented have varying rates**, from 3% (France) to 7% (Czech Republic). The bases of these taxes in many cases draw from the approach outlined in the draft European Commission Directive on DSTs (European Commission, 2018[4]) and sometimes take account of the guidance provided by the OECD Interim Report to Address the Tax Challenges of Digitalisation (OECD, 2018[3]). For example, the UK proposal covers social media platforms, internet search engines, and online market places, while the French proposal covers digital intermediary services and advertising services based on user data.

**In many instances, countries have postponed the effective implementation of these measures pending the outcome of the work of the Inclusive Framework**. For example, Hungary has reduced the rate of its advertising tax to 0% from 1 July 2019 through to December 31, 2022. France has suspended the collection of its DST for one year, pending a consensus-based solution at the OECD level in 2020.

## Table 3.9. Unilateral measures on digital taxation, 2019-2020

| Country Name | Date | Announced/Implemented | Measure |
|---|---|---|---|
| Austria | 1 January 2020 | Implemented | 5% digital tax on online advertising services levied on digital interfaces or any type of software or website rendered in Austria. |
| Czech Republic | 22 January 2020 | Proposed | 7% DST on revenues from i) targeted advertising on a digital interface; ii) the transmission of data about users and generated from users' activities on digital interfaces; iii) making available to users a multi-sided digital interface that may facilitate the provision of supplies of goods and services among users. |
| European Union | 27 May 2020 | Announced | The European Commission has announced that it will put forward in the first semester of 2021 a proposal on a digital levy, with a view to its introduction at the latest by 1 January 2023.1 |
| France | 1 January 2020 | Implemented (with suspended collection) | 3% DST on portion of taxable services income related to France after the application of the "French digital presence" ratios to the corresponding worldwide digital services receipts: 1. Provision of a digital interface enabling users to enter into contact and interact with others ("intermediary services"). 2. Provision of services to advertisers that aim at placing targeted advertising messages on a digital interface based on data collected about users and generated upon the consultation of such an interface ("advertising services based on users' data"). |
| Hungary | 24 February 2020 | Implemented | 7.5% tax on advertising revenues exceeding HUF 100 million per year. However, as a temporary measure, the advertisement tax rate has been reduced to 0%, effective from July 1, 2019 through to December 31, 2022 |
| Indonesia | 31 March 2020 | Implemented | Electronic Transaction Tax imposed on e-commerce sales, when the digital PE cannot be applied due to the provision of a Tax Treaty. Further provisions on the rate, object and calculation will be addressed in a government regulation. |
| Italy | 1 January 2020 | Implemented | 3% DST on gross revenue derived from: i) advertising on a digital interface; ii) a multilateral digital interface that allows users to buy/sell goods and services; and iii) the transmission of user data generated from using a digital interface. When a taxable service is supplied in Italy in a calendar year, the taxable revenue is the percentage of worldwide revenue from digital services that is represented by services linked to Italy. |
| Spain | 18 February 2020 | Proposed | 3% DST on gross revenue from online advertising services, the sale of online advertising, and the sale of user-data. |
| Turkey | 1 January 2019 | Implemented | 15% WHT on payments made to providers of advertising services or intermediaries in return for the provision of services via the Internet. A 7.5% DST has also been implemented, however, the President can reduce the rate to 1% or increase it to 15%. |
| United Kingdom | 1 April 2020 | Implemented | 2% DST derived from UK users from three types of digital activities: 1. social media platforms 2. Internet search engines. 3. online marketplaces. |

1. European Council Conclusions (EUCO 10/20) from its meeting of 17-21 July 2020: https://www.consilium.europa.eu/media/45109/210720-euco-final-conclusions-en.pdf.

Source: OECD Secretariat. Information as of 20 July 2020.

## Value added taxes and other taxes on goods and services

**Overall, this section shows continued stability in standard VAT rates and a mix of VAT base broadening and base narrowing reforms.** The stabilisation of standard VAT rates observed across countries in recent years is continuing, with the exception of Japan, where the standard Consumption Tax (i.e. VAT) rate was raised, and China, where the standard VAT rate was lowered. Instead, the majority of VAT reforms were VAT base changes. The reforms aimed at broadening VAT bases and raising additional revenues focused primarily on the fight against VAT fraud and on ensuring the effective taxation of cross-border online sales. On the other hand, a number of countries have expanded the scope of their reduced VAT rates, effectively narrowing their VAT bases. The increase in the number of VAT base narrowing reforms, typically intended to encourage consumption and/or enhance equity, suggests a slight departure from trends in previous years, where the predominant objective of VAT reforms was to raise additional revenues. Finally, trends in excise duties show continuing tax increases, in particular on tobacco products and sugar-sweetened beverages.

### *Consumption taxes, in particular VAT, are a major source of revenue in most countries*

**Consumption taxes are a major source of revenue across the countries covered in the report**. They ranged from 17.6% of total tax revenues in the United States (the only country in the report that does not have a VAT) to 53.3% of total tax revenues in Chile in 2018 (Figure 3.17). As discussed in previous editions of this report, consumption tax revenues tend to account for higher shares of total tax revenues in emerging countries. A 2018 OECD paper showed that in Africa and Latin America, VAT and other taxes on goods and services were by far the largest source of revenue as a share of total taxation (Modica, Laudage and Harding, 2018[5]), accounting respectively for 50% and 53% of total tax revenues on average. In comparison, consumption taxes accounted on average for 32% of total tax revenues in OECD countries in 2017.

Figure 3.17. Consumption tax revenues as a share of total tax revenues in 2018

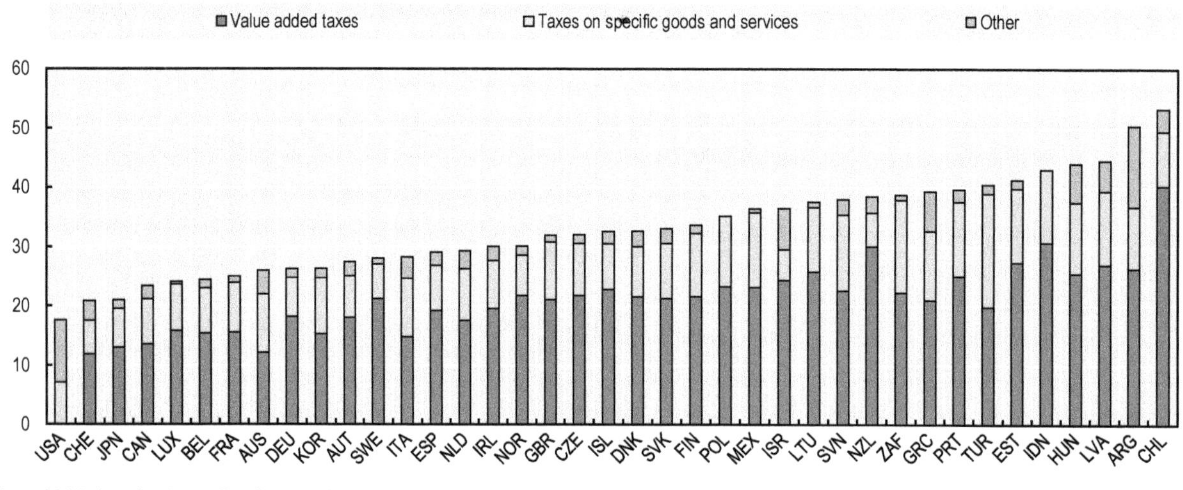


Note: 2017 data for Australia, Greece, Indonesia, Japan, Mexico and South Africa.
Source: Global Revenue Statistics Database

StatLink https://doi.org/10.1787/888934158822

Figure 3.18. General consumption tax revenues (left panel) and specific consumption revenues (right panel) as % of total revenues, 1975-2017

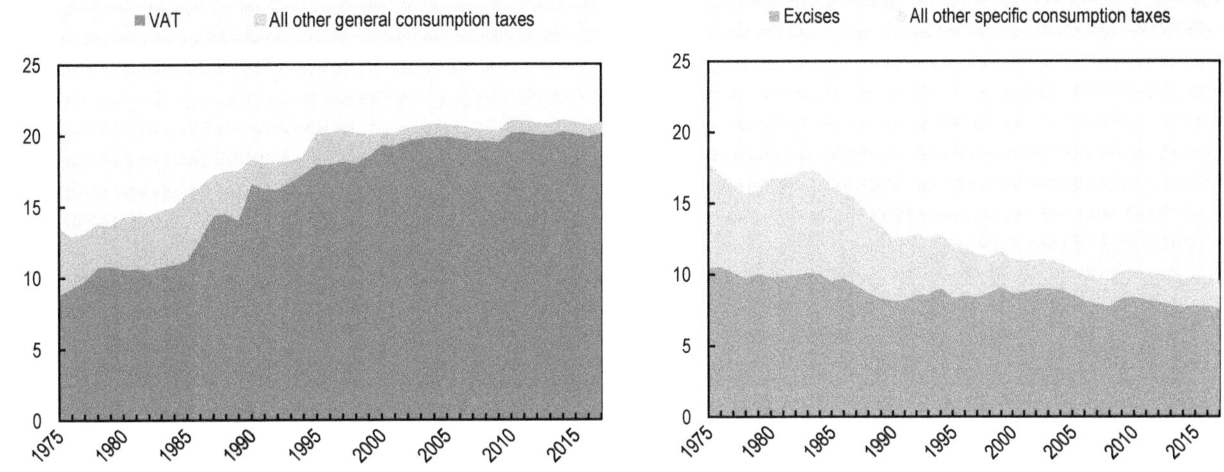


Source: OECD (2019), *OECD Revenue Statistics:1965-2018.*

StatLink https://doi.org/10.1787/888934158841

**VAT is the largest source of consumption tax revenues**. VAT accounts for more than 60% of total consumption tax revenues in 26 of the countries covered in the report. In the OECD, over the last 30 years, consumption tax revenues as a share of total taxation have remained stable but the composition of those revenues has changed (Figure 3.18). Excise taxes and other specific consumption taxes, which made up around 18% of total tax revenues in 1975 across the OECD, now account for less than 10% of total taxation on average. One of the explanations behind this decrease is that tax rates on imported goods were considerably reduced across countries, reflecting a global trend to remove trade barriers. On the other hand, the share of VAT in total tax revenues has grown substantially, from less than 9% in 1975 to slightly over 20% in 2017 on average across the OECD. Recent years have seen a stabilisation of VAT revenues in the OECD tax mix.

**Nevertheless, the amounts and evolution of revenues collected from VAT have varied across countries**. Across the countries covered in the report, VAT revenues ranged from 3.3% of GDP in Switzerland to 9.8% of GDP in New Zealand in 2018 (Figure 3.19). Regarding trends over time, three quarters of the countries have seen increases in their revenues from VAT as a share of GDP between 2000 and 2018, with the most significant increases recorded in Greece and Japan. There were some exceptions, however, most notably Ireland, which experienced the largest decrease in VAT revenues as a share of GDP between 2000 and 2018.

Figure 3.19. VAT revenues as a share of GDP by country in 2000, 2008 and 2018

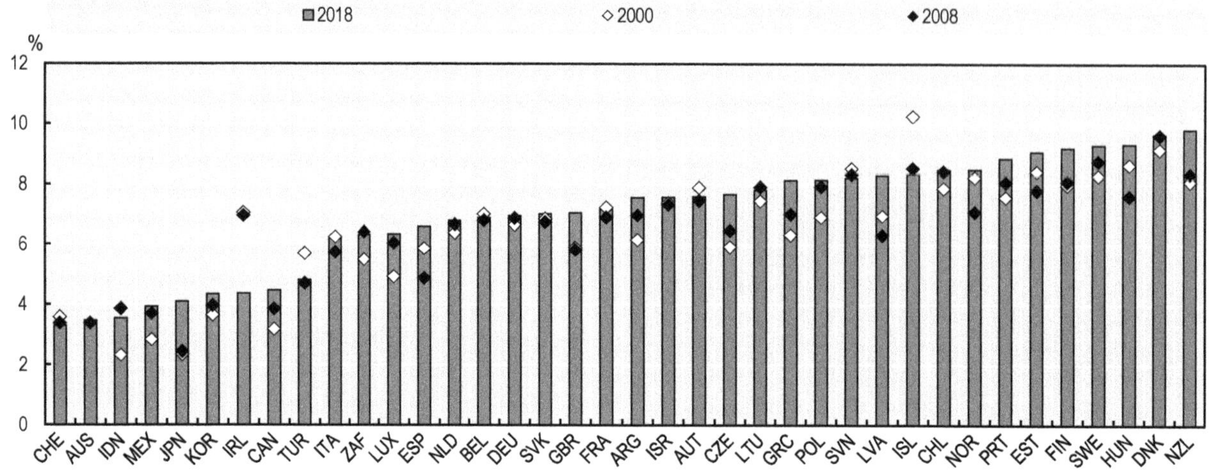


Note: The United States is not included because it does not have a VAT.
Source: OECD Global Revenue Statistics Database

StatLink https://doi.org/10.1787/888934158860

## *Standard VAT rates have seen little change*

**Standard VAT rates have stabilised in recent years**. Standard VAT rates in the OECD reached a record average level of 19.3% in 2015, after years of continuous increases (Figure 3.20). Raising standard VAT rates was a common strategy for countries seeking to achieve fiscal consolidation in the wake of the global financial crisis as increasing VAT rates provides immediate revenues without directly affecting competitiveness and has generally been found to be less detrimental to economic growth than raising direct taxes (Johansson et al., 2008[6]). Among the countries covered in the report, 12 now have a standard VAT rate equal to or above 22%, against only six in 2008 (Figure 3.21). However, the trend towards continuously rising standard VAT rates has come to a halt in recent years. This is explained by improvements in countries' fiscal positions, but also by the fact that standard VAT rates have reached relatively high levels in many countries, limiting the room for additional standard rate increases.

Figure 3.20. Evolution of the OECD average standard VAT rate from 1975 to 2020

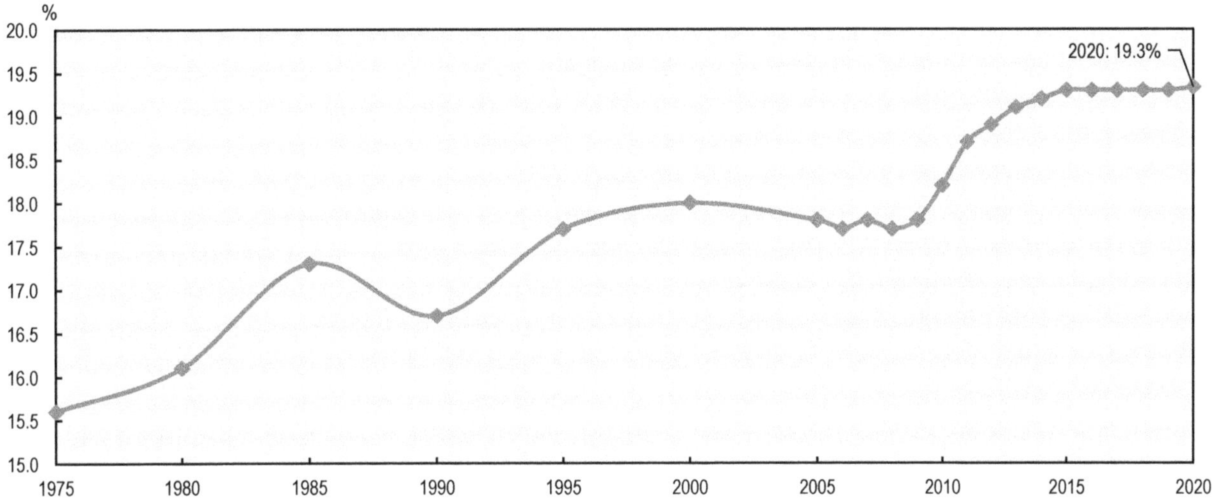


Source: OECD Tax Database and OECD Tax Policy Reform Questionnaire

StatLink https://doi.org/10.1787/888934158879

**With the exception of Japan and China, standard VAT rates have remained stable.** As mentioned in last year's report, after several delays, Japan's Consumption Tax rate increase from 8% to 10% entered into force on 1 October 2019. This Consumption Tax rate increase was accompanied by the introduction of a reduced rate of 8% for basic foodstuffs (see below). The other change in standard VAT rates occurred in China, where the standard VAT rate was lowered from 16% to 13%, following a decrease from 17% to 16% in 2018. The 10% reduced VAT was also reduced to 9%, while the 6% reduced rate remained unchanged. This reform followed successive waves of VAT reform in China since 2016, which have significantly improved the design of the VAT system (see Box 3.6).

Figure 3.21. Standard VAT rates by country in 2008, 2019 and 2020

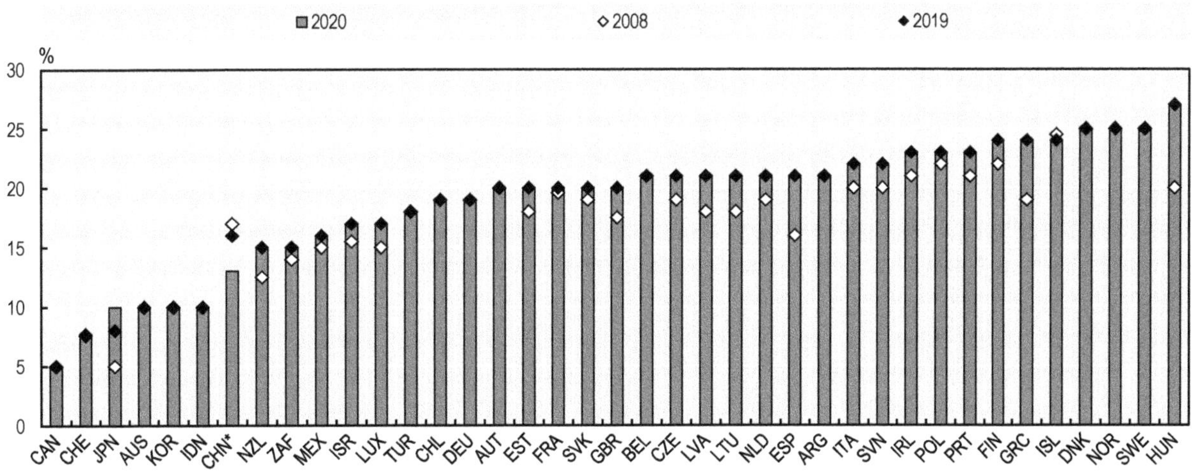


Source: OECD Tax Database and OECD Tax Policy Reform Questionnaire

StatLink https://doi.org/10.1787/888934158898

**Box 3.6. China's recent VAT reforms**

The Chinese government has introduced a series of VAT reforms over the past few years to align its VAT system with internationally accepted principles and adapt it to its level of economic development. Overall, these reforms have considerably improved the design and operation of China's VAT system, in line with the principles embedded in the OECD International VAT/GST Guidelines.

On 1 May 2016, the "Business Tax-to-VAT Reform" was rolled out nationwide, replacing Business Tax on taxable services with a VAT. This reform was notably aimed at minimising the cascading effect of the Business Tax, which was not creditable for taxable businesses, by a VAT that provides for a right to deduct input VAT incurred by taxable businesses on their business inputs. On 1 July 2017, the 4-tier VAT rate structure of 17%, 13%, 11% and 6% was simplified and unified into a 3-tier rate structure of 17%, 11% and 6%.

In 2018, the Chinese government continued to deepen the VAT reform with three measures. First, from 1 May 2018, the VAT rates were lowered from 17% and 11% to 16% and 10% respectively, resulting in a 3-tier VAT rate structure comprising VAT rates of 16%, 10% and 6%. Second, the annual turnover thresholds of RMB 500 000 (EUR 66 800) and RMB 800 000 (EUR 106 900) applicable to small-scale VAT payers engaged in manufacturing and trading respectively were unified and increased to a single threshold of RMB 5 000 000 (EUR 668 400). Third, the scope of refunds of excess input VAT was extended. The existing scope of excess input tax refund for qualified sectors and enterprises was extended to qualified enterprises engaged in modern services (e.g. R&D) and advanced manufacturing (e.g. equipment manufacturing), as well as power grid enterprises. For these enterprises, one-off excess input tax refund was allowed.

In March 2019, the Chinese government announced further measures including a reduction of its "headline" VAT rates from 16% to 13%, and from 10% to 9% and a further expansion of the scope of excess input VAT credits.

### *A number of countries have expanded the scope of reduced VAT rates*

**Many countries apply reduced VAT rates to a wide range of products**. Many of these reduced rates – e.g. on basic essentials, pharmaceuticals, education – are intended to enhance equity. Other reduced VAT rates are in place to achieve non-distributional goals, such as supporting labour-intensive industries, addressing environmental externalities or promoting access to cultural activities. Empirical evidence has shown, however, that such reduced VAT rates are often poorly targeted tools. Where they aim to reduce the tax burden on low-income households by targeting basic necessities, they generally end up providing greater benefits in absolute terms to richer households, even if they might benefit low-income households more in relative terms. Where reduced VAT rates apply to non-essential items (e.g. hotel and restaurant services, theatre, cinema), they tend to be regressive, benefiting the rich more both in aggregate terms and as a proportion of expenditure (Box 3.7).

## Box 3.7. The distributional effects of reduced VAT rates

With the exception of Chile, all OECD countries have one or more reduced VAT rates to support various policy objectives. A major reason for the introduction of a differentiated rate structure is the promotion of equity. Countries have generally considered it desirable to alleviate the tax burden on goods and services that form a larger share of expenditure of the poorest households (e.g. basic food, water). Countries also often decide not to tax medicine, health services and housing at high rates. Reduced VAT rates have also been used to stimulate the consumption of "merit" goods (e.g. cultural products and education) and other non-distributional objectives such as promoting locally supplied labour-intensive activities (e.g. tourism) and correcting externalities (e.g. energy-saving appliances).

In general, VAT exemptions, zero-rates and reduced rates are not a well-targeted tool to support low-income households. Reduced rates that are implemented in countries for the distinct purpose of supporting the poor (i.e. to address distributional goals) typically do have the desired progressive effect. For example, reduced rates for basic food provide in general greater support to the poor than the rich as a proportion of household income or expenditure. However, despite this progressive effect, these reduced VAT rates are a very poor tool for targeting support to poor households. At best, rich households receive roughly as much benefit – in absolute value – from a reduced rate as do poor households. At worst, rich households benefit vastly more than poor households. This result is unsurprising as better off households can be expected to consume more, and often more expensive, products than poorer households. Thus, while poorer households may benefit from reduced VAT rates on "necessities" the wealthier gain even more.

Targeted cash transfer programmes, if well-functioning, are a more effective tool to compensate poor households for the VAT they have paid. If poor households can be compensated directly through a cash transfer programme, it is more efficient and fair to tax all goods and services at the standard VAT rate and compensate the poor directly through cash transfers (and/ or reductions in personal income taxes, etc.), especially if the standard VAT rate is not particularly high. It should immediately be noted, however, that compensating all (and only the) losers of a reform through a transfer programme might in practice be very difficult to achieve. A number of jurisdictions operate or have recently introduced such targeted cash transfers to alleviate the VAT burden on poorer households and/or to replace reduced rates on basic essentials such as Canada (1991), Argentina (2020) and Colombia (2020)[14].

With regard to preferential VAT provisions for social, cultural and other non-distributional goals, richer households benefit considerably more from VAT exemptions and reduced rates. Those tax provisions often provide so large a benefit to rich households that the reduced VAT rate actually has a regressive effect – benefiting the rich more both in aggregate terms and as a proportion of expenditure. For example, reduced rates on hotel accommodation and restaurant food benefit the rich vastly more than the poor, both in aggregate and proportional terms, in all OECD countries in which they are applied. Similar results, but of less absolute magnitude, are found for reduced rates on books, cinema, theatre and concerts.

Finally, VAT rate differentiation might not be the best policy instrument to correct negative externalities. VAT rate differentiation may improve efficiency if it means that the private marginal costs of an activity are brought closer to the marginal costs for society. However, VAT is a blunt instrument for addressing environmental externalities, as it may be hard to target the actual source of pollution.

Source: (OECD/KIPF, 2014[7]).

**Reforms related to reduced VAT rates have accompanied changes to standard VAT rates in Japan and China.** In Japan, in parallel to the increase in the standard Consumption Tax rate (see above), a reduced rate was introduced for the first time, set at 8%, for food items and beverages. In China, along with the decrease in the standard VAT rate from 16% to 13%, the 10% reduced VAT rate on retail, entertainment, hotels, restaurants, catering services, real estate, postal services, transport and logistics was reduced to 9%, while the 6% VAT rate remained unchanged.

**A number of countries have expanded the scope of their reduced VAT rates for equity reasons** (Table 3.10). South Africa introduced additional zero-rated items (e.g. white bread flour, cake flour and sanitary pads) to mitigate the effects on low-income households of the one percentage point increase in the standard VAT rate that took effect in 2018. Greece reclassified a number of basic foodstuffs, which are now taxed at the reduced VAT rate of 13%, and applies the super reduced rate of 6% to the supply of electricity and gas. The 13% VAT rate was also extended to infant food and other baby products, such as diapers and car seats, and to bicycle helmets. In Argentina, basic foodstuffs are temporarily subject to the zero VAT rate. In the Slovak Republic, the VAT rate was lowered on additional basic foodstuffs. In Germany, the VAT rate on feminine hygiene products was reduced from 19% to 7%, while Italy now applies a 5% VAT rate to compostable feminine hygiene products.

**A few changes to VAT exemptions and reduced rates were introduced for environmental purposes**. As part of a broader package of environmental measures (see Box 3.10 in Section 3.4), Germany reduced its VAT rate on long-distance rail travel from 19% to 7% to boost climate-friendly transport. Iceland introduced temporary tax reliefs to incentivise low-emissions transport. These measures include new VAT exemptions (up to a certain value) on bicycles, scooters, electric bicycles and light electric motor vehicles; the extension of existing VAT exemptions for electric and hydrogen vehicles until 2022-2023; a full VAT refund for the purchase and installation of home charging stations at residential properties; and a full VAT exemption on rentals of electric and hydrogen vehicles.

**A few countries have expanded the scope of their reduced VAT rates to support specific industries**. Hungary has reduced its VAT rate on accommodation services from 18% to 5%. The Czech Republic and Greece have reduced VAT rates on catering services. The Czech Republic has also lowered the VAT rate on hairdressing and clothing repair services. Portugal now applies the reduced VAT rate of 6% to assistance services by telephone to the elderly and chronic patients, as well as to admissions to exhibitions, zoos, parks, aquariums, museums and buildings of national interest. A number of EU countries (Austria, Czech Republic, Germany, Finland, Netherlands, Poland and Slovenia) have also reduced their VAT rates on e-publications, following an EU agreement in 2018 allowing member states to cut their VAT rates on e-publications to the reduced or zero rates applied to physical publications. A group of EU countries had already adopted similar VAT rate reductions on e-publications (OECD, 2019[8]).

**On the other hand, reforms narrowing the scope of reduced VAT rates were very marginal.** In Ireland, the VAT rate for food supplements was increased from 0% to 13.5% as of 1 January 2020. Certain products, including some vitamins, minerals and fortified foods, will continue to be taxed at the 0% VAT rate. In Portugal, admissions to bullfighting became standard rated.

**Finally, Poland introduced of a new VAT rate structure with the objective of simplifying and harmonising its VAT system**. This new VAT rate structure is based on an updated classification of goods and services. The VAT rates on a number of goods and services were lowered from 8% to 5% (e.g. soups, tropical and citrus fruits, some nuts), from 23% to 8% (e.g. mustard, spices) and from 23% to 5% (e-publications). On the other hand, VAT rates on a number of goods were raised from 5% or 8% to 23% (e.g. lobsters, octopus and other crustaceans). The reform entered into force on 1 July 2020. Overall, the adoption of this new rate structure is expected to lead to a small revenue decrease.

Table 3.10. Changes to reduced VAT rates

| | General | Food/Basic items | Hotels/ Restaurants | Newspapers/e-books | Culture | Other |
|---|---|---|---|---|---|---|
| Rate ⇧ or scope ⇩ | | | | | | IRL PRT |
| Rate ⇩ or scope ⇧ | CHN JPN | ARG CZE DEU GRC ITA SVK ZAF | CZE GRC HUN | AUT CZE DEU FIN NLD POL SVN | PRT | CZE DEU ISL |

Source: OECD Annual Tax Policy Reform Questionnaire.

### *Increases in VAT registration thresholds have continued*

**OECD countries have very different levels of VAT registration thresholds** (Figure 3.22). The main reason for excluding small businesses (and this notion varies considerably across countries) is that the costs for the tax administration of having all businesses account for VAT may be disproportionate compared to potential VAT revenues and that compliance costs for small businesses may also be disproportionate compared to their turnover. On the other hand, a VAT registration threshold introduces competitive distortions between small businesses under and above the threshold. Thus, the level of the threshold is generally the result of a trade-off between minimising compliance and administration costs and the need to protect revenue and avoid competitive distortions.

**A few countries have raised their VAT registration thresholds, continuing a trend observed in recent years**. As of 1 January 2020, increases in VAT registration thresholds became effective in four countries. As mentioned in last year's report, the Netherlands introduced an optional VAT registration threshold at EUR 25 000 of turnover from 1 January 2020. In Austria, the VAT registration threshold was raised from EUR 30 000 to EUR 35 000. In Germany, it was raised from EUR 17 500 to EUR 22 000. In Portugal, the turnover threshold for compulsory VAT registration was raised from EUR 10 000 to EUR 12 500. These countries' thresholds remain relatively low or moderate in comparison to those in place in other countries (Figure 3.22).

Figure 3.22. VAT/GST registration and collection thresholds in OECD countries in 2020

Annual turnover thresholds expressed in USD ppp

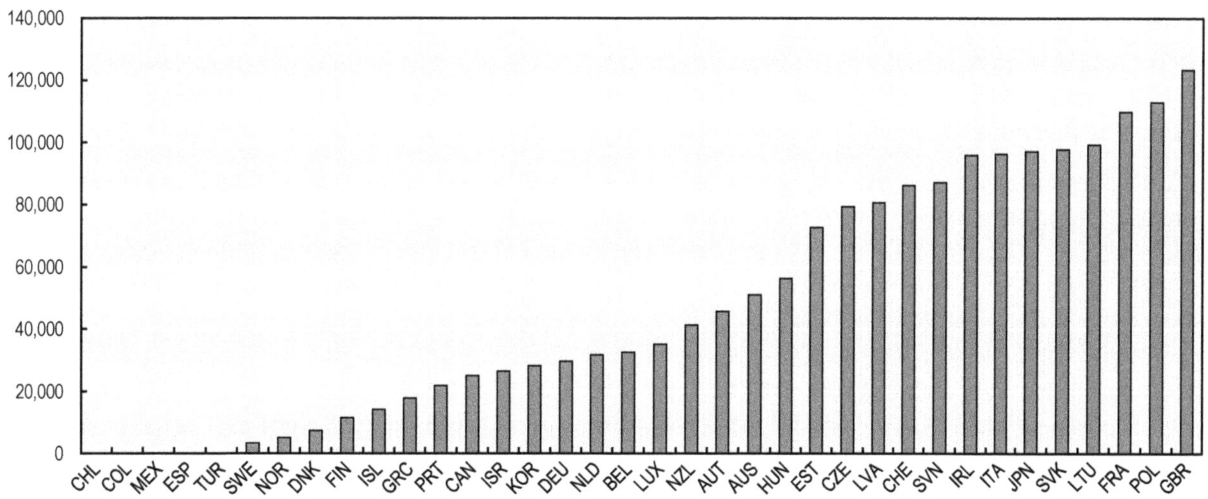


Note: These thresholds still need to be validated by delegates of WP9.
Source: OECD Tax Database and OECD Tax Policy Reform Questionnaire

StatLink https://doi.org/10.1787/888934158917

### *A few countries have introduced measures to increase VAT neutrality and support investment*

**As part of its 2019 package of VAT measures, China has expanded the scope of input VAT credits and is gradually establishing a refund system for excess credits** (see Box 3.6). A VAT refund pilot scheme for excess input VAT credits is being introduced. Previously, most businesses were not able to claim refunds for excess input VAT. Instead, businesses were only able to carry forward the excess input VAT to offset future output VAT liabilities. The 2019 reform has also expanded the scope of creditable input VAT for real estate. VAT taxpayers can now claim input VAT credits for the purchase of real estate and construction services up-front and directly deduct it from output VAT. This means that taxpayers will no longer have to claim input VAT credits over a two-year period. The scope of input VAT credits is also being expanded by allowing taxpayers to claim input VAT credits against output VAT for domestic passenger transport services.

**Chile is seeking to modernise its VAT refund procedures to enhance business cash flow and support investment**. As part of its Tax Modernisation Bill, Chile has reduced the period during which taxpayers must maintain an input VAT credit balance before they can request a refund for purchases of fixed assets. The period is reduced from a minimum of six to two months. The response time for the Chilean tax administration to treat a refund request will be reduced from 60 to 20 days.

**Greece has introduced an optional VAT suspension regime for newly developed real estate to encourage investment in the sector.** From 1 January 2020 to 31 December 2022, building contractors may elect to be subject to the VAT suspension regime. Under this regime, VAT is not levied on sales of real estate, and contractors are not be able to deduct related input VAT. Once elected, the regime must be applied until the end of the period. However, real estate sales are subject to the real estate transfer tax.

### *Administrative improvements and anti-fraud measures have been an important part of countries' VAT reforms*

**As described below, a significant number of VAT reforms have revolved around technical and administrative improvements to enhance tax collection and combat fraud**. Some of these reforms reinforce taxpayers' reporting obligations, including the use of Standard Audit Files for Tax (SAF-T) and real-time data transfers to tax administrations such as VAT invoice reporting. Other measures modify tax collection mechanisms to combat certain types of VAT fraud. These include split payments and the expansion of the domestic reverse charge mechanism to sectors subject to high risks of fraud. Finally, some of these reforms extend VAT accountability to other entities in the value chain (e.g. online marketplaces). Countries generally expect these measures to bring in significant additional tax revenues.

**The VAT Revenue Ratios (VRR) suggest that there is still potential to collect additional revenue by improving the performance of VAT systems**. The VRR provides a comparative measure of how the tax administration's efficiency as well as exemptions and reduced rates affect VAT revenues (OECD, 2018[9]). The VRR is the ratio between the revenues actually collected from VAT and the revenues that could be raised if the standard VAT rate were applied uniformly to the entire potential tax base (i.e. all final consumption) and perfectly administered and enforced. Across the OECD, the unweighted average VRR has remained relatively stable at 0.56 in 2016, compared to 0.55 in 2015, and continues to vary significantly across countries (Figure 3.23). Even if the VRR should be interpreted with care and VAT revenue loss may be caused by a variety of factors, these estimates suggest that there is significant potential for raising additional revenues through base broadening and better tax enforcement in many countries.

**Estimations of VAT fraud suggest that addressing non-compliance remains a key challenge**. In the EU, the total amount of VAT lost because of tax fraud and tax avoidance, as well as bankruptcies, financial insolvencies and maladministration, was estimated at EUR 137.5 billion in 2017. This VAT gap represents a loss of 11.2% of total expected VAT revenues or VAT total tax liability (VTTL) (Center for Economic and Social Research, 2019[10]). In Australia, the GST gap was estimated at AUD 5.3 billion or 7.9% of the VTTL (Australian Taxation Office, 2018, cited in OECD, 2018). In Chile, the VAT gap was found to be around 16.6% of the VTTL (Servicio de Impuestos Internos, 2017, cited in (OECD, 2018[9])).

Figure 3.23. VAT Revenue Ratios (VRRs) in 2016

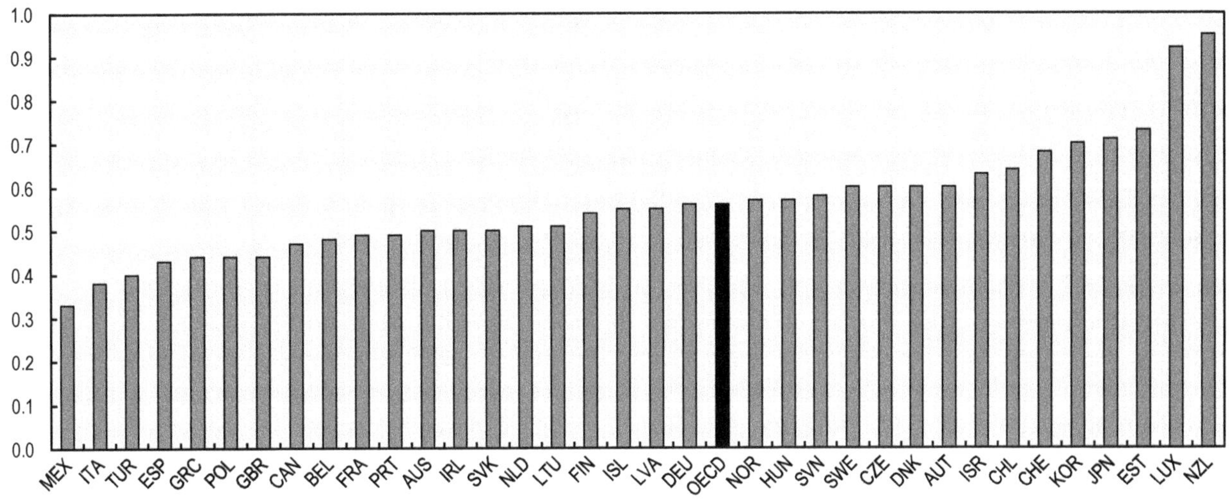


Note: In New Zealand, the very high VRR reflects partly the broad GST base as well as the fact that public services are taxed under GST. In the case of Luxembourg, its position as a financial centre and a hub for European e-commerce has strongly contributed to its high VRR (for a more detailed explanation, see OECD Consumption Tax Trends 2018).
Source: (OECD, 2018[9]).

StatLink https://doi.org/10.1787/888934158936

**Previous editions of this report have emphasised the expanding use of the domestic reverse charge mechanism to address fraud.** The domestic reverse charge mechanism can be used to combat missing trader fraud. A key feature of this type of fraud is that taxpayers charge and collect VAT from their customers and disappear without remitting the VAT to the tax authorities.[15] The domestic reverse charge mechanism – which applies in principle to supplies of specific goods and/or services between VAT-registered businesses established in the same country – aims at addressing this type of fraud by making the customer liable to collect the tax on supplies (instead of the supplier), which prevents the supplier from collecting VAT and disappearing with it. Previous editions of the report have shown that this mechanism was increasingly applied by EU Member States for goods that have been found to be particularly vulnerable to such fraud, often popular high-value goods that can easily be moved around (e.g. mobile phones, laptops, gold, etc.). Trade in certain intangibles, such as carbon credits, gas and electricity and green energy certificates, has also become particularly vulnerable to this fraud type.[16] This year, Portugal was the only country to report a reform in this area, expanding the application of its domestic reverse charge mechanism to certain supplies in the forestry sector.

**Another mechanism to reduce revenue losses from VAT fraud is through split payment.** VAT split payments differ from the standard VAT collection method as the VAT charged by businesses on their supplies is not actually collected by the supplier but remitted separately and directly to the tax authorities. This is typically organised through the intervention of financial and/or payment intermediaries (e.g. banks, credit card companies, online payment service providers), which split the gross amount paid by the customer into a net amount and a VAT amount, remitting the latter to the tax authorities (OECD, 2018[9]). As with the domestic reverse charge mechanism, such a system removes the possibility for a supplier to collect the VAT from its customer without remitting it to the tax authorities. As reported previously, Poland introduced voluntary split payments in July 2018. As of 1 November 2019, it has started implementing mandatory split payments in areas that are particularly exposed to VAT fraud. The mechanism only applies to B2B transactions where invoices are above a gross amount of PLN 15 000.

**To enhance VAT collection and combat fraud, some OECD countries are also reinforcing taxpayers' reporting obligations**. New SAF-T requirements are being introduced in Norway and Poland. SAF-T was developed by the OECD Forum on Tax Administration in 2005 to enable the transfer of accounting data from companies to tax authorities in a standardised electronic format. The main purpose was to allow tax authorities to conduct more efficient tax inspections. Since then, a number of countries have adopted (a form of) SAF-T (OECD, 2018[9]). In Norway, mandatory SAF-T reporting for businesses with a turnover above NOK 5 million became effective as of 1 January 2020. SAF-T files are to be sent to the tax authorities only upon their request. Poland has planned to incorporate VAT returns into a modified SAF-T file. The adapted SAF-T file will contain all the data included in traditional VAT returns, which means that taxable persons will not be required to submit separately VAT returns and SAF-T files.

**Real-time VAT invoice reporting has become an increasingly popular tool to reduced VAT fraud and non-compliance**. This typically includes two different elements: requiring businesses to maintain electronic accounts/electronic invoicing systems and the (near) real-time communication of all invoicing data to tax administrations. Previous editions of this report have reported on reforms introducing (near) live VAT invoice reporting in Italy, Hungary and Spain. In 2019, Italy extended its real-time e-invoicing requirement to include both business-to-business (B2B) and business-to-consumer (B2C) transactions. France and Poland have also announced the introduction of B2B VAT e-invoicing requirements in the next couple of years. In Chile, a first mover in the area of e-invoicing, mandatory electronic invoicing for B2C sales is expected to come into force in September 2020. Italy and Spain have also announced that, based on the information provided in e-invoices, they would introduce pre-completed VAT returns in 2020.

**A few additional measures have been introduced to enhance compliance**. Poland is introducing a "white list" of VAT taxpayers, which is an online register to help business entities quickly identify bona-fide contractors. From 1 January 2020, taxpayers may be subject to sanctions or joint and several liability for VAT purposes if they make payments to accounts of contractors that are not included in the list. Another measure to combat fraud was the introduction of a VAT receipt lottery in Italy. The provisions introducing the VAT receipt lottery, initially applicable as of July 2020, have been postponed to January 2021 due to the COVID-19 pandemic. Such lotteries have already been tested to reduce undeclared VAT on sales to consumers in countries including Greece, the Slovak Republic and Portugal (OECD, 2017[11]).

### *Countries are continuing to make progress in ensuring the effective taxation of online sales of goods, services and intangibles*

**The increasing digitalisation of the global economy has created considerable challenges for VAT systems worldwide**. The rapid development of new technologies dramatically increased the ability of private consumers to engage in online shopping and the capability of businesses such as online marketplaces to reach customers globally without any physical presence in market jurisdictions. To the extent that the market jurisdiction has no right to tax under existing VAT rules or is unable to require foreign online sellers to apply and remit the VAT on supplies to consumers in its jurisdiction, this results in no or an inappropriately low amount of VAT being collected and in an uneven playing field between domestic suppliers, that have to charge VAT on sales to local customers, and foreign online suppliers.

**To ensure the effective taxation of cross-border supplies of services and intangibles, many countries have already implemented the rules and mechanisms recommended by the OECD International VAT/GST Guidelines**. The OECD International VAT/GST Guidelines have been endorsed as the international standard to ensure a coherent and efficient application of VAT/GST to international trade in services and intangibles. As mentioned in previous editions of this report, the elements of the

Guidelines that have received most attention since 2016 are the recommended rules and mechanisms for the effective collection of VAT on business-to-consumer (B2C) supplies of services and intangibles made by vendors that have no physical presence in the jurisdiction of taxation. These rules and mechanisms are particularly relevant for the continuously growing volume of online sales by offshore vendors, made directly to consumers or through the intervention of digital platforms such as e-commerce marketplaces. The Guidelines recommend that the right to tax these supplies for VAT purposes be allocated to the country where the consumer has its usual residence and that the foreign suppliers of these services and intangibles register and remit VAT in the country of the consumer's usual residence. The Guidelines also recommend the implementation of a simplified registration and compliance regime to facilitate tax compliance for foreign suppliers. To date, over 60 countries, including the overwhelming majority of OECD and G20 countries, have adopted rules for the application of VAT to B2C supplies of services and intangibles in line with the Guidelines. Many other countries have announced or are considering reforms to introduce these measures. Notably Mexico has started taxing foreign supplies of digital services and requiring foreign suppliers of digital services to register for VAT as of June 2020. Chile has also started levying VAT on cross-border B2C digital services and introduced a new VAT registration and collection mechanism for foreign suppliers as of June 2020.

**Recent evidence suggests that the implementation of these measures is having a significant impact.** The rules and mechanisms recommended in the Guidelines have greatly enhanced compliance levels, yielded substantial additional tax revenues for market jurisdictions, and evened the playing field between domestic suppliers and foreign online vendors. The EU, the earliest adopter of these principles, reported EUR 14.8 billion of VAT revenues collected from these measures in the first four years of their operation, with revenues showing a constant growth from EUR 3 billion of VAT revenue collected in 2015 to EUR 4.57 billion in 2018. In South Africa, the revenue collected through the application of the OECD principles and collection mechanisms amounted to over ZAR 5.4 billion in the 12 months since the expansion of its VAT regime for online sales of services and digital products in 2019, in line with the OECD standards, thus recording a remarkable growth compared to the previous five years during which ZAR 3 billion (approx. EUR 159 million) were collected in total. New Zealand collected NZD 357 million (approx. EUR 204 million) in the first two years of implementation of its regime for the collection of GST on services and intangibles (as of April 2017). Australia recorded total revenues of over AUD 1 billion (approx. EUR 615 million) of GST collected in the first two years of operating its GST regime for online sales of services and digital products (as of July 2017) and in the first year of its implementation for online sales of goods (as of July 2018; see below).

### Box 3.8. OECD guidance on the collection of VAT/GST on online sales

The OECD has provided guidance in the *International VAT/GST Guidelines* (the "Guidelines") to jurisdictions wishing to collect VAT on cross-border supplies of services and intangibles (OECD, 2017). The Guidelines include recommended rules and mechanisms for the effective collection of VAT on business-to-consumer (B2C) supplies of services and intangibles (including digital supplies) by foreign suppliers. The Guidelines were complemented by further detailed practical guidance to support their effective and consistent implementation. Two reports providing such implementation guidance have been published. The report on *Mechanisms for the effective collection of VAT/GST* (OECD, 2017) focuses on cases where the supplier is not located in the jurisdiction of taxation. The report on *The role of digital platforms in the collection of VAT/GST on online sales* (OECD, 2019[12]) provides guidance on measures to enhance the efficiency and effectiveness of VAT collection on online sales of goods, services and intangibles by involving digital platforms in the collection and compliance process.

**Digitalisation is also pushing governments to revise their VAT rules on cross-border trade in low-value goods**. In the past, most countries introduced VAT relief regimes for imports of low-value goods, as the costs of collecting VAT on those items were often likely to outweigh the VAT actually collected. At the time when most of these relief regimes were introduced, online shopping did not exist and the level of imports benefitting from the relief was relatively small. However, there has been a significant and rapid growth in the volume of imports of low-value goods subject to these VAT relief regimes. This has resulted in large potential VAT revenues not being collected and growing risks of unfair competition for domestic retailers that are required to charge VAT on their sales to domestic consumers. It also creates an incentive for domestic suppliers to relocate to an offshore jurisdiction to sell their low-value goods free of VAT.

**A number of countries are now removing or considering the elimination of VAT relief regimes for imports of low-value goods**. It is no longer considered acceptable in an increasing number of countries that a significantly and continuously growing volume of goods from online sales is imported without VAT as a consequence of the VAT exemption for imports of low-value goods. These reforms follow on from the work carried out by the OECD in the context of BEPS Action 1 on "Addressing the Tax Challenges of the Digital Economy". The Final 2015 BEPS Action 1 Report notably concluded that the efficiency of VAT collection on imports of low-value goods could be increased considerably if online vendors of these goods, or digital platforms that facilitate these sales, were required to collect the VAT from their customers and remit it to the tax authorities via a simplified registration and compliance regime. This was expected to limit or remove the need for customs authorities to intervene in the revenue collection process for imports of low-value goods. This lowers the cost of collection of VAT on low-value goods considerably, and allows customs authorities to allocate their resources and capacity to their other key roles.

**Countries have introduced or are considering reforms in this area.** Australia was the first OECD country to implement a reform to collect GST on imports of low-value goods in July 2018. New Zealand introduced a similar reform as of December 2019. The threshold at NZD 400 below which no GST was collected on imported goods was removed as of that date. New Zealand GST is to be collected and remitted by offshore suppliers for imported goods valued below NZD 1 000 (i.e. the *de minimis* threshold for customs duties). For goods imports below this threshold, foreign suppliers are required to register, collect and remit GST if their annual sales to New Zealand consumers are above NZD 60 000. For imports above the NZD 1 000 threshold, normal customs procedures for the collection of GST, customs and any other duties continue to apply. Similarly, Norway has removed its VAT exemption for imported goods valued below NOK 305 and introduced a simplified scheme for sellers and online marketplaces to register and remit VAT. The EU is also planning to remove its low-value consignment relief of EUR 10-22 in 2021. All these regimes include a liability for digital platforms such as e-commerce marketplaces to collect and remit the VAT on the imports of goods that were sold by online vendors through their platform. The platform is viewed as taking the role of a 'store' with an offering of different supplies and in many cases act as the sole point of contact with the end consumer. The OECD released a report in 2019 providing detailed guidance for the implementation of these measures to make digital platforms liable for the VAT on sales made by online traders, along with other measures that include data sharing and enhanced cooperation between tax authorities and digital platforms (OECD, 2019[12]) (Box 3.9).

**Box 3.9. OECD report on "The Role of Digital Platforms in the Collection of VAT/GST on Online Sales"**

Against the backdrop of the continuously strong growth of online trade to final consumers, the Final 2015 BEPS Action 1 Report on *Addressing the Tax Challenges of the Digital Economy* recognised that digital platforms may significantly enhance the effectiveness of VAT/GST collection given their important role in generating, facilitating and/or executing online sales.

In its 2019 report on *The Role of Digital Platforms in the Collection of VAT/GST on Online Sales*, the OECD provides further detailed practical guidance to tax authorities on the design and implementation of a variety of solutions for enlisting the platforms economy, including e-commerce marketplaces and other digital platforms, in the collection of VAT/GST on digital sales. It complements earlier work carried out on the *Mechanisms for the Effective Collection of VAT/GST*.

The report observes that electronic marketplaces and other digital platforms that facilitate online transactions between buyers and sellers play a central role in online trade. Evidence suggests that about two-thirds of all cross-border e-commerce sales of goods are made through online marketplaces. This reality presents significant opportunities for a more efficient and effective collection of VAT/GST on online sales of goods, services and intangibles, particularly sales to private consumers. Against this background, the report includes detailed guidance on measures to make digital platforms liable for the VAT/GST on sales made by online traders through them. This is complemented with other measures that include data sharing and enhanced cooperation between tax authorities and digital platforms. The report also sets out a range of measures beyond possible VAT obligations for digital platforms that tax authorities can implement to further enhance the effectiveness of VAT collection on online trade.

This report was developed through an inclusive process, involving representatives from OECD members and a large number of partner countries as well as through the active engagement of the business community. It was endorsed by the representatives from over 100 jurisdictions and international and regional organisations as well as from the business community at the fifth meeting of the Global Forum on VAT in Melbourne, Australia in March 2019.

**As of 1 January 2021, online marketplaces in EU countries will be responsible for charging and remitting VAT on sales from non-EU sellers using their platforms under certain conditions** (for goods up to a value of EUR 150 and where the seller uses fulfilment centres). However, some countries have already introduced domestic measures, in particular imposing new recordkeeping obligations. In Austria, as of 2020, platforms are to provide tax authorities with transactional data from third parties on their platforms, while France is now requesting online marketplaces to verify the VAT status of foreign sellers using their platforms.

### *Excise duties have continued to be raised*

**Excise taxes have been a powerful tool to raise revenues and encourage behavioural change.** Excise taxes can cover a wide range of products, but the ones that are common to all countries and raise significant revenues for governments are excise duties on alcohol, tobacco and hydrocarbon oils. In recent decades, governments have increasingly used these taxes not only to raise revenues, but also to influence behaviours and deter harmful consumption. This sub-section covers non-energy excise duties (for energy excise duties, see Section 3.4).

**Taxes on tobacco products are particularly high**. The relatively low price elasticity of demand, the small number of producers and high consumption levels initially made tobacco products particularly attractive targets for excise taxation to raise revenue. In light of the negative health consequences of tobacco use and the effectiveness of tobacco taxation in reducing tobacco use (World Health Organization, 2015[13]), tobacco taxation has also increasingly been used as a tool to reduce tobacco use. As a result, in 2017, the total tax burden on cigarettes was above 50% of the consumer price in almost all OECD countries and reached 80% or more in eight countries (OECD, 2018[9]).

**Excise duty increases, especially on tobacco products, have continued this year.** Increases in excise duty rates on tobacco products have been reported in Denmark, Estonia, Finland, Hungary, Ireland, Lithuania, Poland, Slovenia and South Africa. As in previous years, increases in excise duties have been more popular for tobacco than alcohol. Increases in excise duties on alcohol were reported in Lithuania, Poland and South Africa. On the other hand, Estonia and Latvia introduced a decrease in the excise duty rate on some alcoholic beverages.

**Soft drinks continue to be an area of interest for countries, with new taxes being introduced and existing taxes being raised.** Previous editions of this report have confirmed the increasing popularity of taxes on sugar-sweetened beverages, with many countries introducing such taxes in recent years (e.g. Ireland, Portugal, South Africa, United Kingdom). This trend is continuing. Italy introduced a new consumption tax on soft drinks of EUR 10 per hectolitre for finished products and EUR 0.25 per kilo for products prepared for use after dilution. The tax, initially applicable as of October 2020, has been postponed to January 2021 due to the COVID-19 pandemic. Poland is considering a new sugar levy, but examination in Parliament has not started yet. The proposal consists of a levy on beverages with added sugar or other sweeteners, as well as caffeine and/or taurine, and another levy on alcoholic beverages sold in packages of up to 300 ml. Most of the revenues collected through these taxes would go to the National Health Fund to improve healthcare financing. In addition to these new taxes, Finland and South Africa have both raised their taxes on soft drinks.

### *Other taxes on specific goods and services have been introduced*

**In Chile, a new contribution was introduced to promote regional decentralisation and incentivise the expeditious issuance of administrative permits for investment projects**. A new one-time contribution will be levied on investment projects carried out in Chile exceeding USD 10 million and that require permits from the Environmental Impact Evaluation Service. This contribution will be levied after the investment project has obtained all the permits and begun operations and will be equal to 1% of the acquisition value of fixed assets associated with the investment projects on the part that exceeds USD 10 million, payable in five yearly instalments. The contribution will be fully deductible from the CIT base. Funds will be used to promote regional decentralisation.

**Turkey introduced a new accommodation tax and Hungary expanded its tourism development contribution to accommodation services.** Turkey's new tax is levied on accommodation services rendered by hotels, resorts, guesthouses, and other accommodation service providers, as well as all other services provided in those accommodation facilities (such as food and beverage, entertainment services, use of pools and similar areas). The accommodation tax rate will be 2% and the tax will be declared and paid on a monthly basis by accommodation service providers. The basis of the accommodation tax is the total value of payments for services (excluding VAT). The accommodation tax will enter into force in 2021. Similarly, Hungary extended the application of its tourism development contribution, applicable to restaurant services since 2018, to accommodation services. This reform was introduced in parallel to the VAT rate reduction on accommodation services (see above).

## Environmentally related taxes

**Overall, this section shows that environmentally related tax reform have continued at a slow pace in 2020**. While the number of reforms increased compared to 2019, they were concentrated in a few countries and their scope generally remained limited. Most of the reforms were related to energy use, but transport fuels were not the focal point as opposed to previous years. Instead, changes were made to carbon taxes and taxes on electricity consumption. There were also fewer energy tax cuts compared to last year. Tax reform in the transport sector, aside from energy use, was limited to vehicle registration tax adjustments and tax reductions for vehicles running on alternative fuels. Reforms related to taxes on waste and plastic have also increased this year, but their overall number remains limited.

### Box 3.10. Environmental tax policy reform and climate action in Germany and the Netherlands

#### Germany

Germany is introducing a broad package of environmental measures, which go beyond environmentally related taxes. The package of measures includes an increase in the national aviation tax rates, a VAT reduction for long-distance rail travel and tax incentives targeted at increasing buildings' thermal insulation and energy efficiency (including for smaller-scale modernisation measures such as the installation of new energy-efficient windows or the insulation of roofs and walls).

Furthermore, a national ETS system (nEHS) covering the transport and heating sectors will be introduced in 2021 and complement the EU ETS. The revenue will be used to finance climate-related as well as social measures such as the reduction of electricity levies, increased commuter allowances and housing subsidies.

#### Netherlands

The Coalition Agreement of the new Dutch government (2017 to 2021) includes a number of environmental tax policy changes. Dutch climate and energy policy actions are driven by the national commitment to implement the UN Paris Climate Agreements of 2015. Moreover, as a member of the EU, the country must abide by EU agreements on emissions reductions. The EU ETS covers electricity and industrial companies and allow prices to fluctuate based on supply and demand. The Dutch government has decided to introduce a minimum carbon price of EUR 12.30 per tonne of $CO_2$, increasing to EUR 31.90 per tonne of $CO_2$ in 2030. If the EU ETS allows prices to fall below this threshold, the difference will be levied in the form of a national-level carbon tax.

In addition to the carbon price floor, the Netherlands will promote environmental sustainability by shifting the tax burden from electricity to natural gas to better account for the carbon content of fuels. Additionally, the tax rate on landfilling and waste incineration was increased with plans to broaden the base to include sewage sludge and renewable waste. There is also a parallel reallocation of the tax burden from households to enterprises, with increased rates of the surcharge for sustainable energy for the higher brackets of electricity consumption and higher energy tax credits per electricity connection. These are examples of how environmental tax reform can promote equity. Furthermore, a new tax on air travel tickets was announced for 2021, but preference would be given to an EU-wide tax on air tickets. Last but not least, the Netherlands plans to introduce a carbon tax in the industry sector in 2021. The model they are working on is a tax on emissions above a diminishing tax-free base at a relatively high tax rate. The objective is to generate a strong incentive to reduce carbon emissions and at the same time limit the tax burden to prevent substantially damaging the competitiveness of national industry sectors.

Source: OECD Annual Tax Policy Reform Questionnaire

**Countries differ in the degree to which they rely on environmentally related taxes to achieve climate objectives**. Environmentally related taxes are defined as any compulsory, unrequited payment to general government levied on tax bases deemed to be of particular environmental relevance. They encompass all taxes that are likely to have a strong environmental impact – regardless of the reason why they were introduced – and cover a broad range of areas, including agrochemicals, energy, road use, vehicles, waste, water abstraction and water pollution. Among these, energy taxes, in particular fuel excise and carbon taxes, are particularly effective tools to curb climate change. Germany and the Netherlands are two countries that are stepping up their climate efforts with varying degrees of environmental tax policy reform components as showcased in Box 3.10.

### *Environmentally related tax revenues vary widely across countries and continue to be dominated by taxes on energy use*

**Revenues from environmentally related taxes in 2017 varied significantly across countries**, ranging from 0.7% of GDP in the United States to 4.5% of GDP in Slovenia (Figure 3.24). Between 2000 and 2017, environmentally related tax revenue measured as a share of GDP fell in about half of the countries covered in the report and remained stable in eight of them. Iceland, Denmark and Ireland experienced the largest decreases in revenues as a share of GDP. Revenues rose in eleven countries, with particularly sharp increases in Greece, Slovenia, Latvia and Estonia. The former three are now among the four countries exhibiting the highest environmentally related tax revenues as a share of GDP. On average[17] across the countries covered in the report, environmentally related taxes raised revenue amounting to 2.3% of GDP in 2017, a level comparable to those reached in 2010 and 2000 (2.4%).

Figure 3.24. Revenues from environmentally related taxes as a share of GDP in 2017 by country

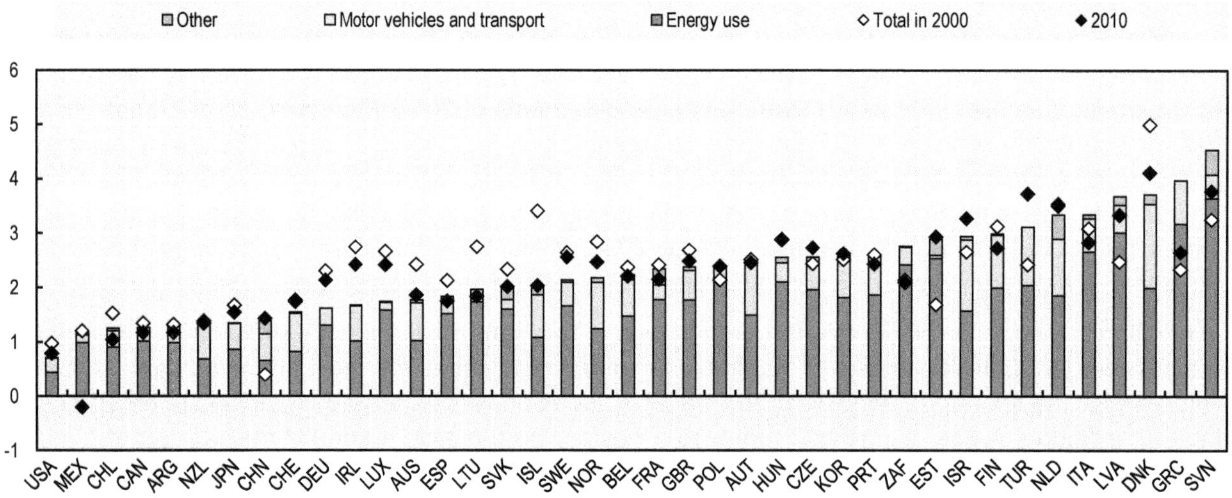


Note: Data for Australia and the United States are from 2016 (not 2017). Data for Israel and Korea are from 2014 (not 2017). Data for China are from 2012. Transport data for South Africa are from 2015. Indonesia missing.
Source: OECD Database on instruments used for environmental policy, http://stats.oecd.org/.

StatLink https://doi.org/10.1787/888934158955

**Taxes on energy use accounted for more than 50% of total environmentally related tax revenues in all countries except China (48%) in 2017.** On average, energy use taxes yielded 72% of environmentally related tax revenues. Taxes on energy use are principally fuel excise, as well as carbon taxes where applicable. They also drive changes in revenues from environmentally related taxes measured as a share of GDP over time in most countries. This is because high energy tax rates in the long run may lead to behavioural changes that result in a decrease in fuel demand – particularly transport – thereby reducing tax bases and potentially the revenues stemming from them. A recent study on road transport in Slovenia investigates the balancing act of seemingly contradictory objectives: using environmentally related taxes to raise government revenues and, at the same time, steering behaviour towards reducing harmful activities (OECD/ITF, 2019[14]). Using scenario analysis and simulations for Slovenia to 2050, the analysis finds that a substantial decline of tax revenue from diesel and gasoline use in private cars is likely to occur, but gradually. A comprehensive and similarly gradual tax reform via taxes on distances driven and higher fuel or carbon taxes on fossil fuel use that accounts for their external costs could facilitate the smooth evolution of future tax revenues.

**Motor vehicle taxes and other taxes on transport are the second largest component of environmentally related tax revenues**. Mainly consisting of one-time registration taxes on motor vehicles and annual taxes on users or owners of vehicles, they range from 2% of environmentally related tax revenues in Estonia to 47% in New Zealand, and account on average for 24% of environmentally related tax revenues across the countries covered in the report. Before 2008, a few countries like Iceland, Ireland, Norway and Switzerland, collected most of their environmentally related tax revenues through motor vehicle and other transport taxes, but this is no longer the case.

### *Carbon price signals remain low and narrow*

**In 2018, nearly all carbon emissions from energy use in road transport were subject to a tax** in the 44 OECD and G20 countries for which comparable data is collected by the OECD and which together account for 80% of carbon emissions from energy use (Figure 3.25). Effective tax rates surpassed those for other fuels and sectors by far and exceeded a low-end estimated climate benchmark of EUR 30 per tonne of $CO_2$ for roughly 84% of emissions. However, this does not necessarily mean that road fuels are excessively taxed, as this low-end benchmark only takes into account climate costs. When other negative externalities are factored in (e.g. congestion, air and noise pollution, road accidents, use of urban space for parking), higher taxation of road transport fuels may be warranted. It is worth noting that carbon price signals can stem from policy instruments other than fuel excise and carbon taxes, namely Emissions Trading Systems (ETS), which sometimes cover additional greenhouse gases and emission sources, especially in electricity generation and industry.

Figure 3.25. Carbon emissions from energy use subject to different levels of effective tax rates in the road and non-road sectors, in 2018

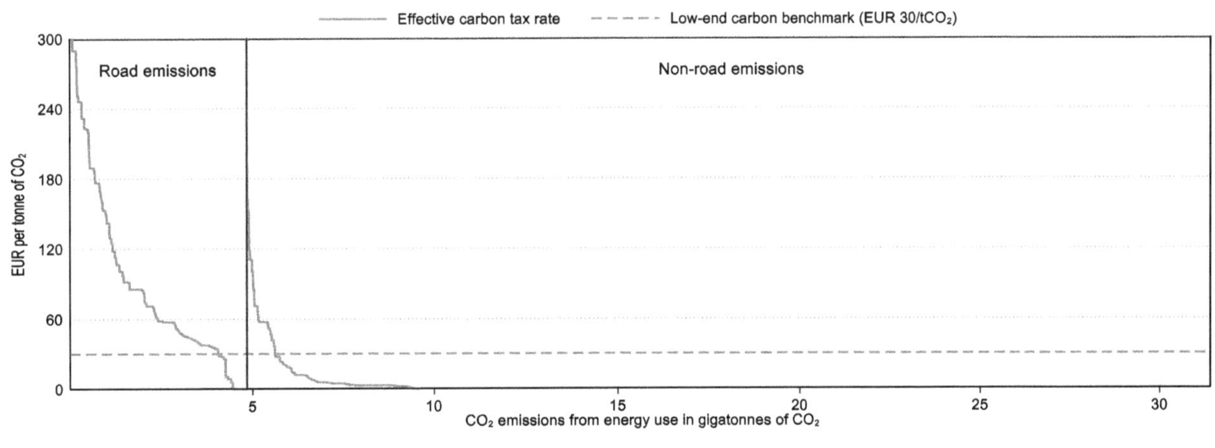


Note: The countries included are the 36 OECD countries and Argentina, Brazil, the People's Republic of China, Colombia, India, Indonesia, the Russian Federation and South Africa plus international transport.
Source: (OECD, 2019[15]).

StatLink https://doi.org/10.1787/888934158974

**Outside the road sector, carbon emissions are largely untaxed, which is disconcerting as 85% of energy-related $CO_2$ emissions do not originate from road transport.** Only 18% of non-road emissions were effectively taxed and a mere 3% were taxed above the low-end climate benchmark of EUR 30 per tonne of $CO_2$ (Figure 3.25). Moreover, changes in tax rates between 2018 and 2015 were modest and did not modify the landscape significantly (Figure 3.26). Accounting for emissions trading systems would make the picture less bleak (OECD, 2018[16]), but the key message would remain the same.

Figure 3.26. Average effective carbon tax rates by country

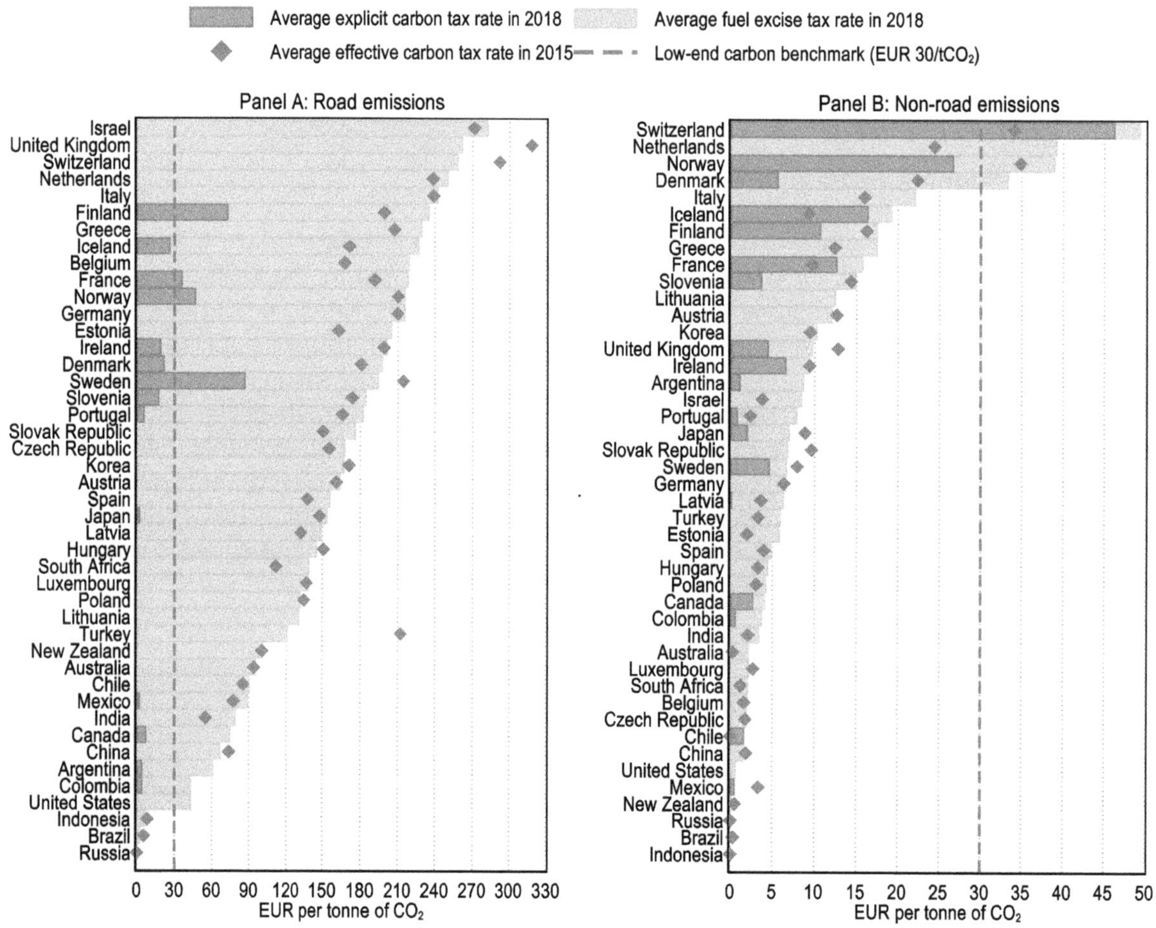


Note: "Explicit" tax rates refer to explicit carbon taxes rather than fuel excise taxes in the legislation. The scale of the horizontal axis differs between Panel A and Panel B. Note that changes in average effective tax rates over time are also affected by inflation, exchange rate fluctuations, and changes in the composition of the energy mix. The comparison excludes 2015 rates for the United States and Canada as data on subnational taxes was not available for 2015. 2015 data for Colombia and Lithuania are missing because they were not yet covered in the previous vintage of Taxing Energy Use. Argentina is missing because no inflation data was available.
Average effective carbon tax rates are weighted by carbon emissions.
Source: (OECD, 2019[15]).

StatLink https://doi.org/10.1787/888934158993

**Momentum for carbon price signals via ETSs has been increasing.** Emissions trading systems and carbon taxes can be equally effective and efficient, depending on the details of their design. As mentioned in Box 3.10, Germany will introduce a national ETS, covering the transport and heating sectors and complementing the EU ETS in 2021. In the Netherlands, the government has decided to introduce a national carbon price floor for emissions covered by the EU ETS including a price path (Box 3.10). Overall, however, ETSs remain a comparatively small component of carbon pricing: in 2015, ETSs accounted for approximately 6% of carbon price signals in OECD and G20 countries (OECD, 2018[16]). The extent to which countries deploy taxes or ETSs to price carbon emissions also varies significantly. The EU ETS, for instance, covers most emissions from electricity generation and industry, and intra-European flights. Allowances traded at approximately EUR 25 per tonne of $CO_2$ equivalent at the time of writing and have risen substantially since 2017 levels as a result of reforms, including the Market Stability Reserve.

**Overall, the energy tax landscape remains widely misaligned with key principles of environmental taxation**. Figure 3.27 reveals in finer detail where CO2 emissions stem from and the associated effective carbon tax rates. Besides the pronounced difference between road and non-road sectors, the Figure highlights that industrial energy use remains mostly untaxed. Another issue concerns the lack of taxation on coal and solid fossil fuels across sectors (e.g. industry and electricity), when other less carbon intensive and polluting fossil fuels like natural gas are taxed. These inconsistencies show the need for efforts towards better aligning taxes with environmental costs.

Figure 3.27. Effective carbon taxes in OECD and Selected Partner Economies differ substantially across sectors

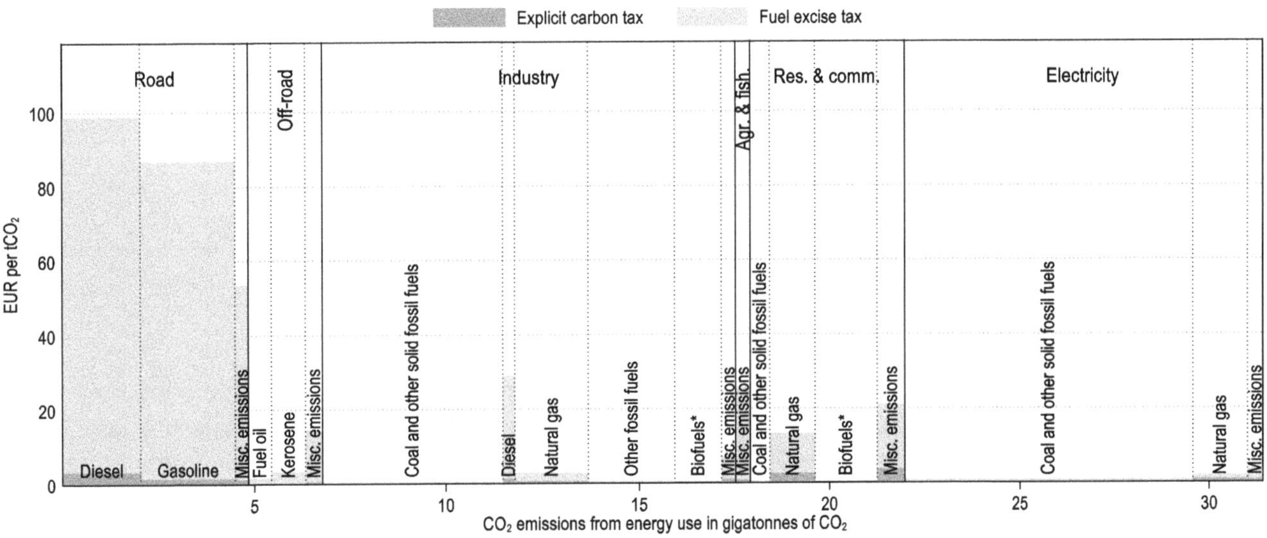


Note: Tax rates applicable on 1 July 2018. The countries included are the 36 OECD countries and Argentina, Brazil, the People's Republic of China, Colombia, India, Indonesia, the Russian Federation and South Africa plus international aviation and maritime transport included in off-road. Biofuels are marked with an asterisk as under the IPCC Guidelines for emissions from energy use, emissions from the combustion of biofuels are not included in the national total. The figure groups energy categories that represent less than 1% of the horizontal axis into "miscellaneous emissions".
Source: (OECD, 2019[15])

StatLink https://doi.org/10.1787/888934159012

## *Countries renew interest in energy taxes in 2020, shy away from reductions*

**Most energy tax reforms involved increases in fuel and carbon taxes** (Table 3.11). After a break in 2019 when strengthening fuel and carbon taxation received attenuated attention, energy tax reforms were again more frequent than other types of environmentally related tax reforms. Six countries raised taxes on fuels. In Lithuania, where tax rates for diesel and gasoline were increased by over 7%. In Latvia, tax reform continued and tax rates on transport fuels were increased by 7% for gasoline and by 11% for diesel. South Africa raised the general fuel levy at a rate slightly below inflation. France is gradually phasing out the preferential tax treatment of diesel used for public works. The Netherlands increased the excise duty on diesel by one eurocent per litre. Sweden abolished the tax exemption for diesel in mining activities. In the transport sector, Finland increased the tax on transport fuels to counteract the effect of inflation by 2023. As announced in previous editions of this report, a carbon tax of EUR 7.42/t$CO_2$[18] came into force in South Africa to help the country meet its Paris Climate Agreement goals. Ireland increased the rate of its carbon tax from EUR 20 to EUR 26 per tonne of $CO_2$ and Sweden raised both the energy and carbon taxes on fossil fuels used for heating in combined heat and power plants (CHP). The Netherlands also reported plans to step up its carbon tax rates after 2020.

**Electricity consumption tax increases emerged as a secondary but novel trend in 2020**. Specifically, the Netherlands increased the sustainable energy surcharge, a levy on the supply of energy, for higher consumption brackets, shifting the burden from households to enterprises. Ireland also raised the rate of electricity tax for businesses. On a different note, Latvia introduced a new maintenance fee to raise revenues as part of a reform of the support provided to electricity producers.

## Table 3.11. Changes to taxes on energy use

| | Rate/Base ⇧ | | Rate/Base ⇩ | |
|---|---|---|---|---|
| Into effect in | **2019** | **2020 or later** | **2019** | **2020 or later** |
| Fuels, with sector specification: | | | | |
| Agriculture | | LTU LVA | SWEca | |
| Electricity production | KOR | | KOR | |
| Heating | FIN | SWE | DNK | |
| Transport | LUX ZAF | FIN | FRA GBRi MEX | MEX |
| Fuels, all sectors | | FRA LTU LVA NLD SWE ZAF | EST SWE | |
| Carbon tax | ISL ZAF | (CHL) IRL (NLD) SWE | FRA | USAb |
| Electricity consumption | | IRL LVA NLD | EST GBR NLD POL | NLD |

Note: Countries in brackets have only announced reforms. ca: carbon tax; b: tax related to biofuels; i: taxes indexed to inflation.
Source: OECD Annual Tax Policy Reform Questionnaire.

**Energy tax reductions were infrequent in 2020**. Preferential tax rates for specific sectors are available in many countries (OECD, 2018[17]).They weaken the incentive for polluters to take part in a country's overall emissions reduction effort. The low number of energy tax reductions for specific energy users, which effectively take the form of preferential tax rates, is thus a welcome improvement. Moderate oil prices may have also reduced the pressure to reduce road fuel taxes. As in previous years, Mexico is extending for another year the operation of a price smoothing mechanism for diesel and gasoline, which serves as a budget neutral buffer for international oil price fluctuations on the domestic market. The United States is extending tax incentives and credits pertaining to bio and alternative fuels. Poland reported in 2020 a big reduction in the electricity excise tax (from 20 to 5 PLN/MWh) that came into force already in 2019. The change came as a response to price hikes in the electricity market since 2018. The Netherlands is gradually lowering the energy tax rate on electricity in the first bracket shifting the tax burden from electricity to natural gas. It will also raise substantially the basic tax credit per electricity connection as a means of promoting equity and redirecting the tax burden from households to businesses. Electricity taxes often fail to differentiate across energy source, making all of them more expensive irrespective of the climate damage resulting from their use. Overall, in 2020 energy tax decreases did not contradict environmental objectives. This is a positive change compared to 2019, where a number of reforms involved extending preferential tax rates to specific sectors and postponing fuel duty increases (United Kingdom, Sweden) or cancelling them altogether (France) (Table 3.11).

**Efforts to reduce the diesel discount in road transport and to index energy taxes to inflation are lacking.** With existing equipment and technology, diesel results in higher emissions of harmful air pollutants and $CO_2$ per litre compared to gasoline. To account for these externalities, diesel should in principle be taxed at higher rates than gasoline. However, Figure 3.28 shows that in road transport only three of the countries covered in this report (Mexico, Switzerland and the United States) tax diesel at higher rates than gasoline on a per litre basis. Additionally, no country that had not already done so previously attempted to automatically index tax rates to inflation, leading to falling real tax rates in the majority of cases.

Figure 3.28. Average effective energy taxes per litre of diesel and gasoline in road transport in 2018, by country

Countries are sorted by average effective energy tax on gasoline in descending order

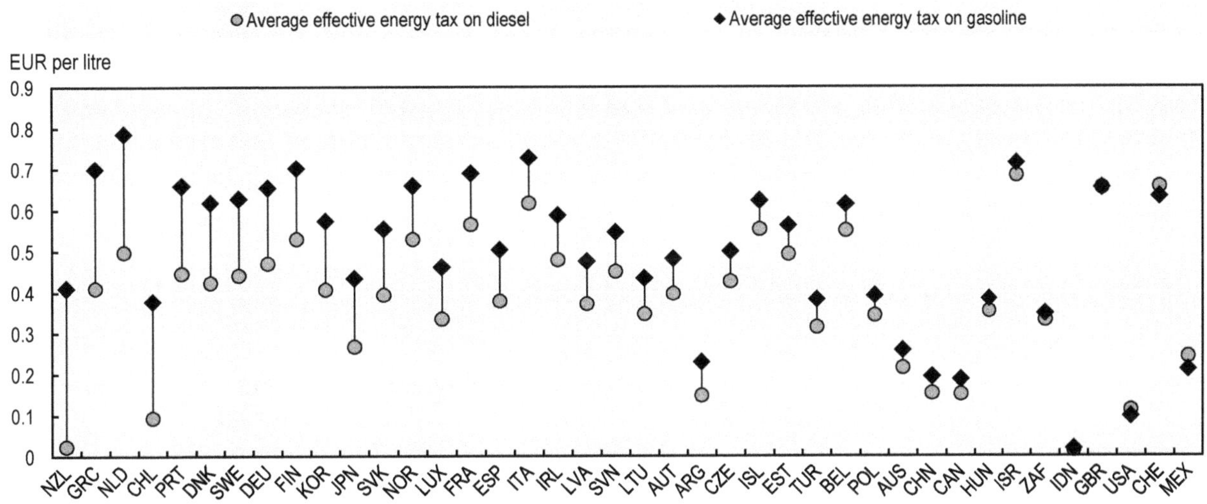


Note: New Zealand is a special case because diesel vehicles pay distance-based road-user charges, which are not included because they affect different behavioural margins than energy taxes.
Average effective energy taxes are weighted by energy use.
Source: Adapted based on data from OECD (OECD, 2019[15]).

StatLink https://doi.org/10.1787/888934159031

### *Transport and vehicle tax reform slowed down further in 2020*

**Changes to traditional motor vehicle taxes, namely recurrent vehicle and registration taxes, were rare in 2020** (Table 3.12). Ireland replaced the 1% surcharge on the vehicle registration tax for diesel passenger vehicles with a nitrogen oxide based surcharge, in an effort to tax more accurately the environmental and external health costs of diesel vehicles. The Netherlands abolished the full refund of car registration for taxis and Lithuania introduced a new pollution tax on vehicles registered or reregistered from 1 July 2020 to incentivise the replacement of its old and polluting fleet. Turkey revised its special consumption tax rates on motor vehicles downwards to encourage the purchase of new and less polluting vehicles.

**Three countries have implemented changes to the taxation of alternative fuel vehicles**. Ireland extended the registration tax relief for hybrid and plug-in hybrid vehicles for another year until the end of 2020. It also introduced a $CO_2$ basis for calculating the rates of benefit-in-kind for company vehicles in order to encourage the use of alternative fuel vehicles as employer-provided cars. The Netherlands extended exemptions from registration tax until 2024 for zero emission vehicles. Poland reduced excise tax rates for hybrid-fuelled vehicles as of 1 January 2020. On the other hand, Israel announced the gradual elimination of the preferential tax treatment for hybrid, plug-in and electric vehicles with the aim of raising revenues and simplifying the tax system. Preferential tax treatment for electric vehicles can provide strong signals to switch to less polluting vehicles, although it depends on how clean electricity production is and the amount of revenue foregone can vary greatly with the design of incentives (German, 2018[18]). It is also likely to be regressive because low-income households are less likely to invest in expensive electric vehicles (Borenstein and Davis, 2016[19]).

**Minor changes to the taxation of less conventional tax bases, such as air travel, were observed in 2020**. Specifically, the Netherlands intends to tax airline tickets from 2021, although it would prioritise an EU agreement. Germany has increased the aviation tax rates in all three of its distance bands. Flights within the European Economic Area are also covered by the European Emissions Trading System, unlike other international flights, which are generally not subject to energy taxes or carbon pricing. However, the severe impact of the COVID-19 crisis on aviation travel may have an impact on recently proposed changes.

**Finally, the Netherlands adjusted motor vehicle taxes to account for the new Worldwide Harmonised Light Vehicle Test Procedure (WLTP)**. The WLTP measures fuel consumption and $CO_2$ emissions from passenger cars, as well as their pollutant emissions and is based on updated laboratory tests using real-driving data. The new test protocol is supposed to match road performance better than previously with the New European Driving Cycle (NEDC). Several countries (Finland, Ireland and Portugal) introduced similar measures in 2019.

Table 3.12. Changes to taxes on motor vehicles and other transport taxes

| | Rate/Base ⇧ | | Rate/Base ⇩ | |
|---|---|---|---|---|
| Into effect in | **2019** | **2020 or later** | **2019** | **2020 or later** |
| Vehicle tax | ARG | | TUR FIN JPN | TUR |
| Registration tax | GBR[1] IRL NOR | IRL LTU NLD | GBR[1] IRL JPN | |
| Vehicles running on alternative fuels | TUR | (ISR) | IRL | IRL NLD POL |
| Road use | DNK LUX NLD SWE | | | |
| Air travel | NOR | DEU (NLD) | | |
| Other (e.g. company cars, road accidents) | ZAF | | IRL | IRL |

1. Taxes indexed to inflation.
Note: Countries in brackets have only announced reforms.
Source: OECD Annual Tax Policy Reform Questionnaire.

### *Interest in other environmentally related taxes is increasing, but remains overall low*

**Environmentally related tax reforms related to other tax bases (e.g. plastic, chemicals or waste) typically attract little attention, but the number of reforms in this area increased in 2020** (Table 3.13). Denmark increased taxes on shopping bags and disposable tableware. Italy introduced a consumption tax on plastic packaging materials, exempting plastic medical devices and compostable plastics. The tax, initially applicable as of July 2020, has been postponed to January 2021 due to the COVID-19 pandemic. Iceland brought into effect a new tax payable by kilogramme of fluorinated greenhouse gases and adjusted by the global warming potential of the gas. The tax rate will double after the first year of implementation. Latvia raised the tax rates on several natural resources (e.g. sand). Sweden introduced new taxes on plastic carrier bags and waste incineration. Poland was the only country[19] to reduce taxes in this category. It reduced by 15% the tax rate on the extraction of certain minerals like silver and copper to lower the tax burden on businesses.

Table 3.13. Changes to other environmentally related taxes

| | Rate/Base ⇧ | | Rate/Base ⇩ | |
|---|---|---|---|---|
| Into effect in | **2019** | **2020 or later** | **2019** | **2020 or later** |
| Natural resources | | LVA | POL | |
| Plastic | LVA | DNK ITA SWE | | |
| Waste | NLD SVK | DNK SWE | | |
| Other | | ISL | | |

Source: OECD Annual Tax Policy Reform Questionnaire.

## Property taxes

**Overall, there have been more changes reported in the area of property taxation compared to the previous years and reforms have predominantly involved tax increases**. Previous editions of this report showed limited changes to property taxation in recent years, with some exceptions. This year shows an increasing number of reforms. In addition, while previous years showed a mix of tax increases and decreases, this year shows a clearer trend towards increases in property taxation, although there have also been some reforms aimed at decreasing property taxes. This year has also seen the introduction of new taxes, including new taxes on high-value immovable property in Chile and Turkey, and a planned tax on financial transactions in Spain.

### *Property taxes continue to be a small source of revenue*

**Countries impose a variety of taxes on property**. The most prominent property taxes across the countries covered in the report are recurrent taxes on immovable property, which are typically a key source of revenue for local governments. Property transaction taxes and inheritance and gift taxes are also common. Very few countries impose a tax on some measure of total net wealth.

**Property tax revenues remain low in most countries**. In 2018, the amount of revenues collected from property taxes varied widely across countries, ranging from 0.1% of GDP in Indonesia to 4.1% of GDP in the United Kingdom. However, in a majority of countries, property taxes remain a small source of revenue. Trends in revenues in the last fifteen years have differed across countries but a majority have seen increases in their property tax revenues. Between 2000 and 2018, 23 countries reported increases in property tax revenues as a share of GDP, while 16 recorded revenue falls. The largest revenue increases in percentage points were recorded in Belgium (largely due to an increase in revenues from registration duties, driven by housing prices), Argentina and South Africa. On the other hand, Iceland and Sweden experienced the most significant property tax revenue falls in percentage points.

Figure 3.29. Property tax revenues as a share of GDP in 2000 and 2018

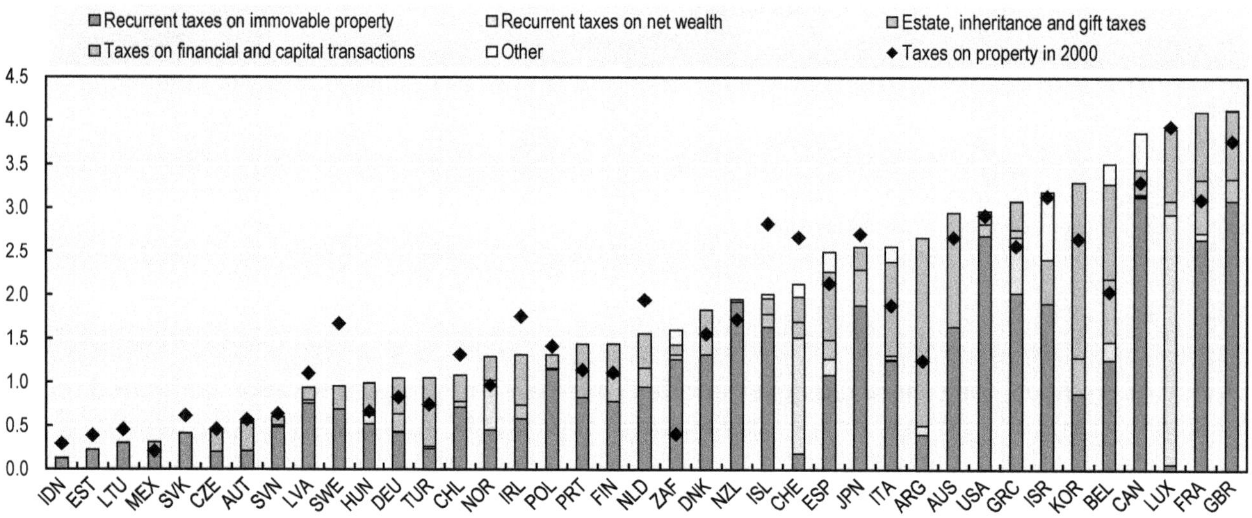


Note: 2017 data for Australia, Greece, Indonesia, Mexico and South Africa.
Source: Global Revenue Statistics Database.

StatLink https://doi.org/10.1787/888934159050

### *Property tax reforms have been more significant than in previous years*

**There has been a marked increase in the number of property tax reforms compared to previous years**. Table 3.14. shows that the vast majority of property tax changes introduced in 2020 were tax increases, through either increases in tax rates or tax base broadening measures. There have also been some measures aimed at lowering property tax burdens.

**Italy and Germany are revising their immovable property tax systems.** Italy unified its local property taxes, by abolishing the municipal service tax TASI ("*Tributo Servizi Indivisibili*") and merging it with the IMU ("*Imposta Municipale Propria*") local property tax. The sum of TASI and IMU rates will remain the same. Moreover, the IMU deduction from business income taxation has been increased up to 100% as for 2022 (instead of 70%). Italy also introduced an annual property tax on marine platforms for the extraction of hydrocarbons. Germany legislated an overhaul of its property valuation rules to comply with the requirements of the Federal Constitutional Court. Indeed, in its ruling dated 10 April 2018, the Federal Constitutional Court declared the way in which properties are valued for the purposes of real property tax to be unconstitutional, as the tax is calculated on the basis of property values that are decades old. The values determined in accordance with new law will be used to calculate the property tax from 2025 onwards. Overall, the reform is expected to be revenue neutral.

**Changes to existing recurrent taxes on immovable property were also reported in France, Greece and Lithuania.** Greece is reducing its property tax (ENFIA) by providing a tax rebate amounting to 30% for properties valued below EUR 60 000 and progressively decreasing to 10% for properties exceeding EUR 1 million. At the same time, the government abolished a property tax cut that was introduced by the previous administration and benefited property owners whose tax liability was below EUR 700. In France, the housing tax ("*taxe d'habitation*") will be gradually removed between 2021 and 2023 for the remaining 20% of French taxpayers who still pay the tax. On the other hand, Lithuania is increasing its property tax by reducing the tax-exempt threshold for non-commercial property from EUR 220 000 to EUR 150 000. It has also increased the minimum tax rate for immovable property used for commercial purposes from 0.3% to 0.5%.

Table 3.14. Changes to property taxes

| | Rate/Base⇧ | | Rate/Base⇩ | |
|---|---|---|---|---|
| Into effect in | 2019 | 2020 or later | 2019 | 2020 or later |
| Estate duties, inheritance and gift taxes | | DNK | IRL | |
| Transaction taxes on movable and immovable property | IRL PRT | ARG (ESP) NLD | IDN IRL | KOR POL |
| Recurrent taxes on immovable property[1] | KOR | CHL DEU LTU TUR | FRA GRC | FRA GRC |
| Recurrent taxes on (net) wealth | ARG ESP | ARG ESP NOR | ARG NOR | |

1. Italy's property tax reform is not included in the table as it has neutral tax rate and tax base effects. Countries in brackets have only announced reforms.
Source: OECD Tax Policy Reform Questionnaire

**New taxes on high-value immovable property were introduced in Chile and Turkey**. In Chile, a new progressive surcharge applies to taxpayers whose combined real estate fiscal value in Chile exceeds CLP 400 million (regardless of Chilean tax residency). The surcharge rate schedule is as follows: 0.075% for the part of the combined fiscal value of real estate properties that ranges between approximately USD 485 000 and USD 846 000; 0.15% for the part of the combined fiscal value that ranges from approximately USD 846 000 to USD 1 088 000; and 0.275% for the part of the combined fiscal value of real estate above USD 1 088 000. This tax entered into force on 1 April 2020 and is added to the ordinary real estate tax that is payable on a quarterly basis. Similarly, as of 2020, Turkey levies an additional property tax imposed on residential houses located in Turkey that are valued above TRY 5 million. The tax rates are progressive (between 0.3% and 1%) depending on the value of the residence.

**Several changes were made to property transaction taxes, generally involving tax increases**. The Netherlands increased the transfer tax rate for non-residential real estate from 6% to 7%. Similarly, Ireland raised the stamp duty on non-residential property from 6% to 7.5%. To increase fairness and limit tax avoidance, Ireland also introduced a new 1% stamp duty where a cancellation scheme of arrangement is used for the acquisition of a company (i.e. where the target company's existing shares are not transferred but cancelled and directly reissued to the bidder). Argentina introduced a 30% rate on foreign currency purchases or any purchases of goods and services nominated in foreign currency and paid in local currency. In Spain, a draft law on the establishment of a financial transaction tax has been submitted before Parliament. The financial transaction tax would be levied at a rate of 0.2% on the acquisition of shares of Spanish companies with a market capitalisation exceeding EUR 1 billion, irrespective of the jurisdiction of residence of the parties to the transactions, provided that the companies are listed on regulated markets. On the other hand, Korea reduced its securities transactions tax to reduce transaction costs for stock trading and encourage investment and Poland reduced the rate of the tax on civil law transactions from 2% to 0.5% for loan agreements from 1 January 2020.

**Finally, a few changes to taxes on net wealth and wealth transfers were reported**. Regarding net wealth taxes, Spain extended the application of its wealth tax until the end of 2020. In Argentina, significant changes to the wealth tax were introduced. The tax rates to be applied to Argentine individuals were raised and now range from 0.5% to 1.25%. For assets held abroad, higher tax rates apply, ranging from 0.7% to 2.25%. For non-resident taxpayers, the tax rate applicable to assets located in Argentina was also raised from 0.25% to 0.50%. Finally, the tax rate on equity interests in Argentine companies was increased from 0.25% to 0.50% for both residents and non-residents. Norway increased its net wealth tax base by eliminating the special valuation provisions for shares of newly established companies. This measure eliminates the possibility to reduce the taxable values of unlisted companies via simple changes to company structure. Regarding inheritance and gift taxes, Denmark repealed the inheritance tax reduction for business owners. On the other hand, Ireland increased the tax-free threshold that applies primarily to gifts and inheritances from parents to their children from EUR 320 000 to EUR 335 000.

## References


Borenstein, S. and L. Davis (2016), "The Distributional Effects of US Clean Energy Tax Credits", *Tax Policy and the Economy*, Vol. 30/1, pp. 191-234, http://dx.doi.org/10.1086/685597. [19]

Center for Economic and Social Research (2019), *Study and Reports on the VAT Gap in the EU-28 Member States: 2019 Final Report*. [10]

European Commission (2018), *Proposal for a Council Directive on the common system of a digital services tax on revenues resulting from the provision of certain digital services {SWD(2018) 81}-{SWD(2018) 82}*, European Commission, Brussels, http://www.mef.gov.it/inevidenza/banner/170907_joint_initiative_digital_taxation.pdf (accessed on 27 April 2020). [4]

German, R. (2018), *Vehicle Emissions and Impacts of Taxes and Incentives in the Evolution of Past Emissions. Report to EEA, European Topic Centre on Air Pollution and Climate Change Mitigation*, https://acm.eionet.europa.eu/reports/EIONET_Rep_ETCACM_2018_1_vehicle_taxes. [18]

Johansson, Å. et al. (2008), "Taxation and Economic Growth", *OECD Economics Department Working Papers*, No. 620, OECD Publishing, Paris, https://dx.doi.org/10.1787/241216205486. [6]

Modica, E., S. Laudage and M. Harding (2018), "Domestic Revenue Mobilisation: A new database on tax levels and structures in 80 countries", *OECD Taxation Working Papers*, No. 36, OECD Publishing, Paris, https://dx.doi.org/10.1787/a87feae8-en. [5]

OECD (2019), *Addressing the Tax Challenges of the Digitalisation of the Economy – Policy Note*. [2]

OECD (2019), *Tax Policy Reforms 2019: OECD and Selected Partner Economies*, OECD Publishing, Paris, https://dx.doi.org/10.1787/da56c295-en. [8]

OECD (2019), *Taxing Energy Use 2019: Using Taxes for Climate Action*, OECD Publishing, Paris, https://dx.doi.org/10.1787/058ca239-en. [15]

OECD (2019), *The role of digital platforms in the collection of VAT/GST on online sales*, OECD, Paris. [12]

OECD (2018), *Consumption Tax Trends 2018: VAT/GST and Excise Rates, Trends and Policy Issues*, OECD Publishing, Paris, https://dx.doi.org/10.1787/ctt-2018-en. [9]

OECD (2018), *Effective Carbon Rates 2018: Pricing Carbon Emissions Through Taxes and Emissions Trading*, OECD Publishing, Paris, https://dx.doi.org/10.1787/9789264305304-en. [16]

OECD (2018), *Tax Challenges Arising from Digitalisation – Interim Report 2018: Inclusive Framework on BEPS*, OECD/G20 Base Erosion and Profit Shifting Project, OECD Publishing, Paris, https://dx.doi.org/10.1787/9789264293083-en. [3]

OECD (2018), *Taxing Energy Use 2018: Companion to the Taxing Energy Use Database*, OECD Publishing, Paris, https://dx.doi.org/10.1787/9789264289635-en. [17]

OECD (2017), *Technology Tools to Tackle Tax Evasion and Tax Fraud*, OECD, Paris. [11]

OECD (2011), *OECD Tax Policy Studies – Taxation and Employment – No. 21*, http://dx.doi.org/10.1787/19900538 (accessed on 29 March 2018). [1]

OECD/ITF (2019), *Tax Revenue Implications of Decarbonising Road Transport: Scenarios for Slovenia*, OECD Publishing, Paris, https://dx.doi.org/10.1787/87b39a2f-en. [14]

OECD/KIPF (2014), *The Distributional Effects of Consumption Taxes in OECD Countries*, OECD Tax Policy Studies, No. 22, OECD Publishing, Paris, https://dx.doi.org/10.1787/9789264224520-en. [7]

World Health Organization (2015), *WHO report on the global tobacco epidemic: Raising taxes on tobacco*, http://dx.doi.org/ISBN 978 92 4 069460 6. [13]

## Notes

[1] In Latvia, there was a decrease in CIT revenues reflecting a transitional period after a major CIT reform, which came into effect on 1 January 2018. Authorities expect a gradual rebound in CIT revenues when the transitional period is over.

[2] This section draws on previous work by OECD Directorate for Science, Technology and Innovation.

[3] For additional information on the design of R&D tax incentives and magnitude of government tax relief for R&D (GTARD) in OECD countries and partner economies, see https://oe.cd/rdtax.

[4] Implied tax subsidy rates on R&D (1 minus B-Index) provide a measure of the notional R&D tax subsidy rate firms of different size (SMEs, large firms) and profitability (profitable, loss-making). The figures in the main text focus on large firms which account for the bulk of business R&D investment (see: http://www.oecd.org/sti/rd-tax-stats-tax-expenditures.pdf). For estimates of implied marginal R&D tax subsidy rates for the four firm scenarios (Large profitable, Large loss-making, SME profitable, SME loss-making), see OECD R&D Tax Incentive database (https://stats.oecd.org/Index.aspx?DataSetCode=RDTAX).

[5] Contract research can be funded if the contractor (third party or affiliated company) is based in Germany or in any other EU/EEA member state.

[6] Unused tax credits are payable in three instalments over a period of three years. For a description of the 2019 R&D tax incentive see: http://www.oecd.org/sti/rd-tax-stats-ireland.pdf.

[7] Capped at NZD 255 000, and to qualify, firms must satisfy certain criteria, including an R&D intensity threshold (see http://www.oecd.org/sti/rd-tax-stats-new-zealand.pdf).

[8] For a description of 2019 R&D tax incentive see: http://www.oecd.org/sti/rd-tax-stats-italy.pdf.

[9] The benefits repealed include a 100% CIT exemption for the first ten years; instant asset write-off for new fixed assets during the first 8 years; a 25% additional deduction for expenses on training; a credit equivalent to 30% of expenses for R&D; a credit equivalent to a 50% of the health and maternity social security contributions for 10 years (and 25% for the subsequent 5 years).

[10] The regime may not apply for the reinvestment of retained earnings in the fishing, aquaculture and primary agricultural production sectors.

[11] On 15 March, the MLI covered 87 jurisdictions: 85 Signatories and 2 jurisdictions covered by their Parent State's signature (Curacao and Hong Kong).

[12] https://www.oecd.org/ctp/exchange-of-tax-information/CbC-MCAA-Signatories.pdf.

[13] http://www.oecd.org/tax/beps/beps-action-14-peer-review-assessment-schedule.pdf.

[14] See https://www.oecd.org/economy/surveys/Policy-note-on-the-introduction-of-VAT-compensation-for-vulnerable-households-in-Colombia.pdf.

[15] This issue is particularly significant in the European Union, where there are no customs controls at the internal borders. Indeed, the B2B intracommunity supply of goods is VAT-free in the member state of origin and VAT is collected in the member state of destination according to a cross-border "reverse charge mechanism" where the customer in the member state of destination accounts for the VAT on the supply in its VAT return rather than paying the VAT to customs at importation. When the goods are used to make an onwards taxable transaction (e.g. a domestic supply of goods), the input VAT on this "acquisition" is entirely deductible and triggers no payment obligation. This deviates from the traditional design of a VAT, where the tax is collected through a staged collection process. Fraudsters have used this system to run "missing trader" schemes where the purchaser that has acquired the goods VAT-free resells the goods on the domestic market, collecting the VAT from its customer and vanish without remitting the VAT so collected. The same goods may be resold again several times through a network of companies across member states with a chain of VAT-free cross-border supplies, reverse charged acquisitions and resales with collection (and no remittance) of VAT creating a "carousel" fraud.

[16] European Court of Auditors 2015
https://www.eca.europa.eu/Lists/ECADocuments/SR15_24/SR_VAT_FRAUD_EN.pdf.

[17] Arithmetic (unweighted) country averages, unless otherwise specified.

[18] Converted based on annual exchange rates. The statutory rate of the carbon tax in South Africa stood at ZAR 120/t$CO_2$.

[19] France extended tax incentives (tax income credit CITE) for efficiency improvements in buildings in a budget neutral manner.

# 4 Special Feature: Tax and fiscal policy responses to the COVID-19 crisis

This Special Feature takes stock of the tax measures that have been introduced to mitigate the impact of the COVID-19 crisis from the beginning of the virus outbreak up to mid-June 2020. This Special Feature focuses on tax measures, but it also touches upon the broader fiscal policy responses that countries have introduced. It covers all OECD countries as well as Argentina, China, Indonesia and South Africa, based on a database compiled by the OECD on tax and fiscal policy responses to the crisis.

**Governments have taken rapid and unprecedented action to address the health crisis and the drop in economic activity caused by the outbreak of COVID-19.** Containing and mitigating the spread of the virus has rightly been the first priority of public authorities. With containment measures in place, the immediate policy reactions focused on alleviating hardships and maintaining the productive capacity of the economy. As the duration of the pandemic lengthens and uncertainty about its development remains high, countries have begun extending and expanding emergency policy measures. Some countries have recently relaxed their containment rules, announcing recovery and stimulus packages to forge a new path towards stronger, more inclusive and resilient economies.

**This Special Feature takes stock of the tax measures that have been introduced to mitigate the impact of the COVID-19 crisis, as well as early steps that countries have taken towards economic recovery**. This Special Feature focuses on tax measures, but it also touches upon broader fiscal measures that countries have introduced. It covers OECD countries as well as Argentina, China, Indonesia and South Africa, based on a database compiled by the OECD on tax policy responses to the crisis.[1] The first section outlines the policy phases that countries are expected to go through as they respond to the crisis. The second section gives an overview of the policy measures implemented or announced from the beginning of the virus outbreak up to mid-June 2020. The third and fourth sections provide more detail on policies to support business and households, respectively. The final section discusses the measures taken to support the healthcare sector.

## Policy phases during and after the pandemic

**Although uncertainty about the development of the health and economic crisis is high, the crisis can be broken down into different phases, each requiring its own policy responses**. While they may overlap and vary across countries, Figure 4.1 presents a schematic view of these different phases and how policy responses may be expected to evolve. In the initial phase (Phase 1), countries confronted with a virus outbreak have implemented containment and mitigation measures, where the aim has been to halt the outbreak. In this phase, tax and broader fiscal policies have tended to focus on liquidity and income support. As the health crisis continues and containment measures remain in place, tax and fiscal measures may evolve gradually into a more sustained effort to reduce the adverse impacts of containment (Phase 2).

**The focus of tax and fiscal policies have shifted where containment measures have been gradually removed**. As countries have begun to relax containment and mitigation measures, the focus on keeping businesses and households afloat and on limiting hardship has begun to shift towards an emphasis on economic recovery, including through fiscal stimulus policies (Phase 3). However, the progression towards recovery may not be linear. There may be some overlap with Phase 2, where containment and mitigation measures are only being removed gradually or partially. There also remains the possibility of containment measures being reinstated to respond to a second wave of the pandemic. Where this occurs, it will present policy makers with complex fiscal policy challenges given the need to limit the economic hardship from containment in conjunction with stimulating recovery. The timing of repayments or delayed payments linked to the liquidity support measures introduced in Phases 1 and 2 will also be critical and should not compromise firms' ability to recover. Once economies have recovered, a shift towards restoring public finances can be anticipated, during which there may be renewed attention on strengthening resilience to health risks but also to other known risks, including climate change and declining biodiversity (Phase 4).

**As the epicentre of the pandemic has shifted between regions, countries have moved at different paces through containment and recovery phases.** The outbreak that began in China in late 2019 first spread to neighbouring Asian countries in January 2020. As the epicentre of the virus shifted to Western Europe during the months of March and April, a number of Asian countries were able to carefully ease containment measures. In an effort to flatten the pandemic curve, European countries entered into lockdowns, which they started cautiously easing in May and June. By this time, the epicentre of the virus had shifted to the United States and a number of middle-income countries, which have also taken steps to slow down the spread of the virus. In early June, a number of the countries that were easing lockdowns and gradually removing containment measures announced stimulus packages to help businesses and households recover from the crisis.

Figure 4.1. Schematic policy phases during and after the pandemic

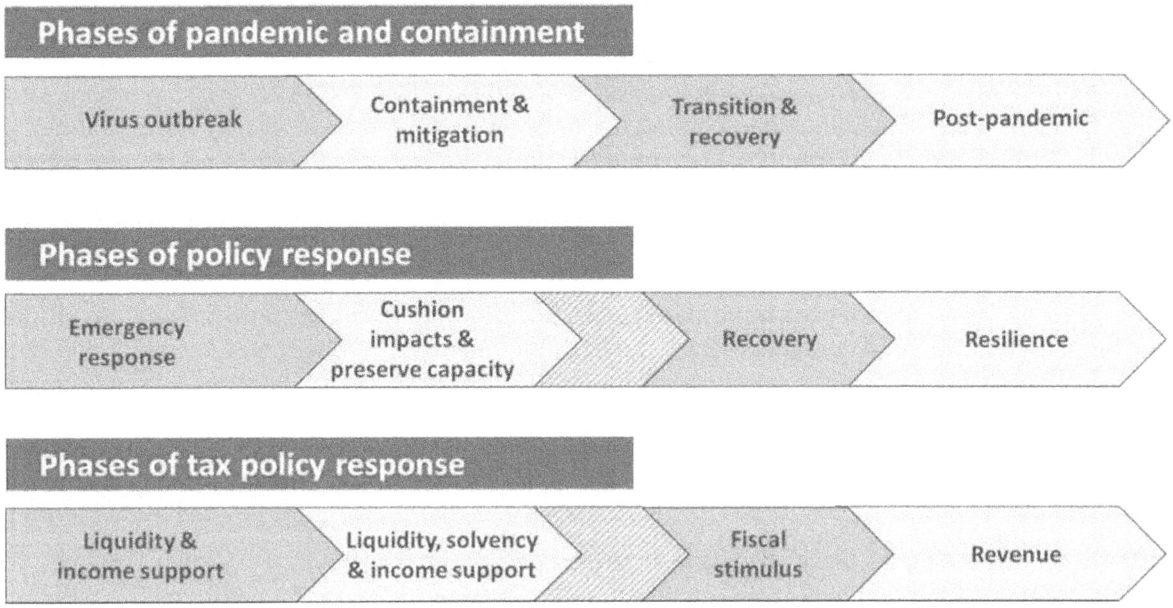


Source: Based on (OECD, 2020[1]).

## Overview of tax policy measures during the COVID-19 pandemic

### *Countries initially focused on emergency responses to the crisis*

**The first measures introduced by countries focused on cushioning the immediate impact of the crisis**. The fiscal packages have had very similar objectives across countries: cushioning households and businesses from the impact of the containment measures and ensuring that households and businesses are able to resume economic activity when the worst of the health crisis has passed. For businesses, this has generally meant providing liquidity support to help them stay afloat. For individuals, the priority has been to provide income support to the most directly affected households. A number of countries have also introduced measures to enhance the funding and functioning of the healthcare sector. These rapid responses may sometimes have been introduced based on the assumption that containment phases would be shorter than what has proved to be the case. Most of the measures introduced in the emergency phase have taken effect immediately and have been time-bound.

**In that sense, initial response packages have differed from traditional fiscal stimulus measures**. A traditional fiscal stimulus package to boost the economy by encouraging investment and consumption would have been ineffective while containment measures were in place, given the policy restrictions imposed upon economic activity, and could have even encouraged the spread of the virus in some countries where social distancing measures or lockdowns may have been harder to implement.

### *Countries have strengthened support packages as the crisis has continued*

**As the crisis has continued, countries have retained their focus on keeping businesses and households afloat and have often expanded their initial packages of measures.** Some countries have prolonged existing crisis measures and expanded support to groups that were not covered by the initial measures. The majority of extended and expanded tax measures for businesses have included deferrals for tax filing and payment. Household support has remained centred on expanded access to social security benefits and job retention schemes. These measures, which are relatively simple to expand once implemented, have proven effective at maintaining liquidity for businesses and households.

**A few countries have also clarified eligibility for emergency measures, halted tax audit activity, and delayed tax reforms**. For instance, Canada has clarified who is eligible for the Canada Emergency Wage Subsidy (CEWS). Several countries have halted tax debt recovery and audit activity for all but high-risk cases (e.g. Canada, the United Kingdom). Some countries have also decided to wind back or delay tax reforms, in particular with a view to easing the tax burden on businesses (e.g. Poland). The United States temporarily relaxed certain provisions put in place by the Tax Cuts and Job Act, including the Section 163(j) interest expense deduction limitation and the net operating losses taxable income limitation.

**Some countries have made government support conditional upon certain criteria, to address longer term issues.** Several countries, including Belgium, Denmark, France, and Poland, have denied assistance or restricted the types of support available to companies that are registered in non-cooperative tax jurisdictions. Several countries have also seen the potential to address climate and sustainability goals in their pandemic response and recovery. For example, Canadian companies receiving government support have been asked to commit to future climate disclosures and environmental sustainability goals.

### *Discussions have begun on stimulus packages to support recovery*

**Recent announcements and discussions suggest that the recovery phase will be supported by expansionary fiscal policy.** Discussions have begun both in countries that are removing containment measures and in countries that are still in mitigation and containment phases. Most countries have signalled that government stimulus will be a key pillar of a recovery effort that aims to be inclusive and sustainable. This includes measures to support investment and consumption and ongoing support for households and businesses.

### *New tax policy issues will emerge in the post-pandemic era, including the need for resilience and restoring public finances*

**Uncertainty around the health and economic crises remains high, but new questions are already arising.** As countries enter the early stages of recovery, several have signalled a desire to strengthen their ability to absorb or respond to future shocks. This may include, but is not limited to, strengthening capacity in the healthcare sector, providing greater social protection to non-standard workers, and enhancing the resilience of supply chains.

**Tax policy will also be an important part of countries' strategies to restore public finances in a fair and sustainable way after the crisis**. Countries are expected to explore a wide range of options, including revamping old tools and introducing new ones. This may include efforts to address the international tax challenges posed by the digitalisation of the economy (Pillar 1) and to introduce a minimum corporate tax (Pillar 2) (see section 3.2), to enhance the progressivity of tax systems, and to strengthen the role of carbon taxation. Some countries have already announced their intention to pursue new sources of revenue, including through schemes that price carbon. The unprecedented nature of the crisis has also prompted reflection on exceptional tax measures, as has been the case after major events in the past, like wars and economic crises (Landais, Saez and Zucman, 2020[2]).

### *Across countries, the types and size of fiscal packages have differed, but most have been comprehensive and significant*

**There have been similarities as well as differences between fiscal packages across countries**. The measures introduced to support businesses have been similar across countries, with a strong focus on tax payment deferrals and other measures that support business cash flow. The introduction or expansion of job retention schemes and other employment support measures has also been common. There have been more significant differences across measures to support households. For instance, many European countries and the United States have extended support for families with children and expanded income support by enhancing eligibility and access to paid-sick leave and unemployment benefits, including for non-standard workers. The United States also provided direct cash transfers to low and middle-income households. In emerging economies, social assistance measures such as cash transfers to low-income households, informal workers, and beneficiaries of social benefits have been more common than social insurance or job retention schemes. A number of emerging countries have also introduced tax payment deferrals and tax waivers, particularly for SMEs.

**Different factors may explain the differences in policy responses across countries**. Differences in the scope, size, and type of responses across countries are due partly to available fiscal space, the existence of automatic stabilisers and the characteristics of the welfare system, as well as administrative capacity. The characteristics of country responses also relate to the severity of the containment and mitigation measures implemented by countries, which have varied from strict lockdowns to lighter measures focused on social distancing.

**There have been large variations in the size of fiscal packages, but some countries have taken unprecedented action.** The size of fiscal packages has varied across countries. Figure 4.2 shows that particularly significant packages have been introduced in Germany, Italy, the United Kingdom and the United States. It should be noted that these estimates focus on the revenue costs of the short-term relief measures, and do not take into account the lower revenues that will be collected from taxes as a result of the crisis, nor the costs of subsequent support packages and the expected fiscal stimulus measures during the recovery phase.

**The budget effects of different types of measures have also varied widely.** For instance, some measures involve permanent losses, even if only for one year (e.g. job retention schemes). Other measures will likely have a temporary impact on budget balances (e.g. deferrals, filing extensions) as deferred taxes should be expected to be paid later on. Finally, state loans and loan guarantees, which appear to have been among the most significant measures in fiscal packages, do not represent a direct fiscal cost. However, they create contingent liabilities which, in some cases, could turn into actual expenses either in 2020 or later.

**Most countries have implemented successive fiscal packages, as the scale of efforts required to combat the crisis has become clearer.** Initial support packages were implemented at a time when uncertainty about the development of the pandemic and the duration of the efforts needed to contain and mitigate the virus was large. As mentioned above, as the crisis has continued, many countries have expanded the size and scope of their fiscal packages. An escalating policy response has necessarily been accompanied by rising costs. In some cases, however, lower-than-expected numbers of claimants have resulted in lower costs. For example, Australia's short-time work scheme will cost less than forecast, as fewer businesses claimed the support than projected.[2]

## Figure 4.2. Estimated scale of fiscal packages in response to COVID-19 in selected countries

Fiscal packages announced or implemented before mid-June 2020, as a percentage of GDP

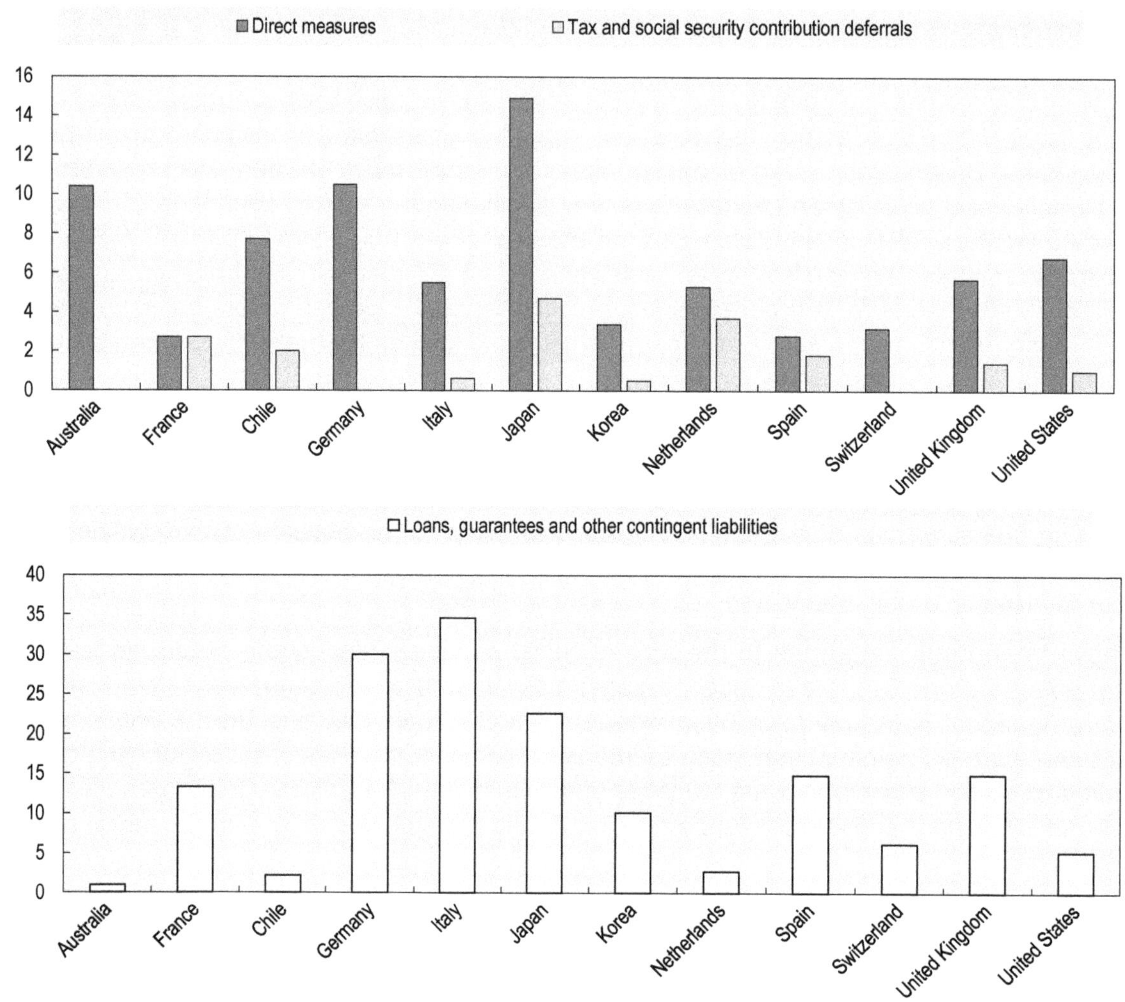


Note: Shows official estimates, when available, of financial assistance included in emergency packages announced by governments in response to the COVID-19 crisis, as of mid-June 2020. In many cases, they are highly uncertain due to the unknown duration of the crisis and take-up of various programmes by the private sector, and may not be comparable across countries.
Source: OECD Secretariat compilation based on official estimates.

StatLink https://doi.org/10.1787/888934159069

## Support measures for businesses

### *The main priority for countries has been to support business cash flow*

**The majority of measures in OECD and partner economies have sought to ensure that businesses have sufficient cash flow**. Many businesses experienced a sharp decline in liquidity during the immediate virus response, particularly in countries that imposed a lockdown, and their ability to return to pre-crisis activity has been limited by physical distancing measures that are a core part of safely reopening economies. The decline in liquidity has hindered businesses' ability to pay for wages, rents, intermediate goods, interest on debt, and taxes. Measures have therefore focused on alleviating cash flow difficulties at each stage of the pandemic response, to help avoid escalating problems such as the laying-off of workers, the temporary inability to pay suppliers or creditors, and, in the worst cases, closure or bankruptcy. Cash flow issues can also cause the failure of connected businesses through a domino effect and could ultimately impact countries' abilities to recover from the pandemic. Overall, around half of the measures reported by countries in the emergency response phase have been aimed at enhancing business cash flow.

**Liquidity support has been provided through a mix of tax and non-tax measures**. The most common non-tax instrument used by OECD and partner economies throughout the crisis has been loan guarantee schemes, where the government guarantees all or part of the value of loans granted to eligible businesses. Other measures have included small interest-free loans and cash grants, typically targeted toward small businesses or businesses in the most affected sectors. Other non-tax measures have included the deferral of payments of wage and non-wage business costs such as rent or interest (e.g. the Slovak Republic, Sweden, and the United States). A number of governments have required that companies receiving support and major banks refrain from paying dividends, undertaking share buy-backs or paying bonuses to senior staff.

**The most common type of tax measure to enhance business cash flow has been the deferral of tax payments** (Figure 4.3). Over three quarters of OECD and partner economies have introduced deferrals of tax payments. These measures have generally applied to taxes that require frequent (monthly or quarterly) payments, including advance payments of corporate income tax (CIT) or personal income tax (PIT), value added tax (VAT) and social security contributions (SSCs). In some cases, the tax liability has been calculated based on present revenue estimates, rather than relying on tax returns from previous years that could have led to overpayment (e.g. Spain). There are also a number of cases where property tax payments have been deferred. During the first stage of the pandemic response, around a third of countries also introduced measures to provide business taxpayers with additional time to file tax returns. Additional time to file tax returns may be particularly helpful where taxpayers require the assistance of intermediaries or specialised staff and systems to file returns.

**Other administrative measures have been introduced.** A common measure, introduced in a third of countries, has been the acceleration of tax refunds (VAT and other taxes) where taxpayers are owed money (e.g. Colombia). A few countries have halted audit activity for all but high-risk cases and around half of the countries have introduced more flexible tax debt repayment plans. Less common measures have included lifting the threshold for access to VAT simplification (e.g. Korea) and increasing the threshold for income tax prepayments (e.g. New Zealand).

**Changes to loss-offset provisions have been another important tax policy tool.** Some countries have introduced or have announced measures allowing loss carry-back for the 2020 tax year, which will allow taxpayers to carry back their 2020 tax losses against profits earned in previous fiscal years (the Czech Republic, Norway, Poland, and the United States). Other countries have increased the loss-carry forward period for losses incurred in 2020 (China, the Slovak Republic).

**Some countries have introduced tax cuts for businesses**. These measures have typically focused on tax categories where the tax base does not necessarily vary with the immediate economic cycle (e.g. property taxes) and where, in the absence of tax cuts, the outcomes could be unduly punitive for businesses facing sharp losses in revenue. About one fifth of countries have introduced a waiver or reduction of employer SSCs (e.g. Greece, Hungary, Spain), in some cases restricted to sectors or businesses affected by the crisis. Other examples have been waivers of property taxes and presumptive taxes for small businesses. A few countries have also waived specific levies on tourism and airline companies, and some have reduced or exempted inputs used in certain sectors (including tourism and manufacturing) from import taxes. Other measures to reduce the tax burden on companies have included a tax credit for workshops and shops in Italy amounting to 60% of rental fees related to the month of March, April and May 2020.

### Figure 4.3. Main tax measures to support business cash flow in OECD and partner economies

Number of OECD and partner countries reporting selected measures

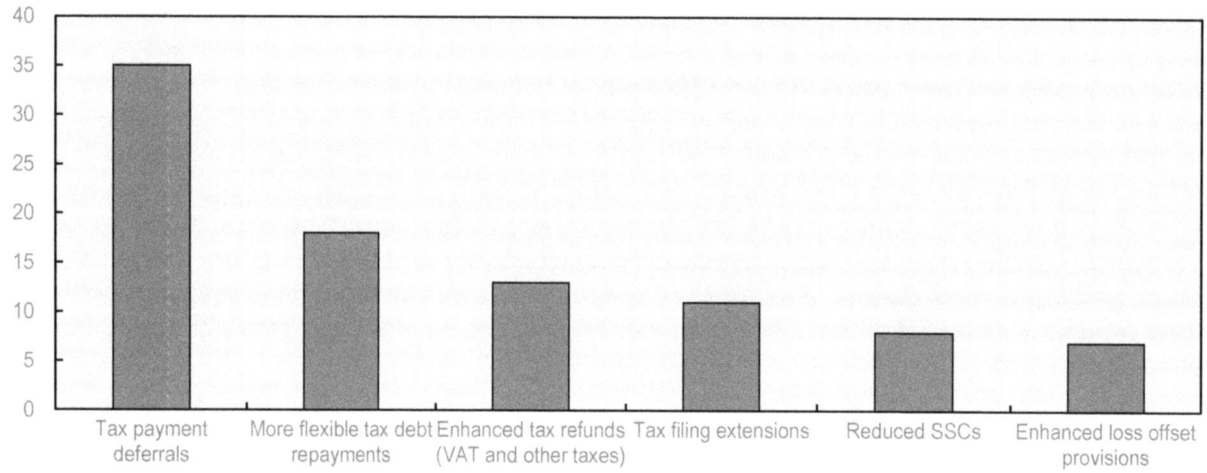


Source: OECD Database on Tax Policy Responses to COVID-19.

StatLink https://doi.org/10.1787/888934159088

**The process for obtaining relief and the degree of policy targeting have varied across countries.** In some countries, measures have been made available automatically to all firms (e.g. Israel). In other countries, the measures are granted to specific sectors (e.g. tourism, commercial air travel). Some countries have required businesses to apply for relief and to prove to the tax authority that they have experienced a significant drop in revenues or have a reasonable justification (e.g. Finland). Instead of targeting the sectors or businesses that have been most affected by COVID-19, some countries have targeted small and medium sized enterprises (SMEs) or self-employed businesses as it is expected that these businesses will face higher liquidity constraints than others.

**As the crisis has continued, countries have expanded initial emergency measures and introduced new measures for businesses, some of which have been targeted at specific sectors.** To deliver more support during the ongoing crisis, some countries have expanded eligibility to a wider group of companies including larger businesses, allowing a larger portion of taxes to be deferred, and permitting more categories of taxes to be deferred. For example, the United Kingdom has expanded tax deferrals to include import duties and South Africa has doubled the turnover threshold for a Pay As You Earn (PAYE) deferral, so that larger businesses are eligible for the tax relief. Countries have also extended the roll-back date of emergency policies and the due date for deferred tax filing and payment. For example, Italy initially extended some tax payment dates to June, but has since pushed this back to September and Austria has automatically extended tax deferrals for businesses to January 2021. Among the new measures for businesses are policies targeted at sectors that have been badly impacted by the crisis, such as the tourism and hospitality sectors, airlines, and extractive industries. These targeted measures include tax filing and payment deferrals but also sector-specific measures like higher limits for tax-free meal vouchers in restaurants (Austria), payroll support for air carriers and contractors (United States), and tax credits for providers of vacation accommodation when low-income families holiday with them (Italy). Non-tax measures have included loan programmes targeted at large businesses who are big employers (e.g. Canada, the United Kingdom), or small businesses, to provide pay check protection and enhance liquidity (United States).

**The protracted crisis and prolonged liquidity shortages could lead to solvency risks, which a few countries have already moved to address.** The nature of the risks caused by the pandemic are evolving due to the ongoing nature of the crisis. In addition to collapsing revenues, the pandemic has led to growing debts, both loans and deferred taxes, which may create problems for firms' solvency. As with liquidity constraints, insolvency could affect not just individual firms but also connected businesses through a flow-on effect. Some countries have shifted support to addressing business solvency challenges. In their second support package, the Netherlands allowed companies to create a "corona reserve" and deduct their expected losses in 2020 against profits made in 2019. Under normal rules, companies would be able to carry back their 2020 losses to 2019, but only after the 2020 tax return is filed, in early 2021. Belgium will support companies rebuilding the equity lost during the crisis by allowing them to allocate part of their profits to a tax-exempt "reserve fund for equity reconstruction", capped at the size of losses in 2020 or EUR 20 million.

**Some countries have delayed tax reforms that were due to be implemented.** This has included delaying the implementation of e-filing, the introduction of new taxes and changes to existing taxes. For example, small retailers in Italy have until next year to begin reporting their daily sales electronically and Poland pushed back an excise tax increase on novelty tobacco products and liquids used in electronic cigarettes and the collection of its retail sales tax.

**In contrast, some countries have implemented new taxes to fund the pandemic response effort**. These typically target large businesses that are expected to fare well during the pandemic due to sustained demand for their products. For example, Hungary has introduced a levy on large retail firms and Indonesia will tax the value added on digital products sold by foreign platform services with a significant economic presence in the country.

**As countries have started easing restrictions, measures to support economic recovery and investment have been announced and introduced.** In the early stages of the health crisis and during confinement periods, a few measures to support investment were introduced. For instance, temporary increases in thresholds for asset write-offs were introduced in Australia and New Zealand, Italy introduced a corporate tax credit for sanitation costs in workplaces, and Norway accelerated deductions for investments in the oil industry for investments decided by the end of 2021. As countries have started easing restrictions, a few countries have announced new measures to encourage investment and boost economic recovery. For instance, Denmark will temporarily increase R&D tax credits in 2020 and 2021. Some countries are also encouraging or directly funding environmentally sustainable investments. For instance, Denmark has announced plans to frontload energy renovation of social housing and France has announced funding for local investment in construction projects that support environmental transition. France and Germany have announced generous subsidies for purchases of electric vehicles. In Chile, a national agreement between the government and political parties has led to a new emergency plan to support economic recovery for the forthcoming two years. The plan includes a reduction in the SME CIT rate from 25% to 12.5% for years 2020 to 2022, a transitory immediate expensing regime applicable to the whole territory for investments in new or imported fixed assets acquired between 1 June 2020 and December 31 2022, the payment by the Treasury of the new one-time contribution on investment projects (see section 3.3.9), the accelerated refund of accumulated VAT credits for SMEs, the immediate amortisation of investments in certain intangibles acquired between 1 June 2020 and 31 December 2022, a hiring tax credit, and the extension of the suspension of monthly advance CIT payments.

### *Many countries have introduced measures to help businesses keep their workers*

**Among OECD and partner economies, many countries have introduced, extended or expanded eligibility for job retention schemes**. A major concern throughout the crisis has been the threat of considerable job losses. Many countries have been helping businesses retain their workers by introducing or enhancing the generosity and availability of job retention schemes (OECD, 2020[3]), which proved successful in reducing job losses during the global financial crisis (Hijzen and Venn, 2011[4]). These measures typically provide public income support to workers whose working hours have been reduced or who are temporarily not working because of the crisis, but where firms maintain their connection with the employee. This is intended to allow employers to hold on to workers' talent and experience and enable them to quickly ramp up production once economic conditions improve. The generosity and duration of job retention schemes varies widely across countries. Many European countries have particularly generous, ongoing schemes, while schemes in some Anglo-Saxon countries are set to expire after several months. Job retention schemes typically cover a certain percentage of wages, are often capped, and have strict rules around businesses' use of workers during this time.

**Some countries have encouraged labour retention by expanding unemployment benefits to those who are still employed but may be working reduced hours**. On the condition that employees remain employed by their employers, firms in Iceland and the Netherlands, for example, can request unemployment benefits for their workers. Like job retention schemes, expanding unemployment benefits to employees that are not working but that remain employed by their employees allows firms and workers to maintain contact throughout the crisis.

**As is the case for liquidity support measures, in some countries, these measures have been broadly applied, while in others they have been more targeted**. In a number of countries, the measures have been targeted at small employers (e.g. Canada). In other countries, these measures have been targeted at the most-affected businesses (e.g. Lithuania, Sweden).

**Job retention schemes and other employment support measures have been far less common in emerging market economies.** This may be related to these schemes' high cost and administrative complexity. However, there have been some exceptions: in South Africa, for instance, an existing tax credit allowing businesses hiring young workers to reduce the amount of Pay-As-Your-Earn (PAYE) tax payable, has been expanded to include all workers below 65 and conditions for accessing the scheme have been relaxed.

**Job retention schemes have been maintained or extended during the ongoing crisis and some countries have begun adjusting the schemes for the recovery period**. Several countries that introduced job retention schemes during the initial phase of the crisis have extended the date that the scheme was due to be rolled back (e.g. Italy, the United Kingdom). Countries that already had job retention or partial unemployment schemes have maintained expanded access, which in some cases includes self-employed workers (e.g. Belgium, the United Kingdom). Countries looking to the recovery period have announced adjustments to short-time work schemes. In some cases, rules guiding businesses' use of workers have been loosened, allowing businesses to gradually bring their workers back without losing the full wage subsidy. For example, the United Kingdom will allow furloughed workers to return to work part-time from July, with firms paying the hours worked and the job retention scheme covering the remaining hours.

## Support measures for households

### *Measures to enhance households' cash flow*

**A number of countries have introduced measures to enhance households' cash flow**. Several countries have extended tax filing deadlines, tax payment deferrals or extended payment plans for households unable to make their tax payments. These measures are provided mostly for personal income taxes (PIT), but in some countries have involved property taxes. In some cases, tax payment deferral measures are targeted at low-income households or property below a certain value (e.g. Chile). Other tax measures have included accelerated refunding of excess payments from PIT, and flexible arrangements for tax debt repayments (sometimes targeted at low-income households). Non-tax measures have included the early release of superannuation in Australia and the deferral of interest payments on mortgage debt for primary residences (e.g. Spain). Some deferrals for tax filing and payment have been extended as the crisis has continued, but tax deferrals have remained less common at the household level than at the business level.

### *Most income support for households has taken the form of increased cash benefits for households directly affected by the crisis*

**Most countries have introduced measures to provide income support to households, generally through enhanced cash benefits targeted at the most vulnerable households**. Many OECD and partner economies have social protection systems in place that provide income replacement for households affected by sickness or job loss. These systems cushion income losses for many workers and act as automatic stabilisers. Given the severe nature of the crisis, many countries have taken steps to expand these systems, to cover groups of individuals that were not covered previously (independent workers, families with unexpected caring needs including parents that had to stay at home to take care of their children because of school closure), to simplify access, and to increase levels of protection.

**Support to households has largely been provided through direct transfers rather than through the tax system.** While the choice between providing income support through direct cash transfers or through the tax system will typically depend upon the architecture of each country's tax and transfer systems, most countries rely primarily on transfers to redistribute income. Given the immediate need to provide financial support to the most vulnerable households in the crisis, transfers have generally been preferred as payments can be made more quickly and are often easier to target.

**The households targeted and the design of tax and transfer measures have varied across countries**. In some countries, cash transfers have been specifically targeted to those households that have been directly affected by the virus (e.g. sick workers) or its immediate economic consequences (e.g. temporarily unemployed workers). Countries have also introduced measures for certain workers, for example, a PIT exemption for overtime workers in critical sectors (Belgium). Some measures have specifically provided support to the self-employed (e.g. Italy, Lithuania, and the United Kingdom). Other countries have provided cash payments to low- and middle-income households more broadly, as these may be the most severely affected by the crisis and will likely have less savings to draw from to support themselves. Chile has introduced a cash bonus for people without formal work, which is expected to benefit two million people, and the United States has provided a broadly based cash payment to work-eligible U.S. residents, in the amount of USD 1 200 for singles, USD 2 400 for married couples, and USD 500 per dependent, which is phased out at higher income levels. Some benefits have also been aimed at families (e.g. Slovenia). In some cases, benefits have been provided as one-off payments, while in other cases they have been provided as temporary increases in regular benefits. New Zealand made a temporary change to its in-work tax credit by removing the hours' threshold, so that workers who see their hours in work reduced below the hours' threshold will still be able to claim the payment. Australia has added a temporary coronavirus supplement to some social benefits, including unemployment benefits.

**In emerging market economies, some countries have reported cash transfers for households including individuals who operate in the informal economy.** Some have been targeted at households directly affected by the pandemic (e.g. Argentina) and at vulnerable households via existing social programmes (e.g. Indonesia).

**Most ongoing payments implemented in the emergency phase are yet to expire, but some countries that made one-off emergency payments have provided additional support.** During the initial phase of the crisis, several countries implemented special benefit payments or supplements to existing benefit payments. As these programmes were implemented for a period of months, many will still be available during the transition and early recovery phase. For example, the Canadian Emergency Response Benefit (CERB) will be available until October 2020. Other programmes have been extended, such as the Pandemic Unemployment Payment (PUB) in Ireland. Due to the lengthening crisis, some countries that opted for cash payments have extended these benefits to provide even more support. For example, Poland initially provided a one-off cash benefit to self-employed workers who had experienced a decrease in turnover, but later increased this to three payments.

**While a few countries implemented measures to guarantee the affordability of consumer goods during confinement, measures to support consumption may become more common during the recovery phase**. In the early stages of the crisis, support for consumption had the potential to undermine the health objectives of confinement, so very few temporary reductions in VAT rates were implemented (e.g. China, Norway). Other tax measures have included the doubling of the tax deduction rate for personal credit and debit card spending in Korea. Emerging countries have favoured non-tax measures to support affordability, such as preventing unjustified price hikes and 'panic buying' (e.g. Argentina, South Africa). Measures to encourage consumption may gain greater momentum as countries ease confinement restrictions. Several countries have announced (mostly) temporary reductions in consumption taxes, including VAT, to stimulate consumption. For example, Austria, Germany and the United Kingdom have introduced temporary VAT rate cuts set to expire at the end of 2020 or the beginning of 2021. While Germany temporarily lowered its standard and reduced VAT rates, Austria and the United Kingdom have targeted their VAT rate reductions, particularly towards the hospitality sector and cultural activities.

### *Many countries have expanded access to paid sick leave and unemployment benefits*

**Around a quarter of OECD and partner economies have expanded sick leave benefits**. Some countries have introduced less restrictive access conditions, such as eliminating or reducing the waiting period before becoming eligible to receive benefits (e.g. Canada, Ireland, Sweden), or removing the need for medical certificates (e.g. from the 8th day of illness in Sweden). Eligibility has also been expanded in a few countries, including to self-employed workers (e.g. Finland, Ireland) and employees who self-isolate (e.g. Latvia, some states in the United States) (OECD, 2020[3]). Some measures have been targeted to specific sectors where many workers are self-employed or informal and lacking social insurance, such as domestic workers. In some countries, governments have covered a larger portion of benefits, reducing the burden on employers, who usually cover the initial period of sick leave. For example, in Slovenia, sick pay for all workers will be covered by the state, not the employer, from the first day of sick leave. Where there are no generally applicable obligations for employers to provide sick leave, new requirements have in some cases been imposed on employers. For example, in United States, public agencies, and small and mid-sized private sector firms (with some exceptions) are temporarily required to provide employees with paid sick leave or expanded family or medical leave for specific reasons related to COVID-19. The federal government has provided employers and the self-employed with refundable tax credits to offset the cost of providing this leave.

**More than a third of OECD and partner economies have expanded the coverage of unemployment benefits**. A common measure in response to the crisis has been to expand the coverage of unemployment benefits to self-employed workers. Workers in non-standard forms of employment (e.g. temporary, part-time or self-employment) are often significantly less well protected against the risk of job or income loss than workers in standard forms of employment. Some countries have also expanded unemployment benefits to workers in quarantine (e.g. Canada, Switzerland). Many countries were already exploring how to shore up access to out-of-work benefits for non-standard workers before the crisis, and many have done so on a temporary basis in response to the crisis.

**On the other hand, emerging market economies outside of the OECD have not reported any expansions in sick leave or unemployment benefits**. This may be explained by the fact that these countries tend to have less well-developed social protection systems and primarily rely on cash transfers to provide income support to households.

**Enhancements to benefits that were implemented during the emergency phase are still available in many countries, while some measures have been extended and some new measures introduced.** Countries that broadened availability of unemployment benefits and sick leave during the emergency phase of the crisis typically implemented these measures for several months. In many cases, these measures will still be in place during the transition and early recovery period, though several countries have publicly discussed ending or gradually withdrawing this support. For example, New Zealand announced a permanent increase in benefit payments in April and Australia will continue paying the coronavirus supplement to unemployed workers until September. The roll-back date of some measures has been extended, such as the sickness benefit for the care of children and the disabled in Lithuania. The scope of some measures has been expanded during the ongoing crisis, including the Temporary Employer and Employee Relief Scheme (TERS) in South Africa, previously restricted to employees that had contributed to the unemployment insurance scheme, but since expanded to all workers affected by the lockdown.

## Support measures for the healthcare sector

**Beyond measures to mitigate the impact of the crisis, countries have adopted responses to strengthen patient care and reduce the pressure on healthcare systems** (OECD, 2020[1]). Several OECD and partner economies have introduced measures to facilitate imports of medical inputs to combat COVID-19. A common measure has been the temporary removal of import duties on medicines and health devices and equipment (e.g. Colombia). These exemptions have often been accompanied by measures to simplify and expedite customs clearance procedures.

**Some OECD and partner economies have also provided preferential tax treatment to stimulate health-related spending and investment**, including measures to safeguard the deduction of input VAT on items donated by businesses (e.g. Belgium, China, Slovenia), to avoid a donation triggering any VAT or income tax liability, and the full or increased deductibility for CIT and PIT purposes of donations made by enterprises or households to healthcare institutions (e.g. Belgium, China, Italy). China has also introduced specific CIT incentives for enterprises engaged in producing key supplies related to COVID-19 protection and containment. This includes 100% expensing for investment in equipment to expand production capacity. In contrast to standard tax rules, there is no limit to the scale of the investment such that larger scale investments also benefit from immediate expensing. China has also introduced PIT exemptions for bonuses and subsidies paid to medical staff working in combatting COVID-19. The United States has issued a technical amendment that enables businesses, especially in the hospital industry, to write off immediately costs associated with improving facilities.

**Measures to support the healthcare sector have been common in emerging market countries**. Most of the measures have consisted in removing or lowering import duties and other taxes on medical equipment. Additional measures have included a reduction of the bank debt tax for companies that provide healthcare-related services (Argentina) and a higher tax-deductible limit for donations to the Solidarity Fund (South Africa).

**A few countries have announced investment and funding packages for the healthcare sector, as part of measures to strengthen resilience.** For example, Germany has announced a stimulus package that includes investments in health, accompanied by measures to allow for a swift investment of these funds by fast-tracking projects and simplifying of public procurement law. The United States has provided funds for hospitals to prepare for and respond to the coronavirus, and funds for expenses to research, develop and expand capacity for COVID-19 tests.

## Conclusion

**Overall, this Special Feature has shown that countries have acted decisively to support businesses, households, and the healthcare sector during this crisis.** In addition to enacting measures to contain and mitigate the spread of COVID-19, countries have focused on alleviating hardship and preserving the productive capacity of the economy. Although the severity and duration of the health crisis and the accompanying drop in economic activity remain highly uncertain, countries can now draw on several months of experience of delivering support in unprecedented times.

**The OECD will keep monitoring countries' responses to the COVID-19 crisis.** Monitoring tax policy measures is crucial to informing tax policy discussions and assisting governments in their response to the crisis. Regularly updating the OECD database of COVID-19 tax measures and providing timely information on the measures that countries introduce as they move into new phases of the crisis is all the more important given the high degree of uncertainty and the need for agile and rapid policy response.

## References

Hijzen, A. and D. Venn (2011), "The Role of Short-Time Work Schemes during the 2008-09 Recession", *OECD Social, Employment and Migration Working Papers*, No. 115, OECD Publishing, Paris, https://dx.doi.org/10.1787/5kgkd0bbwvxp-en. [4]

Landais, C., E. Saez and G. Zucman (2020), *A progressive European wealth tax to fund the European COVID response | VOX, CEPR Policy Portal*, https://voxeu.org/article/progressive-european-wealth-tax-fund-european-covid-response (accessed on 21 July 2020). [2]

OECD (2020), *Supporting people and companies to deal with the COVID-19 virus - OECD*, https://read.oecd-ilibrary.org/view/?ref=119_119686-962r78x4do&title=Supporting_people_and_companies_to_deal_with_the_Covid-19_virus (accessed on 24 June 2020). [3]

OECD (2020), *Tax and fiscal policy in response to the Coronavirus crisis: Strengthening confidence and resilience*, http://www.oecd.org/coronavirus/policy-responses/tax-and-fiscal-policy-in-response-to-the-coronavirus-crisis-strengthening-confidence-and-resilience-60f640a8/ (accessed on 24 June 2020). [1]

## Notes

[1] The information has been collected through delegates from the Inclusive Framework on BEPS and delegates to Working Party No.2 on Tax Policy and Statistics and WP2 No.9 on Consumption Taxes of the Committee of Fiscal Affairs. The OECD Centre for Tax Policy and Administration will continue to update the database regularly.

[2] https://www.ato.gov.au/Media-centre/Media-releases/Joint-Treasury-and-ATO-statement---JobKeeper-update/